UPSCALING DOWNTOWN

UPSCALING DOWNTOWN

FROM BOWERY SALOONS TO COCKTAIL BARS IN NEW YORK CITY

RICHARD E. OCEJO

PRINCETON UNIVERSITY PRESS
PRINCETON & OXFORD

Jacket photograph: *Love in the Lower East Side* © Reny Preussker.
Jacket design by Chris Ferrante.

press.princeton.edu

ISBN 978-0-691-15516-6

Library of Congress Control Number: 2014933832

British Library Cataloging-in-Publication Data is available

This book has been composed in Minion Pro and Avenir LT Std

Printed on acid-free paper. ∞

Printed in the United States of America

10 9 8 7 6 5 4 3 2 1

FOR CHANTAL AND RITA
the hardest-working and most beautiful girls in Brooklyn

CONTENTS

PREFACE

MILANO'S IS A TINY OLD BAR ON HOUSTON STREET in downtown Manhattan, a block and a half from Bowery. Stuffed in the commercial storefront of a tenement building, the bar is long and narrow, and the decor is a messy mishmash of dusty objects, posters, signs, and old photographs of past and present customers. I first went there as a graduate student on a cold Tuesday night in February 2004. I had been having a drink with a friend at Botanica, a newer, "hipster" bar with DJs and secondhand furniture a few doors down. After my friend left, something about Milano's compelled me to go in and have one more for the road. I have always had a romantic affinity for old bars—ones with old men, cheap booze, and a smoky atmosphere. Based on what I had heard about the place, I assumed that is what I would find at Milano's. I was only half right.

When I walked in it was nearly midnight, and there were ten customers sitting at the bar. I ordered a beer and sat at one of the back tables. To my surprise, young revelers in their twenties were sharing the space with a couple of old men in their seventies. The older customers were sitting alone, staring into their beers, while others were in pairs, slightly intoxicated, playing the jukebox, and clearly enjoying their night. The bartender, a woman who looked to be in her early thirties, was friendly and talkative with all of them, making it hard to tell who was a regular customer. The bar clearly showed signs of a past, but it was also clear that something was different. I was intrigued by the place and its people, and decided to keep going back.

I studied Milano's over the next couple of years. I hung out at the bar often and got to know its regular customers and bartenders well. I also met dozens of patrons whom I never saw again and who were the way I was on my first night there: young, curious about visiting an old bar, and at their second bar of the night, or on their way to it. But the more I focused on the people and activities inside the bar, the more I was drawn towards its outside urban context. I identified three types of customer: older men who lived on the nearby Bowery, the city's most notorious skid-row district, and had been coming to the bar for many years; a group of younger regular customers, many of whom had moved to or often visited the neighborhood early on in its gentrification; and even younger visitors, in their twenties and thirties, who either recently moved to or lived outside the neighborhood and visited the bar infrequently. They all only shared the bar at the same time occasionally, and when they did they remained spatially separated. I recognized how each group represented a different stage in the bar's and neighborhood's history, and how each group held different perspective towards both. As a result of my experiences at Milano's, I became intrigued by the idea of studying the transformations of downtown neighborhoods like the Bowery area and the nearby Lower East Side and East Village, especially how their changes affected their people, through an analysis of their bars.

These neighborhoods—being among New York City's most storied and historic—have been common sites for academic research, with their gentrification in particular serving as a popular focus.[1] These studies have traced their history through the nineteenth and twentieth centuries as places for numerous immigrant and working-class groups, to rundown and crime-ridden slums and skid rows, to countercultural and avant-garde arts scenes, and, finally, to popular, gentrifying places for young urban professionals to live. From them we have learned much about the political economy of the gentrification of downtown neighborhoods, the roles of culture and images in their transformation, and the reactions of their residents to gentrification's onset. But these studies possess two shortcomings that I want to address in this book: their analytical time frame stops before the economic boom of the 2000s, when these neighborhoods transformed into destinations with large nightlife scenes; and they do not consider how the commercial dimension of gentrification, particularly new bars and nightlife, have affected them. Given how it had changed, Houston Street just off Bowery was a strange place to still find an old bar for old men in the mid-2000s. The fact that Milano's was still around, but with a tremendously varied clientele, amid a popular nightlife scene, and in an area that was becoming more and more upscale in terms of its residential and commercial exclusivity, inspired me to explore the relationship between downtown Manhattan's bars and their surrounding urban context.

Downtown streets clearly show the mixture of the old and the new, the signs and symbols of the past and the present, in everyday social life and in the built environment. I was always struck by the social contrasts I found at different times of day. During the daytime, lifelong Latino and new, young white residents pass each other on sparsely populated sidewalks. Inexpensive bodegas sit next to upscale hair salons and storefront galleries showing high-priced artworks by internationally recognized artists. Sunbeams bounce off the shiny facades of new condominiums. The grungy bricks of the revalorized nineteenth-century tenements from across the street are reflected in their mirrored glass. In Tompkins Square Park, in the heart of the East Village, homeless people huddle on benches and form a line for food from a nearby church, while young residents chat with their neighbors in the busy dog runs and sip expensive coffees at sidewalk cafés.

If downtown Manhattan features a quiet balance of old and new during the day, the nighttime tells a different story. At night the area teems with activity as the population swells. The narrow streets become crowded thoroughfares for vehicles and pedestrians. The people are overwhelmingly young, some are stylishly dressed and others casually so, and most are white. I regularly overheard revelers talking about which bar to go to next and where it is located, people in groups telling each other stories of previous nights of revelry, and couples bickering. It turns out that the steel barricades blocking so many of the storefronts during the day do not signify failed businesses in a blighted area, as they once did in many downtown neighborhoods. At night the barricades are up, and light and sound pour out from bars, restaurants, lounges, and clubs onto the sidewalks. Lured by nightlife establishments, the city's youth turn downtown into a place for nighttime consumption and amusement. Today when the sun goes down, these neighborhoods come alive in a dramatic way, and the notion that downtown has become a destination comes through, clear and loud.

I observed this nighttime loudness—music blaring from jukeboxes and performance stages, shouts coming from the mouths of cigarette-smoking patrons standing outside bars, street din emanating from sidewalks crowded with revelers walking to and from establishments and from gridlocked cars and taxis—all the time when I was studying Milano's (or when I was one of those shouting revelers). In doing so, I paid little attention to its impact on residents and local groups. But when I left the bar to study people in the surrounding neighborhoods, I learned that the loudness and action of the night was the ultimate symbol for the tensions and conflicts that their transformation into destinations with a large nightlife scene caused. Studying the neighborhoods from this angle revealed to me that bars, nightlife, and the social conditions they produce were among both the signs and the consequences of gentrification, and of a turbulent postindustrial era in which abandoned downtowns like that in Lower Manhattan have been revitalized and service, consumption, and investment have become a city's economic foundation.

The postindustrial era has had major impacts on cities and urban life, and this book is not the first one to tackle its effects through an analysis of bars and nightlife. David Grazian has examined the producers and consumers of contemporary nightspots from two different angles. First, he has looked at how the commercialization and globalization of blues music has led people to search for authentic representations of the art form, which then leads them to the places from which they originate, like blues clubs in Chicago.[2] He focuses on how different actors in blues clubs—musicians, regulars, and tourists—define authenticity in blues music and seek out their interpretations of its authentic forms by examining their practices within the bars. These include jam sessions among local musicians, nights when only knowledgeable regulars are present, and weekends when tourists take over. Second, Grazian shows how in Philadelphia, as in many postindustrial cities around the United States, nightspots and nightlife scenes have helped revitalize abandoned downtowns and former industrial areas.[3] In these increasingly themed and branded environments, he argues, young men and women use tactics of deception to construct and perform a "nocturnal self." In his work on Wicker Park, an artists' neighborhood in Chicago, Richard Lloyd examines how artists construct understandings of "grit as glamour" while learning how to "live like an artist" in part by building, socializing, performing, working, and generally spending time in bars.[4] Existing old ethnic bars were important for incoming artists' conceptions of the neighborhood as gritty and authentically working class. New bars are an important part of Wicker Park's entertainment infrastructure and contribute to its transformation from a working-class, industrial area to a "neo-bohemian," postindustrial site of cultural production.

Like these recent works, this book also grapples with urban conditions wrought by postindustrialism through an analysis of bars and nightlife, but in a unique way. Along with looking at the cultures and subcultures that are found within bars, I also examine how bars fit within as well as shape the larger urban context of gentrified neighborhoods that are becoming upscale. Lloyd's work certainly looks at where bars fit within the neighborhood's arts scene and the role they play for artists. But in this book I wanted to examine a broader array of local groups with competing interests who are affected by and/or play a role in nightlife scenes. Instead of a book about bars, I present an urban community study of bars and nightlife scenes through an examination of how they grew and what they mean to people—residents, community activists, owners, bartenders, local politicians, consumers—who are trying to coexist in neighborhoods that are becoming an upscale destination.

Overall, today's city leaders and real estate and business actors appreciate bars and nightlife scenes because they represent growth and vitality for the city and the neighborhoods where they are located. As one of the Lower East Side's representatives to the state legislature explains to me, "We see [nightlife] as economic development, which it is. It's a very important industry, it brings people into the city, it's certainly a moneymaker, it generates taxes." As this brief quote suggests, bars' benefits are not just based on their economic impact, such as the tax revenue they generate as businesses. Vibrant nightlife also provides a city with a sorely needed image: as a fun place for young, energetic, and creative residents and visitors.

But studying bars and nightlife scenes reveals many issues beyond other problems commonly associated with them, such as alcoholism, drug abuse, and crime.[5] By analyzing bars within a context of advanced gentrification, we can learn about how residents deal with the growth of a nightlife scene in their neighborhood, how nightlife entrepreneurs construct a collective place identity, how community life within local neighborhood bars has changed, how government regulation and law enforcement address nightlife issues in the postindustrial city, and how the growth of nightlife has bred resentment between multiple local actors, frayed civic trust between citizens and government agencies and officials, and undermined local democracy. Through an analysis of the growth, transformation, and surrounding activities of bars and nightlife scenes, this book tells the story of the lives, conflicts, and contested meanings among people who live in, work in, and visit downtown Manhattan—a place where old-man bars and new cocktail lounges, daytime mundaneness and nighttime action, rooted regulars and rootless newcomers and visitors, and people with diverse understandings of place and community uneasily coexist.

ACKNOWLEDGMENTS

Before starting there are a few people I would like to acknowledge. First, a big "thank you" to all the people who opened their lives and donated their time to my project, especially the people at Milano's and CB3, as well as Rob Hollander, David Mulkins, and Rebecca Moore. Most of you appear in these pages and this book would not exist without your generosity. I would like to thank my editor Eric Schwartz, for believing in and shepherding this book along from the very beginning (a phone conversation when I was still a graduate student), as well as Ellen Foos, Ryan Mulligan, and the other good folks at Princeton University Press for all their great work. Special thanks to Sharon Zukin, my biggest advocate and inspiration, and to my CUNY boys for all their support over the years, especially Randol Contreras, Colin Jerolmack, and Jon Wynn, who all read earlier versions of this manuscript (some of which were quite awful). The Office for the Advancement of Research at John Jay College provided some generous funding towards the end. A quick thank you to Paul Willis, for knocking some needed sense into an earlier draft, and the other reviewers for their helpful comments. I will always thank my mother for the job she and my father did to make my life as good as possible. Tremendous hugs and kisses to my wonderful wife Chantal and our daughter Rita. You both fill my life with enough joy and meaning to last two lifetimes. Finally, I would like to acknowledge Bob Arihood, who passed away suddenly in 2011. A true Lower East Sider and champion of the marginalized, Bob's story, fight, and photographs will live on wherever people struggle for democracy. Thanks, Bob.

INTRODUCTION

NIGHT AND DAY

I BEGAN THIS PROJECT BY WALKING INTO A BAR. Like most people, I always considered bars to be places for relaxation, socializing, and fun. They are places where people go to set aside the stresses and obligations of their everyday lives; where, removed from their work and home they can temporarily step out of normal roles (and perhaps step into different ones). The bar is an "unserious" setting, a place people generally agree is for "play."[1] Bars are also unique sites for interaction and community. Some of their patrons confront one another as strangers, while sometimes exclusive groups call the local bar their second home. Many people have a story of the time they struck up a conversation with a random person at a bar, or when they mistakenly walked into a place that was not "for them." As fixtures in neighborhoods, they are repositories of local memory and sources of identity. A bar that is old enough has walls that can tell the history of its surrounding neighborhood and the people who live there, while its regular patrons will spin yarns about local lore. And for some residents, bars are intertwined with their sense of community—of who they are and where they fit in their neighborhood.

There have been many studies and books on bars as important places of sociability and community.[2] Revealing the important roles that these urban institutions play in the lives of many urbanites, authors have focused on social life in neighborhood bars, what bars mean to their patrons, and what cultures get produced in them. In writing this book, I wanted to examine bars not just as places for socializing and relationships. I wanted to use them as windows for understanding how downtown neighborhoods like the Lower East Side, East Village, and Bowery have transformed from disinvested slums to upscaling destinations with nightlife scenes, how disparate groups react to such a dramatic change, and how they either help make it happen or struggle to stop it. More generally, I wanted to provide an understanding of the role and impact of nightlife's rise in the postindustrial city by examining how bars have become symbols of neighborhood change, specifically gentrification, that different groups experience, interpret, and act upon in a multitude of ways. If we look beyond their brick-and-mortar buildings and the social life within them, we can see bars as part of a larger social ecosystem—an urban context of resident groups, community organizations, government agencies, politicians, consumer subcultures, and entrepreneurs—that contributes to our understanding of the nature and consequences of the massive reinvestment in the downtowns of today's cities.[3] The interrelationships between different elements of this social ecosystem affect life not only within bars but also within neighborhoods. Specifically, an examination of these interrelationships provides us with a new way of understanding tensions and conflicts that people in gentrified neighborhoods experience.

By looking at bars as more than just "unserious" settings or places for sociability, and by using them and their surrounding social ecosystem as an analytical lens for understanding how culture and the economy combine to transform social, political, and community life in neighborhoods, this book explores how fundamental urban processes like city growth and gentrification influence local communities, how the role and nature of commercial establishments in neighborhoods have changed as the latter have become destinations, and how aspects of everyday urban life, such as local identity, public forms of social control, and collective action, have altered as these changes occur. I conduct this analysis from the neighborhood's ground level—the spaces where people live, work, and invest in a community: the places where they cultivate social bonds, the public forums where they display collective action, and the bars where they gather. In other words, after walking into a bar for a drink, I walked out years later with a story to tell of life in today's postindustrial city.

NEIGHBORHOOD BARS IN THE POSTINDUSTRIAL CITY

Once peripheral to the city's economic engine of production and manufacturing, consumption, services, and culture have become significant contributors to the growth and vitality of the postindustrial city. Many cities feature all three in entertainment districts, where locals and visitors alike go for action, distraction, and fun. Ideally, entertainment districts provide people with safe amusements that hide the problems of daily urban life behind their glow and noise.[4] Times Square, for instance, the bustling beacon of light and sound, represents New York City's most famous entertainment district. A true "twenty-four/seven" destination, Times Square is a place where people can find amusement at nearly any time of the day.[5] But the district's true spirit comes alive at night, when bright lights guide thousands of visitors through the streets on an unparalleled urban stage. Today, concentrations of bars, restaurants, nightclubs, theaters, and hotels are often located at the heart of a city's center or downtown. More than just amenities for an area's daytime economy, nighttime attractions lure visitors to the city's core and promote it as a place for safe fun.[6] So important has leisure become in the postindustrial era that some scholars have come to refer to the city as an "entertainment machine."[7] According to this model, consumption, amenities, and amusements, rather than the more traditional factors of production and work, drive urban growth and its policies. Bars and other establishments anchor the city's nighttime economy at a time when these forms of consumption play an important role in its economic and social vibrancy.

At the neighborhood level, bars are also important to the process of gentrification. The "return to the city" of middle- and upper-class professionals has transformed many working-class and low-income neighborhoods and districts. Along with familiar residential changes like increases in real estate prices and rents, gentrification also has a commercial dimension.[8] It is common for young artists and musicians who often move into a neighborhood at the start of the gentrification process to either go to existing working-class bars or open their own.[9] In search of places for going out, these newcomers learn the culture of their new neighborhood at its existing bars, while hanging out among the local population. With the new bars they open, they put their own stamp on the neighborhood.[10] New establishments play an important role for artists who use them for socializing, for displaying and performing their art, and for employment. This transformation occurred in these downtown Manhattan neighborhoods from the start of their gentrification. Herman, for instance, told me how he visited downtown as a teenager in the 1970s and went to "Bowery bars" (skid-row bars for homeless men) like Milano's, as mentioned in the preface. He eventually became a member of the East Village's punk-rock music scene and began performing and working in the new bars that were opening. He described a bartending job he had at one of these places:

> Neighborhood people, regulars, some older jazz guys, and some rock 'n' roll visitors. At that time, there was maybe eighty bars in the neighborhood instead of 300, so there was still a packed bar during the week. I made a fantastic living working there two nights a week. Fantastic, it was great! Perfect rock 'n' roll life. I could leave, go play shows, come home, still have a job.

New bars gave newcomers like Herman places to hang out and flexible employment to sustain their lifestyle. But bars also encourage gentrification. New, hip commercial establishments generate local buzz in a neighborhood and signify that it is transforming. Bars have a mutually reinforcing relationship with gentrification: new businesses like bars accommodate the needs of middle-class residents at the same time as they attract new ones. They are both signposts and catalysts in the process when a neighborhood gentrifies.

Downtown neighborhoods like the Lower East Side, East Village, and Bowery exemplify how local bars are an important piece of these larger stories of postindustrial urban life. After a long period as slums, gentrification has turned them into part of an upscaling downtown: coveted places to live for wealthy urbanites, destinations for visitors, and among the largest and most popular bar and nightlife districts in the city. As contemporary urban entertainment districts, their nightlife scenes provide their visitors with a wide array of safe amusements and consumption options to choose from.[11] But bars have caused problems for many people in the neighborhood. Rather than places for socializing or sources of community, some residents see bars as threats to the social fabric they have built. As Virgil, a longtime resident in his early fifties who moved to the East Village in the 1970s, explained to me,

> My concern is really about the transformation of this neighborhood. Gentrification has done a lot of this work, but the nightlife scene is a subset of gentrification—but it's a special one, like gentrification on steroids. It's just wild and uncontrolled, and it's faster than any other kind of gentrification. And it doesn't just bring in upscale people to reside here. It brings in all these nonlocal folks.

Residents most commonly complain that bars have diminished their quality of life. In community meetings and in my interviews with them, they regularly spoke about the noise that bars cause. For people with bars in their building's storefront, vibrations from sound systems travel through the brick of the old tenements into their apartments, while the voices of patrons hanging out and smoking on the sidewalk rise up to their floors and enter through their windows. For people with bars on their block, passersby constantly carry on conversations to and from their destinations. Cars behind taxis blast their horns as passengers settle fares. If residents return home from a night out of their own, they have to navigate through a sea of young revelers who crowd the sidewalks. These conditions last in some cases until after 4 a.m. and sometimes occur on a nightly basis. The next morning, residents often awake to find vomit on their doorsteps and their property damaged (e.g., broken car mirrors, defaced front doors) that they attribute to the previous night's activities.

But as Virgil's quote shows, residents' problems reflect the social as much as the environmental impact of bars. It is not just the depleted quality of life that concerns existing residents but the fact that young newcomers and new establishments signify to them that their home is no longer theirs. Bars, restaurants, cafés, and other expensive stores like boutiques replace their beloved local shops and hangouts (some of which are older bars). White revelers with no stake in the neighborhood and who use it merely for consumption and fun replace a diverse array of creative local characters whom they admire. Even more frustrating to them is that these young folks were not around for the days when the neighborhood was a disinvested slum. They remember when the now-trendy section of the East Village called Alphabet City—so named because of the west-to-east Avenues A, B, C, and D—could be summed up with the following verse: "Avenue A, you're all right. Avenue B, you're brave. Avenue C, you're crazy. Avenue D, you're dead." Existing residents take pride in having invested themselves and their sweat equity into a place that had been abandoned, and for having remained in the neighborhood throughout its depressed period. To them, the East Village is a special place, and they are a special population living there. Meanwhile, hovering above these issues is the omnipresent threat of rising rents that could displace them. As a result, residents have formed many community groups to protest bars and nightlife and mitigate its harms.

Other people in the downtown neighborhoods, however, disagree. Nightlife owners and younger residents argue that new people and businesses are signs of an area's improvement and success. Entrepreneurs and investors see places like the Lower East Side, East Village, and Bowery as viable locations for such establishments as luxury boutique hotels, where hip guests will pay in excess of $400 a night to stay and where nightlife spaces attract visitors from around the city. They also know that the neighborhood's reputation for bars and nightlife will mean their large nightspots will attract revelers in general. To new bar owners, opening a bar in these neighborhoods is a wise investment.

On a smaller scale, bar owners maintain the attitude that their establishments have made positive contributions to these neighborhoods. They argue that without the taxes, employment, and places they provide for the community, these areas would still be depressed, crime-ridden slums. Comparing today's East Village with that of the past, Dave, a new bar owner in the neighborhood, said to me, "What makes people comfortable to come here, venture here, and eventually start moving in here is going to make it a safe place, and it *is* now." Older owners who opened bars during the neighborhood's early stages of gentrification and who managed to stay open despite shifting clienteles and increasing commercial rents have profited from the nightlife scene's emergence and the new crowds it brings. No bar owner I studied or observed sought to deliberately bother existing residents. Rather, each felt in their own way that by owning a bar they were doing their small part to improve the neighborhood. Young revelers meanwhile, who either live in these neighborhoods or visit their bars, also regard their nightlife scenes as positive to downtown's revitalization. For them personally, going out reinforces the social bonds they have already formed with their friends and satisfies their desire to live in a vibrant downtown neighborhood, where the action is.[12]

Along with gentrification, these conflicts between downtown's daytime communities (residents, resident groups, community organizations) and nighttime communities (bar owners, revelers) emerged as a result of "growth machine" or, we can say, "entertainment machine" policies.[13] Like those of other urban entertainment districts, downtown Manhattan's nightlife scenes developed with the influence of local government and the presence of certain institutional actors, with mediation from key political figures.[14] Liquor license laws vary state by state, and they often have provisions that control the density and concentration of licensed establishments. Recognizing the importance of entertainment for urban growth in the 1990s, New York State lawmakers ensured that bars could open in dense concentrations to form nightlife scenes. Officials of the New York State Liquor Authority (SLA), the state government's agency in charge of liquor license regulation and enforcement, regularly makes licensing decisions that encourage nightlife development in the name of urban growth, as was the case downtown. In addition, the steady institutional expansion of the expensive private school New York University (NYU) eastward from its Greenwich Village base through the opening of large dormitory buildings since the 1990s has provided the neighborhood's bars with thousands of young student consumers seeking the pleasures of living in an urban campus in a hip downtown. Students also rent tenement apartments in these neighborhoods, sometimes forming groups of four or five for a one-bedroom apartment to cover the high rents.

The conflicts over these policies and the expansion of bars in downtown neighborhoods have involved other areas of government, namely politicians and the police. Representatives in the New York City Council and the New York State Legislature face the dilemma of having to balance the imperatives of urban growth and the needs of their constituents while constantly intervening on behalf of residents in various forums. As I found, they regularly speak against nightlife on behalf of the local populations and draft, push, and pass legislation that targets bar owners for various violations. But they do not address the scale and density of the local scenes. Instead they maintain a discourse of neighborhood growth that includes nightlife. The police, meanwhile, must deal with the frequent complaints that residents make against bars and ensure that nightlife scenes remain safe without overtaxing their resources. The "quality-of-life policing" policies that have characterized the regulation of public spaces in the postindustrial city often target groups like the homeless and other vagrants.[15] While not their intended focus, these policies require officers to do something about crowds of loud, young, money-spending revelers and bars that are profitable but noisy without disrupting the scenes' vibrancy. Faced with this task, the police also hold individual owners accountable for their own spaces and the street and encourage the use of private solutions to handle their issues.

THE BARS OF AN UPSCALING DOWNTOWN

The conflicts over downtown bars represent symptoms of the postindustrial urban process of advanced gentrification that is transforming its neighborhoods into destinations for visitors and tourists, not necessarily for local residents.[16] There are many examples in New York, as well as other cities such as Chicago and Los Angeles, of bars, restaurants, hotels, music venues, dance clubs, clothing boutiques, and art galleries that attract new residents and visitors.[17] As gentrification progresses in a neighborhood, new businesses begin appealing directly to visitors and newcomers and not necessarily existing locals, while old businesses either begin attracting new clienteles or suffer. I understand this to be an "upscaling" process, whereby gentrified neighborhoods become destinations for increasingly elite forms of consumption. The new commercial amenities that have opened in downtown Manhattan are increasingly high end in nature, with expensive items and specialized offerings and themes that distinguish them from their competition. They match the area's new luxury housing developments, such as the Avalon Bowery and Chrystie Place complexes, with a swimming pool, fitness center, the largest Whole Foods on the East Coast, a restaurant owned by the world-famous chef Daniel Boulud, and studio apartments with rents starting at $3,300 a month. When gentrification progresses to an advanced stage in neighborhoods, new elements—housing types, residents, commercial establishments, public activities—become more socially and culturally distant from the existing examples. Bars themselves exemplify this neighborhood-wide transformation.

Many of the tensions over this upscaling process arise from the fact that the commercial life in downtown Manhattan is becoming homogenized in terms of the type of establishments opening and the socioeconomic backgrounds and cultural preferences of their patrons while overall its demographics remain diverse. In my own street-by-street, block-by-block counts of businesses in this book's geographic focus,[18] I found that 29 percent of all businesses in the neighborhood are nighttime establishments, either bars, restaurants, music venues, or nightclubs (605 out of 2,097 total businesses).[19] On some blocks, bars and nightlife completely dominate commercial life, such as on Avenues A and B, two narrow fourteen-block streets, where bars and restaurants represent 35 percent of businesses (45 out of 122 total businesses and 30 out of 85, respectively), and on a three-block stretch of Ludlow Street, a narrow one-way street, where they represent 44 percent (17 out of 39 total businesses). Downtown Manhattan features several highly dense mixed-used neighborhoods. Businesses often operate on heavily residential streets and occupy the commercial storefronts of tenement buildings. Most residents thereby constantly pass nightlife establishments of some sort every time they leave home.

In addition to these vast numbers, many of the new bars no longer represent community hangouts that bring together diverse clienteles or integrate strangers.[20] Their themes are often highly specialized, focusing on specific products (natural wines, craft beer, handcrafted cocktails, mescal), nighttime experiences (DJs, crowds, live music, dancing), and subcultures (indie rock fans, foodies, burlesque performers). Their ambience promotes entertainment over casual socializing, and they only open after typical work hours and sometimes only on nights when people most often go out. Their customers often live in the metropolitan area or visit from afar. Downtown Manhattan has historic neighborhood bars that still maintain regular clienteles and a sense of community (such as Milano's) but are regularly overrun by tourists and visitors. The greatest example of these is McSorley's Old Ale House in the East Village. Opened in 1854, when the neighborhood had a large Irish immigrant population, "New York City's oldest bar" today is written about in popular tourist guidebooks and international media sources as a must-see destination for visitors.[21] Right down the street from McSorley's, however, are Burp Castle and Standings, two new bars that are also regularly featured in local media and beer guides for specializing in Belgian and American craft beers, respectively. These bars attract a more discerning clientele than places with typical Budweiser-like fare, and beer aficionados seek them out for their rarefied offerings. They are community institutions, but the communities that seek them out are based on taste, rather than locale, race, or ethnicity of the romanticized neighborhood bar.[22] The New York City Homebrewers Guild, a leisure group of beer lovers who make their own concoctions at home, holds its monthly meetings at Burp Castle. They are not cheap, however. Belgian beers can cost $10 a glass. Patrons at these and other bars have the money to spend on such items, and the cultural wherewithal to know where to go for what they want in a night out.

Despite these patterns, these downtown neighborhoods still have diverse populations. As 2010 census data indicates, 32.4 percent of their residents are white, 33.8 percent are Asian, 6.9 percent are black, and 24.6 percent are Hispanic.[23] Only whites, however, who represent a strong majority of downtown's revelers and recent residents, have increased in population since 2000, in their case by a substantial 14 percent, while blacks have decreased by 2.9 percent, Asians by 4.6 percent, and Hispanics by 9.1 percent. In addition, these neighborhoods are rather residentially segregated. Data shows that census tracts with wealthier and whiter residents are located in the northwestern, western, and central areas of the Lower East Side and East Village; tracts with more Hispanic and African American residents and lower incomes are in their northeastern,

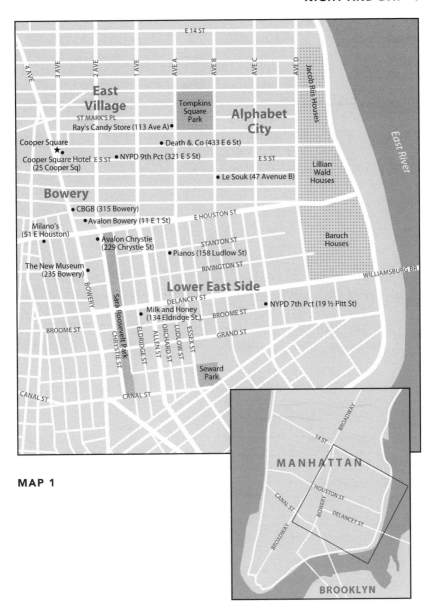

MAP 1

eastern, and southeastern areas, which feature dense concentrations of large public housing projects; and tracts with low-income Asian residents are in the southwestern area, where Chinatown is located.[24] Advanced gentrification and an upscaling process, then, do not mean existing populations, such as people born in the neighborhood and earlier waves of newcomers, and their businesses and cultures disappear from a neighborhood. But a neighborhood's residential and commercial patterns put them at risk. These different racial and ethnic populations contain their own subgroups—for example, lifelong ethnic-white residents such as Ukrainians and Jews of Eastern European descent; longtime white residents who moved into the area at the start of gentrification as artists or students; Puerto Rican, Dominican, and Chinese immigrants of the first and second generation; bohemians, the homeless, and new wealthy members of the professional classes—each of whom have their own material and nonmaterial interests in their neighborhood. Their interests vary by such factors as their social class and the amount of time they have lived in the neighborhood. These groups must coexist with one another within the context of a large, popular, and densely concentrated nightlife scene and endure the transformations of advanced gentrification. Their myriad interests are compromised in different ways by the threats caused by bars. While the primary concerns of most groups are rents and local amenities that are affordable and a decent quality of life, they each have their own unique, symbolic connections to their neighborhood that new bars threaten to sever. The tensions that bars and nightlife cause, I argue, have wider consequences for any community that has been transformed into a popular destination with hip forms of consumption while retaining elements of its past.

EXAMINING TAMED FRONTIERS

Two scholars have famously used the old American frontier as a metaphor to describe phenomena that I examine in this book. First, Neil Smith argued that real estate and government actors saw dilapidated areas like the East Village of the 1980s as similar to the "Wild West": untamed, unpredictable, and dangerous.[25] The downtown slum was full of marginal characters—the working-class, racial and ethnic minorities, the homeless, gays and other sexual deviants— who had to be removed from the (potentially profitable) land to develop it. Groups like middle-class artists served as gentrification's "shock troops," who ventured into the uncharted frontier. The success or failure of their settlement among "native" populations would determine the further investment of capital and the displacement of unwanted groups. Smith saw the East Village as analogous to the American West, with its existing inhabitants treated as the Native Americans were. As gentrification continued, the "frontier line" of investment and displacement progressed deeper and deeper into the neighborhood.

An element of the gentrification process that Smith did not examine invokes Murray Melbin's work on the night.[26] Melbin considers time to be like space, or like a container that we fill with activities and meanings. As daytime has become too packed with work and other obligations, society has gradually started filling up the time of the night. Nighttime has historically been perceived as similar to the frontier: wild, mysterious and unknowable in its darkness, and inhabited by strange creatures. It is also different from the productive day as a time of rest, relaxation, and leisure.[27] But these meanings of night and day are mere social constructions, subject to change. Melbin observes that society is becoming more and more incessant, as companies seek to make goods and provide services at all hours of the day, with profit serving as a key explanation: "A land frontier is turned to for what can be extracted from it, a nighttime for what can be produced in it. The underlying motive is the same, an incentive to exploit the region for economic gain."[28] Meanwhile, people have become more demanding of obtaining anything at any hour, and are shifting many of their daytime responsibilities to the night. As it became colonized, the night would become tamed, or more organized and regulated, less homogeneous in terms of activities and inhabitants, and less tolerant of lawless and deviant behavior.

As we will see, an important aspect of downtown Manhattan's gentrification was the control of its nighttime spaces, including disreputable and illegal bars. But Melbin argued that common daytime phenomena—work, production, order, schedules, services—would gradually seep into the night and replace the behaviors and meanings that typically characterize it. He did not consider how nighttime institutions and their affiliated meanings of leisure and consumption would become significant to the everyday world of the postindustrial city. Smith was also not concerned with what the tamed frontier of gentrified neighborhoods looked like. New bars, as examples of urban nighttime leisure, played an important role in making downtown a place for investment and a destination for upscale consumption. Entrepreneurs and young revelers have successfully occupied its nighttime hours, but these phenomena neither completely resemble nor are completely separate from those of the day.

A central story of nightlife's role in the upscaling process in downtown Manhattan is how the nighttime economy influences the people of the daytime community. This story is about how bars impact the thoughts, actions, and inactions of a group of residents who interpret them and their patrons as real threats to their sociocultural worlds. It tells how old neighborhood bars undergo transformations from local community hangouts to popular destinations. And it concerns local urban growth policies and enforcement agencies whose agendas have become intertwined with the nightlife scene's development and public safety. These are the tensions of everyday social, political, and community life in the neighborhood that bar patrons and visiting revelers rarely see when they are out at night. They are conflicts that reveal the underside of what appears to be successful growth in a postindustrial neighborhood.

But this story of advanced gentrification is also about how bars and their social worlds of the night operate in ways that the daytime communities of residents do not see. It tells how neighborhood bars have changed from places for local social gathering to destinations for revelers and subcultures. It deals with how upscale forms of experiential entertainment have replaced earlier working-class and avant-garde forms of creativity in the neighborhood.[29] And it tells about the strategies that today's nightlife entrepreneurs use for their bars to survive in the nighttime economy. The social worlds of the nighttime economy are far more differentiated than protesting residents imply.

In this book I examine how these two worlds of the day and night in downtown Manhattan neighborhoods conflict with and influence each other. I show how tensions between them emerged as a result of growth policies that favored nightlife development. And I explain how local politicians, the police, and community organizations attempt to mediate between their conflicts, and how they fail to do so.

To tell the story of the impact of the changing role of bars on neighborhood life downtown, I studied people from four general categories:

1 **RESIDENTS** (lifelong and longtime residents, community activists, bar regulars, new wealthy members of the professional classes, college students, and the homeless),
2 **VISITORS** (revelers from outside the neighborhood and tourists),
3 **PUBLIC OFFICIALS** (local elected officials, representatives of the State Liquor Authority, and the police), and
4 **NIGHTLIFE ACTORS** (owners of bars, hotels, and restaurants; bartenders; landlords; real estate agents; and attorneys who specialize in nightlife).[30]

Each group holds a stake in these neighborhoods and has a different position in relation to the upscaling process, bars, and nightlife scene. As I will show, people within each group often vary and differ from one another. Longtime residents who collectively organize to protest bars, for instance, have more in common with older owners of small bars in terms of how they understand upscale nightlife development than they do with wealthier newcomers and students, with whom they regularly conflict. Likewise, older bar owners have little in common with hoteliers or new owners of dance clubs. The neighborhoods represent the terrains upon which each group lays claim in some form, and the groups' struggles over bars, the nightlife scene, and the upscaling process drive the following analysis.

OUTLINE OF THIS BOOK

Looking at the local social ecosystem surrounding bars in the downtown Manhattan neighborhoods of the Lower East Side, East Village, and Bowery, this book examines six aspects of neighborhood life in the postindustrial city that have been affected by the growth of their nightlife scenes. These aspects are all found in these neighborhoods because of their transformation into upscaling downtown areas with large nighttime economies and dense concentrations of diverse groups with competing interests. Each of the following six chapters features one of these aspects as its central theme, with elements of others in the background. In each I also form a dialogue between the dichotomy of the daytime and the nighttime people and phenomena found downtown. Throughout the book I weave the overall story of the consequences that neighborhoods face when they transition into upscale destinations based in part on a large nightlife scene. The different, conflicting material interests and stakes that disparate groups have in these neighborhoods serve as a common thread.

Chapter 1 serves a dual purpose. First, I provide a brief social history of the Bowery as told through the transformation of its bars and nightlife. I discuss how bars and nightlife corresponded to and helped along its eventual gentrification. My goal here is to situate the area historically and demonstrate the different roles that bars have played for people there over time. Second, I focus on how new bars and contemporary nightlife development have shaped community life in downtown neighborhood bars. I begin the chapter with a vignette of the people at Milano's Bar, a bar that has evolved alongside the changes occurring in the area and the nightlife scene. Through an analysis of its multiple generations of customers, its bartenders, and its owners, I examine the tensions that have arisen from its own transformation as a refuge for the homeless to a public gathering place for residents to a "dive bar" for young visitors. The reactions of the people at Milano's to these changes echo many of the book's main themes while demonstrating how urban forces have shaped a fundamental aspect of life for people in these downtown neighborhoods, namely, community socializing.

In chapter 2 I examine the role of the local government in influencing economic development and diminishing civic power in city neighborhoods. It starts with an episode from a public forum on quality-of-life issues held for downtown residents. The vignette shows the open hostility that residents direct at the CEO of the State Liquor Authority (SLA), the government agency that they blame for the development of nightlife in the neighborhood in spite of their protests. The chapter then discusses the policies behind the growth of downtown Manhattan's nightlife scenes, especially the SLA's liquor-licensing decisions that facilitated the proliferation of bars. I show how this policy, which represents "urban entrepreneurialism," or how local governments directly influence private development, created local unrest and led residents to organize and protest bars. Residents understand the SLA and bar owners as complicit perpetrators in the destruction of their neighborhood and sense of community, and understand themselves as victims of these policies.

Building from this point, chapter 3 looks at the social reasons behind collective action against economic development. I focus on how and why residents continue to protest bars despite recognizing their powerlessness to prevent nightlife growth and occupying a role as its victim. I start with a profile of a longtime resident named Bob, who moved to the East Village at the start of its gentrification and spends weekend nights photographing new nightlife activities on a street corner with other characters from the neighborhood's past. With diminished civic power to combat dominant economic development in today's upscale downtown, early gentrifiers like Bob who stayed in their neighborhood through its rough years rely on their own past experiences and definitions of community to contest them as "theirs." This chapter examines how early gentrifiers construct a "nostalgia narrative," or a tale of authentic community that weaves together their experiences with their neighborhood's abandoned spaces, its diversity, and its creativity into a coherent representation of place. Through this narrative they create a community ideology and a new self-identity as their neighborhood's "symbolic owners" that serve as bases for collective action. Since it draws on a past that is both imagined and personal, the residents' narrative presents its own internal contradictions while their sense of community and organized protests exclude certain groups, such as the neighborhood's existing low-income residents, who express different attitudes of how their neighborhood has changed from early gentrifiers.

Chapter 4 analyzes entrepreneurialism in the form of small-business ownership as an example of local place making. It starts with an episode from a community board meeting that shows how residents use their community ideology to act against a Lower East Side bar owner named Sasha. I then segue into the story of my first visit to Sasha's unique, upscale cocktail bar. From there the chapter proceeds to examine who has opened bars in these downtown neighborhoods since the start of their gentrification, how owners understand their role in their neighborhood, and how new bars reinforce preexisting social bonds among groups while supporting rarefied taste communities. Bar owners represent "place entrepreneurs" who collectively construct an image of downtown as a destination for nightlife. While all new bar owners see themselves as purveyors of community and benefits to their neighborhood, they define community differently depending on when they opened their bars. However, in spite of their best intentions, downtown bars mainly attract young clienteles who visit the nightlife scene. Other owners, meanwhile, deliberately open bars to appeal to well-heeled, money-spending revelers. I show how new downtown nightlife has transformed from being for communities of newcomers in the area to being for groups of visitors to the area.

In chapter 5, I examine the issues that arise for policing nightlife scenes. It begins with an episode from one of the special meetings that the police occasionally hold at the precinct for bar owners, at which owners receive tips from officers on how to reduce quality-of-life complaints from residents and prevent crime in their bars. To enhance the quality of life in neighborhoods and provide a sense of safety on streets, leaders of postindustrial cities have enacted policing strategies that target "broken windows," or signs of public disorder. This meeting and other initiatives signify the police department's effort to curb quality-of-life complaints (e.g., noise, litter, and damage from revelers) as well as crimes inside and outside bars by making specific owners responsible for the structural conditions of dense nightlife scenes and targeting those who are "bad" and irresponsible. While residents often petition their local lawmakers to help them in their efforts to fight bars, I also show how elected officials espouse a growth discourse that targets individual bar owners and maintains density and proliferation levels. I then show how bar owners understand these efforts as well as other initiatives by the police and the local state (i.e., new laws and increased pressure and additional responsibility to monitor public space) to be excessive encroachments on their businesses and threats to their entrepreneurial identity as beneficial sources of community in their neighborhood.

Focusing on a final aspect of life in the postindustrial city, chapter 6 examines the limitations of local participatory democracy. It specifically looks at how the competing definitions of community and conflicting understandings of the appropriate use of the neighborhood that residents and bar owners hold play out in community board meetings. In recent years many cities have enacted policies that provide citizens with greater authority over local public affairs, while increasing the accountability of government agencies. My aim in this chapter is to demonstrate the limitations of participatory democracy by analyzing it in action between conflicting groups. I start with one of several episodes featured in the chapter of residents and bar owners debating liquor license applications and quality-of-life issues in their immediate area and surrounding neighborhood. I then examine the strategies that both residents and bar owners use against each other to push forward their definition of community. Early gentrifiers and the community board rely on their past experience in their neighborhood, with the SLA, and with bar owners to hone their arguments and reshape their policies to protest bars. Bar owners, who describe early gentrifiers as irrational for being nostalgic and selfish for not wanting the neighborhood to change, are either frustrated and react emotionally to residents or counter them with their own assurances that they will be different from their predecessors, neither of which changes the image residents have of them. These meetings construct and reinforce the perspectives that each group has towards the other. By documenting these confrontations in a political context of weakened local civic power, this chapter reveals the limits of neighborhood-based democratic processes.

A NOTE ON BOUNDARIES, DEFINITIONS, AND PERIODIZATION

People normally consider downtown Manhattan to be the section of the island south of Fourteenth Street. In addition to the Lower East Side, East Village, and Bowery, downtown Manhattan includes Greenwich Village, the West Village, NoHo, SoHo, Little Italy, NoLIta, Chinatown, TriBeCa, the Financial District, Battery Park City, City Hall, and the South Street Seaport historical district.[31] Historically, the Lower East Side and East Village neighborhoods and the Bowery area combined to form the "Lower East Side" of Manhattan: between Fourteenth Street and the Manhattan and Brooklyn Bridges and between Broadway and the East River. Over the centuries, numerous immigrant groups have divided this "Lower East Side" area into their own smaller ethnic social worlds (e.g., Little Italy, Chinatown, Little Germany, Little Odessa) while coexisting under the general name "Lower East Side." The boundaries between these subworlds have expanded, contracted, and shifted over time, and many have all but disappeared except for scant architectural traces of their onetime existence. But the overall status of the "Lower East Side" as an immigrant, working-class area—until recently—has remained constant.

In the late 1960s, real estate actors coined the name "East Village" to make the area east of Bowery between Fourteenth and Houston Streets more attractive and distinct from the "Lower East Side," which always carried the negative label of being a place for immigrants and the working class. They borrowed from the names of the nearby Greenwich Village and the West Village neighborhoods, which had more middle-class residents and tonier images. The name change succeeded in branding a new neighborhood and limiting the Lower East Side to the area south of Houston Street and east of Bowery. But it failed to prevent the East Village from turning into a slum like Bowery and the Lower East Side. While this nomenclature predominates, some people still use other names for these neighborhoods. Puerto Ricans, who moved to the East Village and Lower East Side in great numbers in the decades after World War II, refer to the area as "Loisaida," a Spanglish or "Nuyorican" pronunciation of "Lower East Side." However, given advanced gentrification, much of the Hispanic presence in terms of businesses and street life is disappearing from most streets (although Avenue C's official alternative name remains Loisaida). Some residents, real estate agents, and media sources call the far-eastern section of the East Village "Alphabet City," in reference to Avenues A, B, C, and D. This name has obscure origins, although it emerged at a time of high crime activity in that section of the neighborhood. Today the western section of the Lower East Side features part of Chinatown, which stretches west through Little Italy to the border of TriBeCa. Finally, Bowery, which I discuss in great detail in the next chapter, has always represented both a street and an area of the "Lower East Side," most especially a skid row area. In short, the various sections of the "Lower East Side" of Manhattan have their own histories and cultural connotations that, as Christopher Mele points out, indicate the struggles of representation that have taken place among the various social actors who have had a stake in them over the past few decades.[32]

The three areas that I focus on in this book make up Manhattan Community District 3, which Manhattan Community Board 3 represents. Jane Jacobs would describe Community District 3 as a "district" in the sense that it mediates between the streets and places in a neighborhood and the larger city.[33] Most important for this book, Community Board 3 serves as the forum for liquor-licensing matters, which I discuss in chapter 2. Compared with other neighborhoods and areas in downtown Manhattan, the Lower East Side, East Village, and Bowery share a similar historical trajectory as places for immigrant and working-class groups that became slums and then underwent gentrification. Throughout the book I carefully examine the uniqueness of different sections within the district and delineate the meanings behind "neighborhood" and "community" and the phenomena they reference when different people use such terms.

In choosing downtown Manhattan as my case, I do not argue that it features representative neighborhoods that resemble gentrified neighborhoods or downtown areas in other cities. I find support in Mario Small's statement that qualitative researchers should not look for "average" cases such as neighborhoods in their research to make generalized statements about their empirical findings.[34] Such selections do not meet statistical standards of representativeness, and qualitative researchers should therefore neither seek to achieve external validity in their work nor use such quantitative language.[35] Qualitative scholars rarely select neighborhoods from random samples, and furthermore their analyses remain based on samples of one. Downtown Manhattan is a "unique case," or an opportunity to make analytically logical inferences on "an idiosyncratic combination of elements or events which constitute a 'case'" through a revelation of contextual processes.[36] Scholars have identified the processes I examine in this book occurring in cities around the world. They have shown how new nightlife scenes and gentrification can look different from place to place, feature different groups, and occur at different paces depending on specific spatiotemporal contexts.

I see downtown Manhattan as an example of an area in a top-tier global city with neighborhoods at an advanced stage of gentrification and undergoing an upscaling process. I examine what happens to neighborhood life under these conditions through an analysis of the conflicts over its many bars to deepen our theoretical understanding of these processes. Perhaps only a few neighborhoods in such cities feature all of these conditions that arise from such densely concentrated diversity, economic developments, and conflicts and actions among their local populations. As the postindustrial transformation advances in other cities, neighborhoods may come to resemble those in this book in terms of the nature of their transition and the conflicts between their local groups. I hope that readers will find my approach of examining the social ecosystem surrounding bars useful for understanding how people experience life in a neighborhood that has become a destination for visitors and a place of upscale consumption.

Finally, I began my fieldwork for this book in early 2004 and completed it at the end of 2008, when the recession that affected the United States had begun. Although I followed the effects of the recession on nightlife in these neighborhoods and conducted several new and follow-up interviews after formally exiting the field, I end the analysis in 2008. I offer several observations and comments on the impact of the recession on the neighborhoods and their nightlife scenes throughout the book.

CHAPTER 1

THE BOWERY AND ITS BARS

Mr. Cunningham remembered a narrow bar called Milano's on Houston Street. It is still there, but it has been transformed. "The college boys go there now," Mr. Cunningham said. "The prices have gone up, and there's not so many veterans any more."[1]

A NIGHT AND A DAY AT MILANO'S BAR

One Saturday night while sitting at the bar at Milano's, I run into Phil Simpson. He comes in at 3 a.m., which is unusual for him. I have been here since midnight and have watched the crowd of three dozen young revelers gradually get drunker as the hour grows later. Leslie and Amber, both in their mid-thirties, are bartending tonight, serving drinks quickly and keeping people in check (at one point someone tried standing up on the bar). Stevie, a musician in his mid-forties who regularly comes in on weekends after his gigs, is also here. He is sitting by himself at the back end of the bar, as usual, and talks to Leslie when she comes down his way. As the crowd thinned, Leslie took a seat in the bartender's chair in the front, getting up to help Amber when she had a few customers at once. Later on they switched. At around 2:30 a.m., Leslie indicated that everyone could smoke, if they want to. (She did not actually say anything; she just started smoking, in defiance of New York State's smoking ban. Others followed her lead.) I am sitting in the middle of the bar when Phil walks in, and we both have to squint through the wisps of smoke to make each other out. We usually only see each other in the mornings and afternoons, so it is strange seeing Phil so late at night.

Phil is a longtime resident of the East Village and a regular customer at Milano's Bar. If you ask him, he is "the best regular this place has." In his mid-fifties, Phil came from Minneapolis and moved to New York City in the late 1970s after receiving a bachelor's degree in fine art from the University of Minnesota. "If you're famous in New York, you're global," he says. "If you're famous in Minneapolis, you're famous in Minneapolis." Such was the mindset of many young artists at the time, and, once they arrived in New York City, one of the areas where they settled was downtown Manhattan. Neighborhoods like the Lower East Side and East Village and areas like the Bowery have long been considered the city's destination for the marginal, particularly immigrants, ethnic and

FIGURE 1   Milano's Bar at night. Photograph by Chantal Martineau, 2011.

subcultural groups, and the working class. After going to a few other bars in the neighborhood with some regularity during the 1980s, Phil eventually settled on Milano's, a short walk from his rent-regulated apartment (for which he pays $750 a month, in a neighborhood where one-bedroom apartments can rent for more than $2,000 a month). At the time, down-and-out men who made their "home" on the streets and in the flophouses of the Bowery, the most notorious skid row in the city, frequented the bar and gave it its reputation. But new residents like Phil were also attracted to it. Artists, writers, filmmakers, musicians, and students living on the cheap in the gritty confines of downtown Manhattan became regular customers at what was one of the few bars in the area.

Phil has stopped in tonight before heading over to Chris's nearby studio loft, which Chris is renting out for a private party. Older than Phil, Chris is also a longtime regular at Milano's. He is a Vietnam veteran who started coming to the bar in the early 1980s, when he was working at a nearby women's shelter and living downtown. He normally rents out his loft space to dancers and artists but is finding it harder and harder to do so affordably due to rising costs. He rents it out for private parties and runs his own fundraising events to offset some of his losses. Phil, who often does odd jobs in the bar and for regulars (and is usually compensated in alcohol), agreed to help Chris clean up and decided to stop in for a drink first, as he usually does before going to a job.

But tonight's crowd and action is not the bar as he knows it. The customers are younger and unfamiliar to him. They are coupled off and in small groups. And they are dressed nicely for a night out, while Phil wears his usual paint-splattered pants, half-buttoned shirt, and raggedy shoes (he only wears his best outfit—a purple suit—once a year, when he flies home to see his family). No one is talking to anyone outside of their company, or to the bartenders for that matter, except Stevie and me. The music is loud. There are not any Bowery men here. Phil is out of his element, and he feels uncomfortable, which is why he usually avoids the nighttime crowd and leaves as the bar's happy hour winds down.

"The nighttime people are very different [from the daytime people]," he told me once. "They get very drunk, and they listen to music until they are unreasonable and dangerous."

"Dangerous?" I asked.

"Yeah, they'll fall on you or barf on you."

Nor is the neighborhood that Phil lives in and walked through to get here the same as he remembers it. From his building—which now houses mostly "young transients," as he calls them—he passes by modern apartments, storefronts filled with new bars, and crowds of revelers—many of whom are similar to those in Milano's at this late hour—going to and from various nightspots. Some of the Bowery's familiar population—homeless people, addicts—are also out on the street. But with all the action, lights, and noise, they are easy to miss despite the contrast they make. For Phil, Chris, and many other regular customers at Milano's, as well as for longtime residents, both inside the old bar and throughout downtown, life is different.

Phil finishes his drink (his usual vodka and grapefruit juice) and smokes a quick cigarette. As he prepares to leave, he asks me, "So will I see you tomorrow?"

"Yep, I'll be there."

"Great!" Phil nods and sets out into the lively night to Chris's loft. I leave shortly afterwards to go home and get a few hours of sleep before coming back to the bar for the Sunday morning routine.

—

The next day, at 9:30 a.m., I find myself back on Houston Street, walking from the subway towards the bar. Unlike a few hours ago, the street is now empty and quiet. The occasional car or taxi passes me, but no one is out walking, and the corner deli and gas station are the only businesses open. The closer I get to Milano's the more clearly I can hear the music from its jukebox piercing the street's rare silence. The door is locked and shaded, and the vertical blinds on the windows are drawn shut. I knock hard and wait. Rachel peaks through the blinds and her eyes bend into a smile. She unlocks the door and lets me in, locking it behind me.

Phil, Mary, Tiffany, and Casey are all sitting next to each other in the front of the bar, with drinks in front of them and lighted cigarettes resting in makeshift ashtrays fashioned out of bent coasters. Casey and Mary are in their late and early fifties, respectively, and Tiffany, among the youngest regulars, is in her mid-thirties. Phil and Tiffany are engrossed with the Sunday *New York Times* crossword puzzle. Casey listens in and offers the occasional guess. I order my customary morning drink, a Bloody Mary, and stand in the small open area between the bar and window that the bartenders use to get out from behind the bar.

Since it is so narrow and long, with a single large window, a windowed door, and old antique lamps, Milano's is an incredibly dark space. It is even more so on Sunday mornings when the blinds are drawn shut. Mornings and days at the bar are usually quiet, with no or little music playing. Since I could hear the jukebox from outside, I knew the regulars had company. Milano's has a reputation for being an "after-hours" bar, or a place that is open for select revelers after bars must legally stop selling alcohol (4 a.m. in New York City) or, in this case, before they can legally sell alcohol (noon on Sundays). Through the smoke and into the darkness, I see a group of eight people in the back of the bar, about twenty feet away from the smaller group in the front. Their hair is disheveled, and their nice designer clothes are a bit unkempt, with shirts untucked, buttons undone, and high heels off. I walk to the back and learn that they have been out all night, having gone to a nearby club. One of them knew about the after-hours policy at Milano's from working as a bartender in the industry, and he suggested to the group that they continue their night there.

At a few minutes before noon, Rachel starts preparing the bar to "open" to the public. She douses the coaster ashtrays with water and throws them in the garbage. She announces, "OK, last call for cigarettes, so smoke 'em if you got 'em. And anyone who is either asleep or showing sleeping symptoms has to wake up and cease doing any sleep-like activities or get out." Finally, she opens the blinds and unlocks the door. Ironically, the group of young revelers leaves when the bar opens, blinded by the daylight as they exit. Tiffany and Phil also leave, each to different construction jobs, and Casey and Mary depart soon afterwards. That leaves Rachel and me. With the jukebox now silent, we spend a few minutes chitchatting about music and gossiping about people in the bar. I eventually pick up the crossword puzzle and then start reading other sections of the newspaper, while Rachel keeps herself busy by wiping down dusty liquor bottles with a damp rag. I occasionally look up to gaze out the window, and two hours fly by before another customer walks in.

—

The above scenes from Milano's exemplify a microcosm of the tensions surrounding these transitions from old to new and from night to day in downtown neighborhoods. Like downtown itself, the bar is a space where multiple generations of customers and visitors coexist. As both individuals and collective groups, the people who go to Milano's and those who work there have constructed different meanings for the bar, and they each occupy and use it for different reasons. More importantly, the story of Milano's, its mix of people, and its place in the neighborhood through time provides a clear example of how the growth of downtown's nightlife scenes have shaped life within many of its community institutions.

Many scholars have recently examined contemporary commercial nightlife spaces like bars. Most prominent among them is David Grazian, who has looked at blues clubs in Chicago and hip nightspots in Philadelphia.[2] Based on his research, Grazian is skeptical that bars today provide the same sense of community as many believe they did in the past:

> It is as if the promise of the gated community as an urban fortress of solitude has been realized on an interpersonal level in the very spaces of public interaction once cherished for their ability to bring strangers together in moments of shared camaraderie, from colonial Philadelphia's City Tavern to McSorley's Old Ale House in New York.[3]

Here Grazian invokes the classic idea that bars are local community institutions, which he also dismisses as an urban myth: "most bars, taverns, and late-night cafés in U.S. cities have *never* really operated as 'social levelers,' and in the contemporary neoliberal metropolis it seems unlikely that we should expect any better from our urban entertainment districts anytime soon."[4] He cites racial and class barriers, normalized gender differences, and a general lack of inclusiveness surrounding local nightlife as reasons to be skeptical of a neighborhood bar's ability to integrate diverse strangers. Furthermore, his research in Philadelphia shows that the city's youth tend to reinforce their existing bonds within their own social circles when they go out with friends, rather than form bridges across social boundaries and networks. In other words, small groups of like-minded friends in the presence of but isolated from other groups, and not intermingled diverse communities, define socializing in today's urban night-spots. Tammy Anderson argues that while some examples of contemporary urban nightlife fit Grazian's claims, his cases point to a homogenized night-time environment that excludes the underground and subcultural ends of the nightlife spectrum.[5] Her research on electronic dance music, rave, and hip-hop scenes shows that there is far greater diversity among alternative nightlife cultures than in mainstream scenes in city centers.

As I will show in later chapters, new bars in downtown Manhattan reflect both Grazian's and Anderson's analyses. Some serve to reinforce existing social bonds among groups of friends, while others allow revelers to develop genuine bonds and feelings of community within nightlife subcultures. But how can we understand old bars like Milano's, with lengthy histories and a group of regulars, in the context of a new nightlife scene and a gentrified neighborhood that is upscaling? In examining Chicago blues clubs, Grazian finds that regulars, or active members of the local blues subculture such as musicians and serious enthusiasts, regard weeknight jam sessions as times when the clubs are "theirs" and they can experience authentic blues music. For them, the club is a "haven" that satisfies their ideals of authenticity in blues music. It is at the club that they develop a "nocturnal self" and go to live out their fantasies of being a member of an authentic blues community. The clubs and their jam sessions are "like therapy," where regulars get their "fix" of playing and hearing authentic music, as opposed to the popular songs heard at tourist destinations, and where they can escape from their mundane, everyday lives. Grazian argues that this group of regulars represents a "brotherhood of strangers," or a (mostly male) grouping that provides its members with social ties that are weak, yet friendly enough to give them the illusion that they are part of a strong community.

Old bars in the upscaling downtown tell a different story. My research at Milano's found that historically the bar was successful at integrating a diverse group of newcomers to the neighborhood into its culture, particularly during the start of the area's gentrification. Without such integration, the bar would likely have closed many years ago. In contrast to blues musicians and fans, its regulars do not go to the bar to experience authenticity, and not all of them go to feel that they are a part of a community or that the bar represents an escape from their everyday lives. Rather, they have made going to the neighborhood bar a routine aspect of their everyday lives in the neighborhood and city. Going to the bar is intertwined with their local identities and provides them with a regular opportunity to maintain friendships and strengthen local ties. At Milano's, they do not manufacture and put on a "nocturnal self" but embrace the freedom the bar gives them to act comfortably, apart from work and family.[6]

Situating Milano's within its surrounding context of an upscaling neighborhood and new nightlife scenes further complicates the picture of life inside the bar. Some of its regulars, namely homeless men from the nearby Bowery, are in peril of being evicted from their residences as the area becomes more and more upscale. However, they are also under threat of being excluded and even barred from Milano's, which is the last of the "Bowery bars" that would accept them, due to shifts in the bar's culture that limit and even prohibit certain behaviors that were once quite normal. Meanwhile, a new group of customers, who have not been integrated into the main group of regulars as other newcomers were in the past, goes to the bar with a different set of meanings and understandings about downtown and about life in a neighborhood bar. There are several old bars like Milano's still open in downtown Manhattan. By analyzing the bar as a local institution within a distinct urban context, we can begin to understand how public socializing in these neighborhoods has been shaped by their transformation into upscale destinations for nightlife.

A BRIEF HISTORY OF THE BOWERY

The name "Bowery" has always referred to a street, an area, and a state of mind. The oldest thoroughfare in Manhattan, it was originally a path for the Lenape, the Native American tribe that populated the islands that would make up New York City.[7] Today it is a mile-long (approximately fifteen blocks), four-lane, two-way, and mostly treeless street that runs from Chatham Square in the south to Cooper Square in the north in Lower Manhattan.[8] The name derives from the Dutch word *bouwerij*, which means "farm." In the 1600s and 1700s, the street and its environs consisted of farmland and country estates for the city's wealthy (including Peter Stuyvesant, the Dutch colony's last governor). In the early nineteenth century it boasted New York City's greatest collection of respectable theaters. Writing in 1888, the eminent New Yorker Walt Whitman reminisces about what, to him, was the "old Bowery" of the 1830s: "For the elderly New Yorker of today, perhaps, nothing were more likely to start up memories of his early manhood than the mention of the Bowery."[9] For Whitman's generation, the Bowery was the center of New York City's nightlife, theater, and performance cultures. Whitman laments that after 1840 (a period that corresponds to the influx of Irish, German, and other immigrants), the Bowery that he loved has given way to "cheap prices" and "vulgar programs."[10] Whitman's nostalgia romanticizes the nature of the Bowery during this period as the place where New York City's working-class culture took public form.

As the nineteenth century progressed and Broadway, a few blocks to the west, began attracting its own varieties of respectable theater and nightlife, the Bowery and its environs became an entertainment district for the dense collection of immigrants on the Lower East Side. The Bowery held dual parallel positions to the upstart Broadway that were geographical as well as cultural. It was the working-class entertainment and nightlife counterpart to Broadway's upper-class setting: "Broadway was rich (or looked it), highbrow (or affected it), and elegant (or tried to be). The Bowery, just to the east, was a world away in atmosphere—poor, but loud, free-spending, and lowbrow—a mob scene to defy Broadway's measured promenade."[11] On the Bowery, New York's Irish and German (and later Chinese, Jewish, and Italian) immigrants made their pleasures and vices manifest.[12] The Bowery's theaters, dancehalls, dime museums, brothels, and music saloons were the largest concentration of popular entertainment venues in New York City, where people formed and openly expressed working-class identities in the bars and basements and on the stages and streets.

Immigrants and the working class filled the Bowery and surrounding Lower East Side. The area became so notorious for its slum-like conditions (e.g., overpopulation, poverty, vice), bawdy amusements, and unusual cultures that the middle and upper classes, who had already migrated uptown, developed a strange fascination with it. New York City's respectable classes often went "slumming" on the Lower East Side, venturing there to witness firsthand the depravation at the bottom of the social ladder.[13] By going down to the Bowery, uptown people could temporarily step out of their own social worlds and even, unlike in their own neighborhoods, participate in its public vices, such as drunkenness, gambling, and sex, including homosexual behavior.[14] Despite its closeted nature, slumming served to reinforce the upper class's sense of moral superiority over the working classes.

By the late nineteenth century, the Bowery became a destination for the disconnected, disaffiliated, and transient. Modern processes in the United States such as industrialization, urbanization, and westward expansion created opportunities for itinerant workers in American cities. On the Bowery, inexpensive hotels (lodging houses or flophouses) and bars sprang up to serve these populations who joined existing and incoming immigrant groups. Hoboes, rootless American-born workers, emerged as admirable folk heroes. With feelings of wanderlust hoboes followed seasonal work and longed for experiences and encounters in new settings.[15] The life of the hobo reflected the pioneering American mindset of movement, ambition, and restlessness, and hoboes "were transformed by journalists, novelists, illustrators, and filmmakers into cultural types, figures of fear and fun."[16] This general image matches portrayals of the early-twentieth-century "Bowery man":

If among these men who filled the flophouses and the police stations there were some fleeing from life, they lost the race. For life on the Bowery caught up with them and was ever present in the crashing, blaring dance around them. Most of the Bowery Men in the first part of the twentieth century were men on the loose, men who needed a cheap place in which to rest, to drink, and to make love on the wing. . . . He was the stuff of legends.[17]

After a period of decline, symbolized by the construction of the Third Avenue El (elevated train) in 1878 that cast a shadowy pall over the street and betrayed its preexisting vice-ridden underbelly, the coming of the Great Depression solidified the Bowery's reputation for lowbrow and seedy forms of nightlife. Cheap bars and flophouses for homeless, down-and-out men replaced the lively working-class theaters and music halls, and the Bowery became the city's most notorious skid row. The Great Depression caused the Bowery's homeless population to swell. The disreputable bum, who was the pathological embodiment of unemployment and alcoholism, replaced the romantic image of the independent hobo, with his natural inclination towards movement and freedom. A more permanent population of homeless men replaced the transient wanderers and working-class groups. The Bowery's homeless population peaked during the Depression at 15,000 in 1930 and 20,000 in 1935, with other estimates ranging between 25,000 and 75,000 men sleeping there each night in more than one hundred lodging houses and on the streets.[18] Many writers documented conditions and people on the Bowery during this period, such as Joseph Mitchell, in the *New Yorker*, and E. B. White, in his classic 1948 essay, *Here Is New York*:

Walk the Bowery under the El at night, and all you feel is a sort of cold guilt. Touched for a dime, you try to drop the coin and not touch the hand, because the hand is dirty; you try to avoid the glance, because the glance accuses. This is not so much personal menace as universal—the cold menace of unresolved human suffering and poverty and the advanced stages of the disease alcoholism. On a summer night the drunks sleep in the open. The sidewalk is a free bed, and there are no lice. Pedestrians step along and over and around the still forms as though walking on a battlefield among the dead. In doorways, on the steps of the savings bank, the bums lie sleeping it off. Standing sentinel at each sleeper's head is the empty bottle from which he drained his release. Wedged in the crook of his arm is the paper bag containing his things. The glib barker on the sightseeing bus tells his passengers that this is the "street of lost souls," but the Bowery does not think of itself as lost; it meets its peculiar problem in its own way—plenty of gin mills, plenty of flophouses, plenty of indifference, and always, at the end of the line, Bellevue.[19]

In this passage we see the city's ongoing fascination with the Bowery. However, by midcentury, "slumming" had more or less ceased as the area sank into depression. The fearful "cold menace" bum replaced the admirable hobo as the neighborhood's chief character type. Visitors experienced the "street of lost souls" as an open-air exhibit from the safe confines of the tour bus rather than through direct interaction with its people and places. The more distant gaze of the tourist replaced the licentious play of the slumming visitor, while moral superiority was a foregone conclusion.

The classic skid row of the industrial city functioned on three important institutions: hotels and lodging houses (flophouses), charity missions (usually run by religious groups), and bars.[20] The first two provided shelter (albeit in tiny cubicles) and food (albeit at the cost of being preached to), respectively. But for men on the Bowery, the bar was the central refuge. Beyond their chief function of providing cheap alcohol, Bowery bars also provided homeless men with basic services, such as banking and mail, employment through social networking, and human contact. The Bowery bar was a private, but not exclusive or expensive, establishment where homeless men were accepted: "The bars of the Bowery are its life—source of its nourishment, meeting ground, forum—miraculous with the power of creating a world without sharp edges, a rounded, hazy, ludicrous, unimportant world."[21]

After World War II, relative economic prosperity, federal programs for returning veterans, welfare agency policy reform, and urban renewal programs decreased the number of homeless people on the Bowery from 13,675 in 1949 to 5,406 in 1966, with evidence of a national trend in the skid rows of cities across the country.[22] Furthermore, a change in New York City's housing code in 1955 prohibited the construction of new hotels with cubicle-size rooms, jeopardizing the expansion of inexpensive housing facilities.[23] But this reduction of skid row homeless populations, and the decline of classic skid rows in the United States in general, did not necessarily mean that there were fewer homeless people or that the conditions for the homeless had improved. A more likely explanation is that the homeless population on the Bowery as well as on other skid rows dispersed to other areas in the city, while overall conditions on the Bowery remained stable as the homeless men aged.[24]

When the section of the Third Avenue El train that ran above the Bowery was torn down in 1955, the street was exposed to sunlight for the first time in seventy-seven years. Although real estate actors saw the tearing down of elevated trains as beneficial for property values and investment and carried some hope that the area would improve, the decision proved to be merely cosmetic.[25] Restaurant and kitchen supply stores, located between Delancey and East Third Streets, and lighting stores, located south of and on Delancey Street, opened as the Bowery's more or less only new businesses. They managed to survive in the economically depressed area because of low commercial rents and because their clienteles did not consist of window shoppers, who avoided the Bowery.[26]

New York City's dire financial conditions of the 1970s struck downtown neighborhoods severely. Deindustrialization, suburbanization, urban disinvestment, and a citywide fiscal crisis caused property values to sink, crime rates to rise, and public drug activity and homelessness to flourish. In the face of rapidly depreciating real estate, landlords abandoned buildings and engaged in the "arson for profit" strategy of setting fire to their tenements to collect the insurance. Vacant and rubble-strewn lots and abandoned shells of buildings pockmarked the neighborhood. Large sections of downtown lacked the basic public services of functional streetlights and fire hydrants because the city government was broke.

Several additional factors during the 1970s and 1980s—the deinstitutionalization of the mentally ill, the crack epidemic, and the lack of low-cost housing, best represented by the sharp decrease in inexpensive single-room occupancy (SRO) hotels—increased New York City's homeless population.[27] While these processes affected all lower-class populations, they had the greatest impacts on African-American communities (especially the crack epidemic). Many of the new residents on the Bowery did not resemble the "old guard," who were mostly white alcoholics. By the 1980s Bowery bars were segregated according to new and old residents, divided along lines of race and type of drug addiction.[28] The new population, along with the depressed economic climate, furthered the Bowery's status as an area at the bottom and on the margins.

Popular nightlife on the Bowery and downtown continued in the postwar decades despite the area's decline. In the 1950s musicians cultivated avant-garde jazz and bebop in the East Village, and the Beat poets flocked to clubs there and in nearby Greenwich Village. In the 1960s artists had begun moving into the large loft spaces of SoHo, the neighborhood to the west of the Bowery, converting the deindustrialized area into an artists' colony.[29] Similarly, new residents during this period also came to live in the inexpensive, industrial lofts and cheap tenements on the Bowery. The street became home for many musicians and artists, including the feminist writer, activist, and filmmaker Kate Millett and the Beat author William Burroughs, with brief stints from the abstract expressionist Mark Rothko and the pop artist Roy Lichtenstein. In addition to these famous names were hundreds of more obscure artists who lived and worked on the Bowery. Downtown Manhattan was also a key location for the countercultural movements of the 1960s, such as Abbie Hoffman's Yippies and the well-known hippies. The performance venues of the Fillmore East and the bandshell in nearby Tompkins Square Park featured iconic rock 'n' roll acts like Jimi Hendrix, Neil Young, the Allman Brothers Band, and the Grateful Dead, all in their youthful prime. It was at this time that real estate actors soon followed these countercultural activities and renamed a large section of the Lower East Side the "East Village." The rebranding strategy capitalized on the popularity of Greenwich Village and dissociated the newly hip area from the immigrant environs, skid-row label, and impending slum-like conditions that characterized downtown.

New, young residents were moving to the dangerous and depressed, but edgy and inexpensive, area during this period, and sowing the earliest seeds of gentrification. Early gentrifiers not only went to the existing nighttime establishments such as the skid row bars, they also opened their own hangouts. The most famous example is CBGB. During the 1960s Hilly Kristal, CBGB's owner, performed and worked in bars in Greenwich Village. He decided to open his own bar to the east, which he found attractive because of its growing reputation as an arts and music scene and its cheap rents. In 1969, Kristal opened in the storefront of a Bowery flophouse, which Bowery men quickly inhabited, to his chagrin. In 1973, he built a stage and renamed it CBGB—Country Bluegrass Blues—for the type of music he wanted to present. Within two years, the bar blossomed into a space for the area's burgeoning subcultural activities. CBGB was a new outlet for expression through musical performance that launched the punk-rock movement and became home to such well-known acts as the Ramones, Patti Smith, Blondie, and the Talking Heads. Although a far cry from the musical genres and styles he intended for the club, Kristal emphasized originality in the acts he booked. CBGB represented a new cultural space as a symbol of edgy creativity that countered the symbols of devastation on the Bowery.[30]

CBGB and other spaces attracted people from around the city, the country, and the world who wanted to be part of the scene as producers, as consumers, and often as both. Musical acts that would achieve global success, such as Madonna and the Beastie Boys, got their starts in such downtown clubs. An arts scene also developed in the neighborhood in conjunction with the music scene. The million-dollar-selling artworks and high-profile commissions of artists such as Jean-Michel Basquiat (who lived in a loft in a building owned by his advocate, Andy Warhol, on Great Jones Street) and Keith Haring drew great national and international attention to downtown that led to an art gallery boom. Something new developed on the Bowery and downtown Manhattan alongside, but also separate from, its working-class, immigrant, ethnic, and homeless populations. These commercial and cultural developments set the scene for a radical transformation in the area.

ON THE NEW BOWERY

The upscale developments on the Bowery during the 2000s were the culmination of several decades of the dismantling of skid row as a supportive habitat for
a large homeless population, and of the increasing gentrification that followed
from the popularity of the art and music scenes and the buzz of downtown living.[31] In 1964 there were twenty-nine bars in the Bowery area, twenty-seven of
which catered to Bowery men.[32] By 1975 there were only seventeen. This number decreased over the next two decades, to seven bars in 1985 and only five
in 1995.[33] Although new ones were not built, the number of existing lodging-
house hotels during this period remained steady. However, mainly Chinese
immigrants came to fill them instead of Bowery men. Chinese businesses also
gradually moved into the area, particularly in the street's southern blocks, as
Chinatown expanded. Since 1995, several flophouses closed, including the Sun-
shine Hotel, where several Milano's regulars lived. Charity missions, meanwhile,
began offering drug and mental health programs to serve the new needy populations while scaling back their religious intent. In short, the three social institutions that sustained the Bowery's homeless population gradually disappeared or
shifted their focus and goals. Al's, the last "Bowery bar" on Bowery (the street)
that specifically catered to Bowery men, closed in 1993, and regulars and longtime residents expressed a degree of nostalgia over this "end of an era."[34]

A key example of the Bowery's development is the building that once stood
at street number 295. During the 1970s, the city government acquired a pleth-
ora of buildings and properties in downtown Manhattan when abandonments,
foreclosures, and arson-for-profit tactics were common.[35] Although the city
gradually sold off or developed many of these buildings and properties as the
area improved, the renewal project for 295 Bowery—where Kate Millett and
several artists were living at the time—was not announced until 1999, when the
street was on the verge of changing.[36] The building was razed to build Avalon
Chrystie Place, a large housing complex containing expensive apartments and
amenities such as bars, restaurants, fitness centers, lounges, and retail stores.[37]

For the most part, the longtime businesses of restaurant-supply and lighting stores remain, but many have closed or their owners sold their buildings
for large sums to new real estate interests. Featured in Scott Elliott's 2002 documentary *Slumming It: Myth and Culture on the Bowery* is Harold Mazer, a
longtime owner of a restaurant-supply store that opened on Bowery in 1946.
Comparing his early memories of the street to today, he says,

> Rents were cheap when I first came down here. That's why all these busi-
> nesses . . . flourished on the Bowery—rents were cheap, labor was cheap.

They're not cheap anymore. This store, if I wanted to rent it out I could get $8,000 to $10,000 a month! On the Bowery! It's unheard of.

A 2002 *New York Times* article also portrays this new era of development:

Say, kid, been down on the Bowery lately? You know, Skid Row, desolation street, the end of the road? It's a sad sight, what with all the designer bags, hipster cocktails and stylish, attractive young people. Look at them: on the corner of Bowery and East Second Street, luxury lofts with 11-foot ceilings and starting prices of $1.295 million. How about across the street, where a 13-story New York University dormitory has just opened, depositing hundreds of fresh-faced students on a strip where every parent once feared their kids would end up.[38]

Note how the author connects nightlife (specifically cocktails) to the Bowery's redevelopment, and also mentions the major institutional impact that New York University (NYU) has had on the Bowery and downtown Manhattan. Mostly located west of the neighborhood in Greenwich Village, NYU was already a presence in the area after it built two dorms near Cooper Square, just to the north of the Bowery, in the late 1980s, that fit a combined total of 1,400 undergraduate students.

New nightlife establishments have played an important role in repositioning the Bowery's status from the city's social and economic margins to the center through the reframing of its images and symbols. Since 1995 a dozen new bars opened on the Bowery, such as the popular Bowery Bar (it later changed its name to B Bar) and Mission Bar, named after the Bowery Mission.[39] A street notorious for alcohol abuse among homeless men now features bars whose names ironically borrow from the institutions that constituted the local support system for those men. There are currently nineteen nighttime establishments on the Bowery in the commercial storefronts of both new and old buildings. An example is DBGB, a restaurant owned by world-renowned French chef and restaurateur Daniel Boulud, which opened in June 2009 in the new Avalon Bowery building. As Samantha, a PR representative of Mr. Boulud, told me prior to its opening, "It's going to have class but not be too classy; French but not too French. He's good at following changes, and with all that is going on in the neighborhood and on the Bowery, with places opening and uptown people buying places downtown, he wants to add that uptown vibe on the Lower East Side." The interior design of the restaurant is a nod to the Bowery's past. As its Web site states:

At DBGB Kitchen and Bar the interiors . . . take their cue from the Bowery's history as New York City's industrial restaurant supply neighborhood. The tone, at once modern and old school, is set by floor to ceiling shelving stocked with the restaurant's own tools, tableware, and dry goods along with a partially open kitchen for all to see. Linking our restaurant to our culinary past is a collection of copper cookware. The braisers, roasting pans, stockpots, and countless other well worn pots and pans have a place of honor on the open shelving, with each piece in this veritable museum of copper cookware generously donated by a world renowned chef. Integrally colored concrete floors and custom furniture in dark stained cerused ash provide an utterly contemporary counterpoint.[40]

While the restaurant's theme selectively borrows from the area's industrial history and mixes it with touches from haute cuisine, the name (which stands for Daniel Boulud Good Burger) is a blatant wordplay on CBGB—which had been located one block north of the restaurant—that latches the restaurant onto the neighborhood's creative past.[41]

Such businesses cater to a middle- and upper-middle-class clientele, many of whom come from other neighborhoods, visit from outside the city, or have recently moved into the area. For these people, the Bowery is a destination for nightlife. Unlike when artists moved into the area, today's revelers have a large number of new nighttime establishments from which to choose. Although the remaining shelters and charitable organizations draw large homeless and substance-abusing populations, none of these new bars on the street cater to them, and revelers have even fewer interactions with the homeless than they once did.

By the mid-2000s many of the older performance venues in downtown Manhattan had closed, and even the stalwart CBGB gradually became more a tourist destination than a creative space. The name became a global brand for countercultural rock music, with its logo appearing on T-shirts, hats, and other memorabilia. Its full transformation into a brand was complete when the actual club closed in 2006 as a result of rising rents and its own rent arrears. A tribute store selling CBGB merchandise opened a few blocks away, while rumors swirled of the club relocating to Las Vegas.[42] In 2007, the commercial space that housed CBGB became a boutique store for the world-renowned men's clothing designer John Varvatos, whose style often evokes downtown rock 'n' roll cool.

Along with new businesses are new buildings for luxury living. Unlike most streets in downtown Manhattan, the zoning code on the Bowery legally permits the construction of high-rise buildings as of right. Larger in scale and uncharacteristic of the street's existing building stock, these new structures are intended to attract people with considerable financial means from outside of the area. A prominent example is the Bowery Hotel, a luxurious, seventeen-story boutique hotel that opened in 2007. Its standard rooms cost $450 per night ($750 per suite), entrees are $30 at its downstairs restaurant, Gemma, and cocktails are $12 at its Lobby Bar. Another example is the twenty-one-story glass-and-steel structure of the Cooper Square Hotel, another boutique hotel on the northern tip of Bowery that opened in 2008 and towers over East Fifth Street's brick tenements. Like other young entrepreneurs, the hotel's owners, Gregory Peck and Matthew Moss, are capitalizing on the neighborhood's status among urban youth as a cool destination for nightlife consumption. Along with minimum room rates of $400 per night, the hotel features an interior restaurant and bar on the first two floors, an outside garden on the ground floor, an exterior dining and lounge area on the second floor, and a basement lounge and club. These spaces combine to accommodate a total capacity of 731 people. With only 146 rooms in the hotel, they intentionally designed their nightlife spaces to be a destination for revelers—people who both live in and visit downtown—and not just amenities for their guests. And in addition to the Avalon complexes, several other tall glass-and-steel luxury condo and apartment buildings that bring new wealthy residents to the street are either finished or under construction.

Developers, hoteliers, nightlife and other new business owners, and the local media refer to the Bowery as a place of "downtown luxury" for savvy, cosmopolitan urbanites who would rather stay and live there than in the staid midtown and uptown areas of Manhattan, with their old businesses and corporate chain hotels and typical tourist spots. Once a laughable, oxymoronic description of downtown Manhattan, especially during its 1970s and 1980s period as a slum, "downtown luxury" has become an expansion of the "downtown cool" label that defined the area when it had a vibrant art and music scene.[43] Peck used "downtown luxury" to describe the Cooper Square Hotel to longtime residents in a community meeting, adding that his hotel will be "an old-world European-style hotel and highly service-focused."

Another important actor on Bowery during the 2000s was the New Museum, a museum for contemporary art from around the world, whose seven-story, state-of-the-art, $64 million building designed by the world-renowned Tokyo-based architectural firm Sanaa (Sejima and Nishizawa and Associates) opened in 2007. In discussing the choice of the Bowery location, the museum's director states, "It wasn't till we saw the empty parking lot on the Lower East Side that we knew we'd found the spot. . . . They [the museum's board] saw right away how consistent it was with the museum's mission. They loved the fact that the neighborhood was rough and the street was languishing."[44] Externally, the building's design of six smooth metal boxes stacked askew like children's blocks beg pedestrians' attention by contrasting with the surrounding low-rise brick tenements while evoking the grit and chaos of the industrial era that once characterized the area. Inside in a special exhibit, the museum acknowledges the artists who lived and worked on the Bowery and the Lower East Side and formed an arts scene. But as a whole, the museum's content focuses mostly on art and artists whose global scope far exceeds the street's history and neighborhood's boundaries. The New Museum has had the effect of making the Lower East Side a destination for the modern art world. Many new galleries have opened on the Bowery and in the area since the building project was announced to capitalize on the art consumers and aficionados that the museum attracts. Very few of the artists whose work is displayed in the museum or sold in the galleries, however, either make art or live on the Bowery or downtown Manhattan. Despite a significant presence of art spaces, then, the Bowery is not an arts "scene" in the productive or collaborative sense as the Lower East Side and East Village once were.

All of these new actors have added an upscale layer to the Bowery that represents a unique urban lifestyle of the postindustrial city. Young workers in the financial industry, elite members of the "creative class," and fun-seeking college students are choosing to live among the specialized amusements and entertainment districts that they seek out in the contemporary city.[45] This layer features the reorganization of industrial spaces and symbols within a framework of consumption, the accommodation of new residents in luxury housing, and the attraction of young professionals and students with such amenities as nighttime establishments. Along with nightlife and housing, the new "upscale downtown" also includes hotels and high-priced modern art. Social class, race, and ethnicity have historically divided downtown and uptown cultures, while a mutual fascination by the members of each have linked them together. Today their differences are transforming as downtown spaces such as those on the Bowery are unprecedentedly characterized by the exorbitant spending on leisure activities such as nightlife by the well-heeled middle and upper classes.

But there is a tension on the Bowery between the postindustrial present and the skid-row and slum past. For example, the Bowery Hotel is located directly across the street from a drug-treatment shelter and from the (ironically named) Whitehouse Hotel, originally a flophouse, which has been converted into a travelers' youth hostel with a small common area on the ground floor and rooms costing $30 per night. Although the Whitehouse advertises as a hostel to attract young visitors to the city, it, along with a few other active flophouses, still has Bowery men as residents. As these contrasting spaces face each other, revelers on their way to new bars, clubs, lounges, and restaurants walk past living signs of the street's past such as the homeless men who still congregate outside of the Bowery Mission. Located on Houston Street, a few blocks west of Bowery, Milano's remains as the last of the local bars in the area that caters to homeless or low-income men. But the inside of the bar has not been immune to the changes that have occurred outside its door.

BEING A REGULAR AT MILANO'S

The history of the people at Milano's and the bar's role in the neighborhood reflect this history of downtown. The Milano family opened Milano's in 1924, when the surrounding area was known as Little Italy.[46] Downtown's tenement apartments are small, and they often have poor ventilation and light. The neighborhood also lacks public spaces like piazzas that Italian immigrants would have been familiar with. Cramped indoors, they went to cafés and bars like Milano's for community socializing. As the decades passed and Italians gradually moved out of the neighborhood, the Bowery solidified into a skid row, and homeless men became the bar's clientele. Most of them were working-class laborers, some were war veterans, some had eventually "ended up" on the Bowery after experiencing ongoing employment issues and struggles with substance abuse, and some once had comfortable middle-class lives with families and steady jobs.[47] They became regulars, but their relationship with the bar and with each other did not reflect that Milano's was an establishment for a tight-knit community.

Longtime regulars describe Tommy Milano, the bar's owner during its period as a distinctly Bowery bar (1950s–1990s), as someone who was friendly with the Bowery men, but who was also cheap (exemplified by his habit of refilling half-empty wine bottles with water).[48] Here Chris recalls one of many stories that demonstrates Tommy's relationship with the men:

> Tommy Milano would give [the Bowery men] tabs and let them drink throughout the month, then they would pay him when they got their monthly checks. . . . One time when [Tommy] was standing in the window and saw one of the old bums coming across the street with his monthly check in his hand, on his way to the bar to pay off his tab and start a new one. Suddenly, he died by the curb of a heart attack. Tommy went outside to grab the check from his hands, but a cop happened to be standing there and he couldn't get it. All he cared about was the check! The guy just died. But he was probably a good customer, considering.

Such a story reflects the lack of communality that characterized the Bowery bar. It also confirms that the Bowery men used the bar as more than a drinking space. Along with cashing their checks at the bar (and promptly paying off their monthly tabs), the men regularly used it to receive mail and to sleep. "I had to step over two bodies on the way to the bathroom," says Denis, who purchased the bar from Tommy Milano in 1988 and owned it for twenty years, about the first time he stepped foot inside.

As skid row changed during the 1980s and 1990s and other Bowery bars closed, Milano's continued to cater to Bowery men and maintained its status as a social institution for the skid row way of life. Aware that the men had fewer and fewer alternatives in the neighborhood, the bar embraced them and tolerated their behaviors. "We got a kick out of the old guys," says Mary, a former Milano's bartender who moved to the Lower East Side in the mid-1980s, when she was in her early twenties. "But we also felt very sorry for them in a very human way. We wanted to take care of them and give them a place where they could feel welcome." Bartenders accommodated the men, and made it a point not to judge them. Part of Bowery bar culture was an early start to the day for drinking alcohol. Stephanie, a Milano's bartender during the 1990s, recalling her arrival at the bar on her first Saturday morning at 8 a.m. in 1993, says, "I was shocked to see a line of old men waiting patiently outside for the bar to open. They all had different stages of broken noses." "They were tremendous people, those old guys," says Denis. "They would never complain about anything. . . . They wanted a drink and that was it."

They did not want just *a* drink. The men were chronic alcoholics, and alcohol was their primary reason for going to the bar. Like the totalizing Bowery with its skid row infrastructure and rampant cases of addiction, Milano's supported the men's cyclical behaviors with cheap beer, whiskey, and wine. Denis describes a pattern that many of the men repeated:

> A lot of the guys, they had to stick it out. They'd get that check the first of the month, they'd be broke by the middle of the month, and then pack up and head to the "holy mountain," they'd call it. There was a retreat up in the Catskills, run by these Brothers for alcoholics and all those. They'd go there, dry out, and at the end of the month, they'd come in the door with the suitcase. They'd throw it right near the back there where the jukebox is now, and suitcases would be piled up there, and the suitcase wouldn't be touched until two weeks later when it'd be time to go up the mountain again. Just this continuous routine.[49]

Each story about the men carries with it the dual message that they were people with interesting personalities as well as sad lives. Their chronic drinking and poor health saddened the bartenders and made conditions difficult for them. Stephanie describes the actions of a Bowery regular:

One time he was drinking screwdrivers [vodka and orange juice] and got quite drunk. So I stopped putting vodka in them and just gave him the orange juice, to sober him up. But after a while I noticed that it wasn't working and he was getting drunker. I followed him into the bathroom and saw that he had a bottle of vodka hidden there.

The emotional difficulty of dealing with the Bowery men—who combined up-close interaction with the weight of alcoholism—was a major reason why some bartenders stopped working at the bar.

The Lower East Side and East Village began gentrifying in the 1980s as artists, writers, students, and musicians began moving into the neighborhood and its artistic scenes grew. Rents near skid row were cheap for young newcomers, and the existing local bars were convenient places for them to hang out. The newcomers from this time claim that the Bowery men at Milano's accepted them and allowed them to use the bar as a local gathering place. Neil, a regular now in his early forties, remembers first visiting Milano's with two of his friends (who also became regulars) when he was in college in the late 1980s:

We would be walking around SoHo, checking out some art galleries, and we came across the bar. Even though we were underage, they served us anyway. There were all these old guys in there. One of them, Victor, came up to us and talked to us about the bar. He told me not to do drugs in the bathroom. But they didn't bother us when they saw we were just there to drink. We liked it. It was a diverse place.

After graduating, the three of them lived in the neighborhood and maintained their connections to the bar, becoming regulars. For some of the young newcomers, the bar fulfilled an idea they had about neighborhood bars in New York City. It had unique characters and stories and an atmosphere that were only found in old bars. Jim, a regular in his early forties, recalls the first time he walked in:

Mary was working then and John Carmody [an old Bowery man] was sitting in his chair passed out with urine all around him. He did this all the time, but I didn't know that. When I came in I told Mary about the mess. She came around the bar and wiped it up, then asked me what I wanted to drink, unshaken! That's when I knew this was my kind of bar. I had never seen anything like that before. The attitude was just so raw. I was new to the city and it was so different.

For young newcomers who came at the start of the area's gentrification, Milano's fulfilled several desires: a convenient, local, and affordable public place where they could develop social ties with people in the neighborhood.

Now older, today's regulars maintain many of these motivations, which have been strengthened and solidified as the neighborhood has transformed beyond what they remember. First, they still appreciate its diversity. "You still see every type of person in there," says Mike, an artist and handyman who has been going to the bar since the late 1980s. "I like that. You see artists, musicians, lawyers, people from New York, people from other places, business people, guys in suits, guys in old clothes. And they're all in there, talking. You don't see that at most bars, especially not now." Second, many of the regulars still live and/or work within walking distance of the bar, making it convenient for them to go regularly. Third, many claim that the bar grants them the "freedom" to be themselves without judgment. Phil explains, "It's fundamentally nonjudgmental. Nobody cares how you smell or look or behave. There's a real freedom of expression there."[50]

Bartenders also do not judge customers' lives, habits, addictions, or behaviors. Instead, they establish themselves as authority figures with problematic customers and avoid emotional entanglements. Leslie discusses how she came to this realization:

> When you cut somebody off, if you don't judge them they feel that. I used to get angry, because I would feel put upon. I would feel angry at them for making me cut them off and them not being responsible enough to stop and making me throw them out. So now I don't see it that way anymore and so it makes it a lot easier. I just say, "This is just the way they are and who they are, and I'm doing them a favor and it's out of love." And that's how I try to do it with everybody, because nobody wants to be judged, especially someone who's drunk and sensitive and needy. The last thing they need is someone to look at them like they're crap.

By refraining from judgment, bartenders maintain social distance between themselves and their customers. This distance also helps them balance their own emotional needs with those of regulars, who often demonstrate a high level of neediness.[51]

Some regulars use the classic term "second home" to describe what the bar means to them and to explain why they go regularly.[52] In doing so, they place the bar in the context of the surrounding nightlife scene, in which many old bars have closed while new ones do not serve as adequate replacements. Alex began going to Milano's after moving to the East Village in the early 1990s, lured there at a young age from his working-class neighborhood in Queens by its punk and hard-core rock scene. As the years have passed, recording music and playing live have become more hobbies than moneymaking or career pursuits for him. But the local nightlife spaces that provided the infrastructure for the neighborhood's music scene to grow remain important to him:[53]

> I lost all my rock clubs this year—CBGB, Continental. I still go to the Continental to drink, but it's not the same. I played over at Delancey, and that new place, Midway. It has a stage like this [indicates a few inches with his thumb and forefinger]. It sucks. I still have Arlene's Grocery, which has a good stage, but I used to be able to go to CBGB and play that night. Now this is it. This is basically my only bar. My home.

Although Milano's is not a performance venue, for Alex, as for many regulars, the bar has been a fundamental element of his life in the neighborhood. The most important reason the regulars give for going to the bar frequently is the personal social relationships they have formed with its people over the years. But these relationships vary considerably in strength and type, and regulars refer to specific people rather than a collective when discussing their relationships. Older regulars recall fondly the old-timers they encountered when they first started going to the bar. They appreciated listening to the stories the old-timers would tell them, even when they heard the same ones again and again and knew most of them were untrue anyway. When I started going to Milano's, in 2004, many of those old-timers had already passed away. When some of the longtime Bowery men died, Denis started putting up framed pictures of them in the front of the bar as a form of remembrance. Some of the regulars had formed strong attachments to the old-timers, and today they reflect on their relationships.

One day as we are sitting in the front of the bar, Mary asks if she could borrow my copy of the *Village Voice*. She wants to look up some plays that she wants to tell her students to see (she teaches at a local college). Mary reads a blurb about the smoking ban in Ireland and the one that passed recently in New York. I mention hearing that the United Kingdom is going to test out a smoking ban in Northern Ireland. Magdalene, today's bartender, who is from Northern Ireland, is elated at the notion.

"Really! I love the idea of smoking bans. Especially in Northern Ireland, the bars are all small and there's poor ventilation and the smoke just cuts your eyes out. I wish they would do it so that my mother and friends quit."

"What did you think about New York's smoking ban?" I ask.

"I love it. The smoke used to bother me, and it might get my friends to quit. Then again, I don't like that the government is telling people that they can't smoke in bars. And it isn't necessary in some places where they have good ventilation."

As Magdalene debates with herself, I notice that Mary has been quiet. I look over and see that she has been staring up at one of the framed photos sitting on a mini-fridge and resting against the wall behind the bar. She has a small smile on her face, and when she hears that we are done with our conversation, asks, "Magdalene, could you hand me Jerry's picture?" Magdalene reaches up and takes it down for her. The photo is a close-up picture of an older man with a mustache and a balding round head.

"Who is he?" I ask.

"Jerry Romero, one of the boys," she says while gesturing to the back of the bar with a wave of her hand, where the Bowery men usually sit. "He was a regular who died a few years back. He always supported me and my writing, and encouraged me to do something with it. He'd be happy to know that I'm teaching at the collegiate level. I'm sure he's happy when he looks down at me."

I nod and smile at her as she continues to stare. She then asks, to herself, "Can I get Jerry to look at me?"

In the photo Jerry is looking away from the camera, to his side, and he appears to be in the middle of speaking. Mary moves the frame around to the side of her head to make it seem like he is looking back at her, and perhaps also speaking to her. She does not hold it there long, and a few seconds later she hands the frame back to Magdalene and goes back to reading the *Village Voice*.

I occasionally heard a regular tell a story about a Bowery man who either is now deceased or simply stopped coming to the bar. But strong emotional sentiments and attachments such as those demonstrated by Mary are case by case; they are not universal. When I asked other longtime regulars of their feelings for Jerry, I got a mixture of responses: some barely remembered him, some remembered him but not clearly , some remembered him as a nice guy, and some did not remember him fondly. I asked Phil once about how people at the bar remember dead Bowery men. "I find it particularly odd that some people's deaths are regarded as important and some not. Their deaths are important to me, but I'll be dead too one day and nobody'll care." In general, some regulars had meaningful relationships with some of the Bowery men, some had weak ones, and some had no real relationships at all. This basic variation also describes most of the relationships between regulars that exist in the bar.

By the 2000s, after most Bowery men had either died or disappeared, regulars already had formed their own relationships with each other and with the bartenders. I often asked regulars how they defined a "regular" customer, and I usually got a wide range of answers. They often began by naming the number of times per week one should go to the bar or how long one should stay. I would ask them how many regulars there were and whom they would include on their list, and their answers always varied (although they always included themselves and their closest friends in the bar on it). Based on my fieldwork I identify two types of regulars: regulars of the bar and regulars of certain bartenders. I find that the main criterion for being a regular is far more qualitative than quantitative; it entails having a relationship with people at the bar.

Being a regular of the bar means you know a few other customers and usually a few of the bartenders. Regulars generally stick to patterns of when they go to the bar. But those who are regulars of the bar know they can go almost any time and either know another customer or know the bartender. "You know me," says Chris, "I don't really have a set time every week when I come here. I don't really care who's here when I'm here. I'll know someone. I'll at least know Magdalene or whoever's working." These regulars have made going to Milano's a meaningful routine in their lives. Some customers, though, are regarded by regulars and bartenders as "irregular" regulars, since they no longer came to the bar frequently but had already established relationships with people and were thereby greeted warmly when they came in.[54] Regulars and bartenders do not hold grudges against irregular regulars for not coming to the bar often enough. "Well, you know, people's lives change," says Fran. "People get married, or have kids, or move back home, or move altogether, or switch jobs and change their lives." Some regulars maintain friendships with other regulars and with bartenders outside the bar, while for others relationships with people are purely contextual and do not extend beyond the bar's doors. Regulars who are musicians sometimes play music together, while others who work in construction and home renovation jobs often hire each other for projects they have. "Yeah, some are my friends," says Neil. "We sometimes go to the movies and stuff, or to [music] shows. But most people, not really. I just see them at the bar and occasionally around the neighborhood. But that's all." Overall there are no obligations to stretch contextual relationships in the bar into friendships outside it, or to even discuss one's personal life outside the bar with other regulars.

Some regulars, however, will usually only go to the bar when certain bartenders are working. Their routine could be such that they could only go to the bar at certain times, or they have simply developed a relationship with a particular bartender and choose to go when she is working. Since they see both types of regular, bartenders are aware of these distinctions. As Amber explains:

> [Someone] could be a regular and [as the bartender you won't] really engage that much with them. They could be a regular of the bar, or they could be your regular. The Friday after work guys, they're regulars of the bar. They're going to go to that fucking bar. I don't care if Attila the Hun's behind the bar.

They're going to go to that bar and sit in those seats no matter what. They're not there for me. They will sit there and that's their bar, so they will always come to that bar.

Amber, however, who works weekend nights, has her own regulars who do not always know other bartenders or other regular customers who go to the bar during the day. These customers are also "irregular regulars." Jeff is a retired fireman in his mid-fifties. Originally from the Bronx, he now lives upstate. He used to work at a fire station around the corner from the bar, which is how he got introduced to it. "I used to come in after my shift. It was back when there were Bowery men and Italian men who still lived with their mothers." Despite the distance, he still makes a point of traveling downtown a couple times a month, mostly to visit Magdalene on Saturdays, when she works. He says there are no neighborhood bars like Milano's where he lives. "People in my town are suburban," says Jeff. "They don't really go out to the bar to sit and have a drink. Instead they have you over at their homes, which I'm not really into." While he never lived in the neighborhood, Jeff formed strong enough attachments with people at the bar, particularly the bartender, to make it an important place for him to routinely visit, even from a great distance.

Regulars distinguish themselves from other customers in the bar in several ways. First, they tend to congregate towards the front of the bar, near the door, the window, the space where the bartender exits from behind the bar, and the bartender's chair in the corner. This area features the most daylight in the bar, and the space and bartender's chair provide regulars with the opportunity to face one another in a small group without turning their heads or moving their chairs. The bartender only allows certain regulars to congregate in these spaces, which in most bars are off limits to customers. Second, regulars leave their money on the bar top, sitting next to their drinks or tucked under a coaster, and bartenders take the requisite amount from the pile when a drink gets ordered. Regulars do so when they use the restroom or go outside to smoke, trusting that other regulars and the bartender are watching it. Bartenders are also more likely to give regulars a buyback, or a drink on the house, earlier in their ordering (the general industry standard for bars that allow the practice is every fourth drink; Milano's bartenders will often buy regulars' first or second) and more often (sometimes every two or three drinks). Bartenders factor their relationships with regulars into their buyback decisions. Leslie explains:

There are people that need it. In order to avoid them getting all pissy-faced, you get them their second one so they feel special, because there are people that need that. Bill needs the second or first drink bought, because then his smile lights up like a little child. "Thank you, sweetie!" But if you wait until the fourth one, he's hurt. And he buys the same amount. And I just know he's going to be there anyway so I just fucking get it out of the way.

In addition to buybacks, in a select few cases (discussed in the following section) the bar allows regulars to run long-term tabs that they need not settle before leaving the bar. Finally, some regulars run errands and do chores for the bartenders, such as changing beer kegs in the basement, retrieving ice from the machine in the back, taking out garbage bags, and purchasing limes and lemons from the corner store (and bartenders buy them drinks for doing so). Each of these behaviors indicates regularity and familiarity that revolve around the consumption of alcohol.

But the regulars at Milano's do not resemble an exclusive club. Neither bartenders nor regulars treat strangers in a manner that is unfriendly, and one may become a regular fairly easily through repeated visits and by establishing a rapport with a bartender or some regulars. And other than the above distinguishing characteristics, being a regular confers few privileges in the bar. The bartender's chair is off limits to strangers, but strangers can and do sit in the front of the bar, without hassle, if they arrive first. Bartenders will not buy a stranger's first drink, but they will buy their third or fourth, provided the customer is tipping them. There are three times of the year when Denis maintains special community-oriented parties: catered trays of hot food on Thanksgiving and St. Patrick's Day, and for a holiday party around Christmas, with a two-hour open bar period for the latter two days. They are not advertised and word spreads among regulars of their occurrence. Regulars maintain their social order of interpersonal relationships during these events, and despite their appearance of being for members only, strangers who happen to be in the bar at those times may partake.

In sum, during the 1980s and 1990s, Milano's transformed from being solely a Bowery bar for Bowery men to being a local bar for people who lived and worked in the gentrifying neighborhood. Newcomers were successfully integrated into the bar culture when it was a place for Bowery men, in the sense that the latter accepted them, and they formed their own relationships with people at the bar, most often with each other. The regulars at the bar do not represent either a tight-knit community or a "brotherhood of strangers" (for reasons not the least of which being that many of them are women). Instead, the group features a mixture of relationships—friendships, contextualized friendships, acquaintanceships, and working partnerships—that vary in strength for each regular and in importance in their lives. Regulars also do not put on new "nocturnal selves" when they enter Milano's, and in few cases do their lives revolve around the bar. Going to the bar and seeing people they know are part of their daily routines and intertwined with their life in the neighborhood.

THE DIVE AND THE SALOON

"Where else in this city can you get a drink at eight in the morning?!" asks Steve in a loud voice, his arms raised and spread widely like antennae. We are sitting next to each other early on a Sunday morning in the back of the bar and have been talking a bit about its history. Mostly, though, he is telling me about his night out last night while his friend is passed out next to him with his head on the bar and his hand still wrapped around his drink. As shown in this chapter's opening vignette, Sunday mornings are times when some regulars congregate and reaffirm that they think of the bar as the living room of their "second home": they read the newspaper, work on the crossword puzzle, drink coffee (with and without whiskey) and other morning cocktails, and watch television. The door is locked and shades drawn, since the practice is illegal, and the mornings are generally quiet.

Often, though, a new, younger set of customers joins them. They are usually in their twenties, come from different neighborhoods in the city, arrive at the bar already intoxicated, and are looking to extend their Saturday night experiences of alcohol and drug consumption. Steve, for example, is twenty-nine and lives on the Upper West Side. He tells me that last night, while he and friends were out at a nearby bar, they heard from a bartender who is a friend of a Milano's bartender that Milano's is open on Sunday mornings. They went to another bar, where they stayed until an hour past last call, around 5 a.m. At that point, only Steve and his currently passed-out friend were still game to continue the evening, so they went to a nearby twenty-four-hour diner for some breakfast and more alcohol before finally heading over to Milano's at 7:30.

Steve asks me if I am a regular, and I tell him that I am, in a way. I explain my project, and he nods along while taking frequent sips from his bottle of Bud. He says that he has been to Milano's a few times before, but only on Thursday, Friday, and Saturday nights when he is in the neighborhood. Sometimes he has made the bar his sole destination, but usually it is his first stop to meet friends for a night out, or the last stop for one more drink before going home. I ask him what he likes most about the bar, and he says the decor, especially the scores of old photos of customers that line the walls, protected behind Plexiglas. In his hazy and inebriated state, Steve then tries to explain that he feels when he is in bars like Milano's that he does not have to be himself. Yes, he says, he is still usually with his friends, but the social situation and context are unlike the types of bars he normally goes to. He does not elaborate much on this point, and takes the end of his bottle as his cue to wake up his friend and leave. I return to the front, where the group is watching an old *Twilight Zone* rerun and working on the crossword puzzle.

In examining new nightlife scenes in the United Kingdom, Paul Chatterton and Robert Hollands describe some bars as "residual" nighttime consumption spaces, left over from an older industrial era and unusual in the contemporary postindustrial context.[55] However, amid the new, sleek nightspots, older bars develop a reputation for possessing grittiness and character that clashes with the glamour and modern casualness of their surrounding environment. The growth of new nightlife scenes such as those in gentrified neighborhoods like downtown Manhattan have created a new type of nighttime establishment: the dive bar. Some of the cultural holdover from the city's industrial era that can be found in the dive bars of the popular imagination includes inexpensive brands of beer and whiskey that reflect working-class drinking culture (e.g., Pabst Blue Ribbon beer, or PBR), jukeboxes filled with artists and songs that are commonly associated with smoky, boozy environments (e.g., Johnny Cash, Willie Nelson), bathrooms that are in poor condition, and even actual old-timers.[56] A bar becomes a dive in the contemporary city if it survives beyond this period, in the sense that it preserves certain physical and social conditions that accurately symbolize a lost era. In New York City, local lifestyle media sources—*New York*, *Time Out New York*, and the *Village Voice*, as well as numerous blogs and Web sites that review and rank nightlife venues—regularly feature dive bars in articles and roundups. Dive bars have even found a place in travel guides that encourage visitors to discover places that are "off the beaten path." These sources measure the quality of dive bars and devise "rules" for what constitutes a dive bar based on how many standards of grit and authenticity they meet. As one states, "If you'd be scared to take your parents there, it's a dive," "[I]f there's a toothless old geezer talking about some guy he offed in the '50s, it's a dive," and "In a real dive, you don't feel weird ordering a drink ten minutes after you ordered the previous one."[57] Dive bars have an air of seediness and debauchery, with just enough dereliction and sadness to make them interesting without being truly scary or depressing. And dive bars decline in status if they commodify their grit, such as by selling hats and T-shirts aimed at tourists, and adopt "non-dive-y" elements, such as trendy drinks.[58] Steve did not use the term "dive bar" to describe Milano's, but some other young revelers whom I met did.

As young revelers, newcomers often exhibit behaviors that betray their status. One Saturday night a young man and three young women, all nicely dressed, walk into the bar and head straight to the back. The three women take a seat at one of the tables while the man goes to the bar to order. Rachel, one of tonight's two bartenders, greets him.

"I'm going to need to see everyone's ID," she says.

The man turns back, collects their drivers' licenses, and brings them to the bar.

"No, I need to see them with all their IDs."

"Why?"

"A fake ID could easily have a different picture, so I have to see them with their IDs to match them up."

"You shouldn't be so uptight!" he says, as he motions to his group that they are leaving.

As they are leaving, one of the women says to Rachel, "I thought this bar was cool!"

Rachel gives a fake smile back at her and waves at them.

"You know that just means that the girls were underage," I say after they leave.

"Yeah, probably only one of them was underage, and they thought they would get away with it."

Meanwhile, Rachel and I both then notice Leslie at the other end of the bar staring blankly at two well-dressed women as they talk to each other. After a few minutes, she walks to our end of the bar to prepare their drinks (two vodka tonics).

"Ugh, these two are taking forever," she says.

Rachel puts on an exaggerated ditzy-sounding voice and says, "'Oh, what do you want?' 'Oh, I don't know.' 'What do you have?' 'Do you have 1–5-1?' 'I don't know what I'm in the mood for.' 'So, is this bar old?'"

"Yes! Exactly! And one of them did ask me if this bar was old!"

As they chat, a young man standing at the end of the bar waves his arm at Rachel. She walks down to him.

"OK, don't do that. Don't wave at me. I can see you. What would you like?"

After serving the two women, Leslie walks over to three young men who just came in and took seats towards the front.

"We'd like three PBRs, please," says one.

"I'm sorry, we don't have it anymore."

They groan and look at each other.

"Hey, I'm sorry, don't shoot the messenger!" replies Leslie.

They ask her what beer she has in bottles, and as she runs off the list, they stop her at Red Stripe.

"I knew you would pick Red Stripe," she says. "People that have PBR generally go for Red Stripe."

Since downtown Manhattan has become a destination for nightlife for young revelers from around the city, and since Milano's represents a unique setting within the surrounding scene, it attracts a greater amount of anonymous customers than it did before. Their ordering style and drink preferences, not to mention their behavior and clothing, create a new and different vibe in the bar. When dealing with these customers, bartenders use "categoric knowing," based on a tiny amount of information that shapes their attitudes and interactions with them.[59] Customers who sneak into the back and have someone order for them may be underage. Customers who are dressed a certain way may act out of their element. Customers who wave money at them must be taught that such behavior is inappropriate. And customers who want a cheap beer they do not serve will probably be satisfied with another cheap alternative. Some newcomers return to the bar often enough to get to know some of the regulars and bartenders, but the vast majority do not. Overall their presence constructs the social environment of a nightspot rather than a local bar.

Unlike new customers, regular customers and bartenders do not consider Milano's to be a dive bar. As mentioned, regulars consider it to be simply a neighborhood bar—a local place that lacks pretension. Neil contrasts the bar with several common images of dive bars, "A dive bar smells like piss, nasty floors. It's not [a dive bar]. It's a comfortable spot; it doesn't smell like piss, the people are very friendly. Dive bars are usually just nasty." Some regulars who encounter strangers at the bar engage in conversations with them, sometimes enough to engage in treating (i.e., buying each other drinks). Usually, though, regulars sit among themselves towards the front and wait and see if someone demonstrates a willingness to develop relationships. Phil provides a common attitude that regulars have towards newcomers:

> Bars are doing the right things. People die and people move and new people have to come, and that's just the way it is. And sometimes that's painful because it takes [new people] a while to learn the culture of the place. But if they become regulars they will learn the culture; if they don't they won't.

Bowery men, meanwhile, refer to Milano's as a saloon and do not concern themselves with the younger clientele. They tend to sit in the back of the bar, either chat with each other or any regulars who know them, and leave before the bar gets crowded. Bartenders, who encounter and interact with the younger clientele the most, have their own interpretation of the new wave of customers that is influenced by the bar's dive-bar classification:

> "You know my 'Tom Waits theory'?" asks Leslie.[60]
> "What's the 'Tom Waits theory'?" I reply.

"I have this theory of these guys. They'll walk in the door, and they're kind of hipsters. They're about twenty-four years old, twenty-five years old, and they'll walk in the bar, and they got a little bit of an attitude, and they sit in the back, usually, or they might sit at the end of the bar, but they're not really chatty. They order whiskey and Bud, and they'll say things like, 'Give me the cheapest shit beer you have,' and I say, 'Whoa, rock-star middle-class boy, okay, you slumming it?' So, okay, 'Do you have PBR in a can?' And I'm like, Oh god, I know it's coming, I know. I'll turn to the regular next to me and go, 'They're going to the jukebox, they're going to play Tom Waits, they're going to play Johnny Cash, they're going to play Nina Simone, and they're going to play Willie Nelson, amongst others. Maybe the Velvet Underground, you know? Oh, and the Pogues, too. And they're going to get this kind of nihilistic, barroom, country-type feeling."

"Like 'Whiskey River'?"

"Yeah, 'Whiskey River,' but the *real* barflies will play Tom Waits. And they'll like get their little drink, their bourbon and their Budweiser, because they'll be bummed that we don't have PBR in a can, so they'll settle for Bud because it's the worst beer we have. It's just this idea of what a bar is, and that's so boring and limited. What's interesting about Milano's is someone plays funk, or some fucked-up disco song, and this sixty-year-old tourist is dancing and someone else down the bar is making out, and that's what's interesting—when you go against the sort of natural downward pull of the bar. I want to say to them, 'It's not romantic and cool to watch someone drink themselves to death. There's nothing sexy, there's nothing "authentic" about it; it's just sad, and boring, and sad. And there's nothing glamorous about it.'"

Perhaps bartenders come across such customers, but in my fieldwork I never met someone who admitted that they came to the bar because old alcoholic men drank there. Leslie's point, however, reflects her attitude towards the overall perspective that young revelers have about the bar and how it satisfies an inaccurate image they have about old neighborhood dives.

The new classification of Milano's as a dive bar that provides young revelers with a unique place for casual socializing creates a clear contrast between the day and night. The memories of a line of Bowery men waiting on the sidewalk early in the morning for a bar to open, and of a packed daytime bar, are a far cry from the deserted street and empty bar that I regularly encountered in the mornings and during the day. When he bought the bar, Denis originally intended to leave it alone. He was a regular customer and knew the Bowery men who went there. But he also recognized that the neighborhood was changing:

The great thing about that time was that you had great business during the day from the old-timers from the Bowery, and then you had a younger crowd at nighttime. It was all day, you know. Whereas now, day business has gone down quite a bit, but the night business has picked up a lot. So it balances out. It used to be the other way.

Today the bar is lucky to get more than a handful of customers during the day. As happy hour approaches in the late afternoon, regulars gradually start coming in as they get off work. By night, most of them have left as the younger crowd comes in. Bartenders are most aware of this dichotomy, which shapes their work experiences at the bar. Kristin, a nighttime bartender in her early thirties, describes her clientele:

When I start my shift, it's the happy-hour crowd. So, it's either people that don't work and want to drink cheaply for a couple of hours, or people that are getting off work. So all those ones are out by like 8, or 8:30. My nighttime crowd kind of varies. My late-night crowd are all musicians and a lot of bartenders. Before that it's young people, mostly young people around thirty.

Amber, however, works daytime and nighttime hours. For workers whose income depends on tips, having fewer customers means less pay. But at Milano's, the daytime customers are not just fewer in number but also higher in maintenance. They are often Bowery men or regulars who are alcoholics. Behind the bar, sometimes with no one else to serve or talk to, bartenders are stuck having to talk to these customers, hear about their problems, and witness their addictions. Amber contrasts the two sets of customers:

Some of the old-time regulars you dread, because these are people that are regular regulars. These are people that can't seem to function outside the bar. The nighttime is more like a hustle, you know? People are going out, they're looking good, they have money. They stop in, then go off to their next destination. So that's good, in a way.

Leslie, who only works at night, refuses to work during the day for these very reasons. She prefers the quick pace and youthful energy of the night to the slow drag and old sadness of the day.

With more nighttime and weekend customers, as well as new residents and developments—new residential buildings and new businesses—in the neighborhood, Denis gradually changed the products that the bar offered. He knew he not only had to pay the escalating rent, but he also had to compete with new bars that were opening up and displacing the Bowery men that had been the bar's main clientele.

> "At first, the only thing we changed was the beer. When I took over there were six taps, all Schlitz. And it wasn't too cold, either."
> "That's what all those guys drank though, was it? The cheap beer?"
> "That was it. I said to Tom Milano, 'Why didn't you put Guinness in here?' He said, 'That's $100 a keg. How am I going to sell it?' He was buying Schlitz for $10 a keg. He was buying three barrels and he'd get one free, on top of that. We put in Guinness, Bass, Harp, some others."

The greater selection beyond cheap beer signaled to customers that the bar was not just a place for homeless men. Denis also added an Internet jukebox and hired young women instead of the traditional men to bartend to attract younger customers.[61] Over time, he began discouraging certain behaviors and ending policies that were once normal at the bar, such as sleeping and keeping long-term bar tabs, for the sake of the business. Some Bowery regulars who had been going to the bar for many years and who relied on it for their basic needs and complex addictions were barred because of their inappropriate behavior.

Tugboat has been going to Milano's for more than thirty years. He is in his late fifties, and he always wears old jeans, work boots, a button-down shirt, lightly tinted sunglasses, a military cap, and several days' worth of stubble. After serving in Vietnam as a marine, he became a dockworker, hence his name. He spent a couple of years in Virginia, where he still works in seasonal construction, and in Florida with his cousin (he claims he lost the keys to their place), and he is now back living in New York. Today he is sporadically employed and housed, sometimes staying in one of the Bowery's remaining flophouses, sometimes sleeping out on the street, and sometimes staying "somewhere in Brooklyn."[62] He splits his days between Spring Lounge (also known as Shark Bar, another old neighborhood bar a few blocks away) in the mornings and Milano's in the afternoons. One day he tells me about the code of tipping. "My mother always told me not to tip the owner, because anything you buy goes right to him anyway. But when I'm at the Spring Lounge and one of the owners is bartending—they have three of them—I always tip him. I always tip Denis, and Denis always gives me the first drink on the bar. But Denis always gives all of the tips to the bartender that comes in next."

Some regulars and bartenders have known Tugboat for many years. On the first of the month, when he receives his government checks that he cashes at the bar—for disability, welfare, and military service—he pays down his bar tab and spends the next two weeks buying people drinks. Some regulars express frustration that he butts in on their conversations, and that he uses buying drinks as a justification for entangling them in a conversation with him that they do not want to have. Tugboat usually enters the bar drunk from Spring Lounge, and proceeds to drink more until he passes out in his chair. The two daytime bartenders, Magdalene and Amber, regularly cut him off and serve him a glass of water or ginger ale, although at that point he is too out of it to even take a sip. A bar can get in trouble by the police if they find someone who is clearly intoxicated sleeping inside, so the bartenders and regulars constantly try to wake Tugboat up when he nods off ("Tugboat, you're sleeping." "What? No I'm not!" goes the refrain). Eventually they call him a cab. "I would prefer if that man never even walked in the bar again," says Amber. "He always stumbles around and defecates and urinates on himself and spits and drools and yells at other customers. It's too much maintenance, emotionally. And for the other customers, you constantly feel like you have to apologize for him to the other customers so they don't leave." One time, she sat and quietly counted the number of customers who left either after being confronted by Tugboat or immediately after entering the bar and noticing his presence.

Tugboat walks in the bar late in the morning on a weekday in April while Amber is working. He is drunk and delirious from lack of sleep, food, and water; smelling from days of not bathing and not changing his clothes; and slurring his speech. He sloppily plops himself down on the first barstool. Knowing she will not serve him and not wanting to deal with his behavior, Amber tells him he has to leave. Tugboat does not put up a defense, but he does not go immediately either. After ten minutes of repeating her demand more and more forcefully, he goes. Tugboat returns the following day in a similar state of inebriation, exhaustion, and disorientation. Returning to his seat from the restroom, Tugboat loses his balance and falls, hitting his head on the bar, which cuts him and knocks him out for a minute or so. A few regulars present try to revive him, while one calls an ambulance. In the time it takes for the paramedics to arrive, he wakes up in as much control as he was before he passed out, and they take him to the hospital. (As Stephanie, one of the former bartenders from the 1990s who knew Tugboat back then, tells me, he sometimes purposefully put himself in this state so that he could spend a night being cared for in a hospital bed.) When Denis hears about this incident after many months of complaints, he immediately bans him. A few days later, after being released from the hospital, Tugboat walks back in the bar early in the morning. Denis, who is opening the bar, scolds him and kicks him out, telling him he is not allowed to return. Denis's son, James, who was also in the bar, says later that he never saw his father as angry as when he kicked Tugboat out. I never saw him again after that.

Tugboat's behaviors of sleeping in the bar, bothering other customers, and achieving intense levels inebriation and self-destruction were once normal aspects of life in the Bowery bar, the saloon for the down-and-out. Today Milano's has a lot of attractive competition in the surrounding nightlife scene and fewer daytime customers to support the business. Regulars had mixed reactions to Tugboat's banishment. Some felt bad for him, since they knew there were few places in the neighborhood left for men like him. Others understood the decision. Many found him obnoxious despite his ties to the neighborhood's and bar's past. Amber, who regularly clashed with Tugboat, reflects on these perspectives:

Tugboat is going to be devastated [that he was banned] because he is a man who's been coming here for years. I mean all of his relationships, the majority of the relationships in his life are in the bar. But at the same time, none of those people respect him or genuinely look forward to seeing him. I see their faces, they're just, "Ugh," they look at him and they're like, "Ugh, he's just a decaying human being." Denis actually held onto these people longer than anyone else I think would have, giving people like Tugboat a tab. Who would give a guy like Tugboat a tab at another bar? They wouldn't even let him in at another bar, let alone let him pay once a month.

The changing culture within old neighborhood institutions in downtown Manhattan like Milano's presents a small example of the effects of advanced gentrification, which features places of downtown luxury in the midst of existing populations and businesses. But to learn more about the growth of downtown Manhattan's nightlife scenes and their impacts on other local groups, we must leave the bar and examine the broader social ecosystem.

CHAPTER 2

GROWING NIGHTLIFE SCENES

... explain why overwhelming community opposition to proposed club
was overbalanced by value or utility of a new nightclub.

**—FLATIRON COMMUNITY ASSOCIATION V. NEW YORK STATE LIQUOR
AUTHORITY (NEW YORK STATE SUPREME COURT, 2004)**

ON A WEEKDAY IN MARCH 2007, New York City Councilwoman Rosie
Mendez, who represents the East Village, holds a "Quality of Life Forum"
for her district in the auditorium of a local public school.[1] Born and raised
across the East River in what was a heavily Puerto Rican community in
Williamsburg, Mendez worked in various capacities of community service,
such as tenant and labor union organizing, before being successfully elected as the neighborhood's representative to the city council. The protégé of
Margarita Lopez, the former councilwoman who was also once a community
activist, she exemplifies the East Village's longstanding tradition of electing
progressive-minded leaders. Councilwoman Mendez organized this public
forum at the request of her constituents, who are fed up with a number of
quality-of-life issues. Dozens of residents and Community Board 3 members
from the East Village and neighboring areas go to listen to the panel that
Councilwoman Mendez has assembled. The speakers include representatives
from the city's Department of Environmental Protection, to discuss the new
noise code; the Department of Buildings, to discuss construction issues; and
two local precincts of the New York Police Department (NYPD), to discuss
enforcement. But most of the audience have come to listen to Joshua Toas,
the CEO of the New York State Liquor Authority.

Named the SLA's first CEO in many years in 2005, Toas travels around the
state and speaks to local groups about liquor license issues. In other regions
he addresses groups that deal with such licensing matters as wholesaling and
manufacturing. But in New York City he deals with residents who care only
about retail licenses and the nightlife in their neighborhoods. For people in
downtown Manhattan, Toas is the first SLA representative to whom they have
been able to personally address their concerns. After a lot of practice from
years of organizing and attending Community Board 3 meetings, they are fully
prepared to voice their complaints.

After being introduced, Toas gets up from the dais, steps to the podium, and begins his presentation. Anticipating the hostile reactions he normally gets at his public appearances before residents, he begins lightheartedly.

"Good evening. First, I'd like to thank all of you for not booing."

[Silence.]

"Tough crowd already."

In a calm but spirited tone, he starts by explaining that over the past year, the SLA has undergone changes to its leadership and its policies. He preempts the audience's complaints and concedes that there have been issues in the past.

"Over the course of years, many of you and certainly your neighbors have complained about the way we treat the 500-foot rule and our attitude towards licensing, and many people think we oversaturated certain places."

A man from the audience abruptly shouts, "Two nightclubs right next to each other!"

Although Councilwoman Mendez said that questions and comments would be reserved for the end, after all the presentations have been made, he acknowledges the complaint and says, "Right, we've saturated certain areas."

A woman then says, "Or four bars in a row! How about that?"

He acknowledges her with a nod and continues his talk.

"So I think if you look at the history, the recent history of the State Liquor Authority . . . ," but several voices from the restless crowd interrupt him again in unison and say that they cannot hear him. He adjusts his microphone and continues with his point.

"So, if you look at the recent history of the State Liquor Authority, you'll see that definitely our policies with regards to licensure have changed. And the reason for this is twofold. The first reason is," he says while stretching out his arms, "you all demanded it. You demanded that we pay close attention to what your interests are and the residents throughout the different communities throughout the state, and certainly New York City. And the second reason is we recognize that licensing decisions have a great impact on enforcement problems. If we put too many licensees in one area, or we license the wrong person without doing proper due diligence with that licensure, we very well may turn into situations which are going to cause enforcement problems for us and certainly enforcement problems for the NYPD. So we really changed the way we look at things."

A few people laugh incredulously in response. He continues his talk, emphasizing these changes and assuring the audience that today the SLA is taking their perspectives on what is in the "public interest" into account.

"We've been working very closely with the community boards to try and determine what is and what isn't in the public interest, and again, we've tried to balance that with the legitimate needs of the businesses and the neighborhoods."

He takes a seat after his talk and waits patiently for the barrage of questions and complaints he knows he will receive at the end. During the talk, I had noticed that a woman sitting two seats from me had been attentively nodding and shaking her head at Toas in equal measure but did not speak or call out like many others. I introduce myself and find out that her name is Samantha. Samantha lives on Thirteenth Street and has been an East Village resident for thirty years. Like other residents, the new bars that have opened have bothered her, and she is getting tired of putting in the effort to fight them, which she has done for years. I ask her what she thought of what Toas had to say.

"Well, I'm glad that he's here. No one from the SLA has ever come. They've never listened to us. But I don't know, I don't know what they're going to do about it. It doesn't sound like they want to do anything."

—

The SLA did not have much responsibility in downtown Manhattan during the 1970s and 1980s, when the area featured disinvested slums and relatively few legal bars were in operation. As figure 2 shows, there were sixty-seven bars on the Lower East Side, East Village, and Bowery in 1975; and in 1985, after New York City's fiscal crisis and recession took a considerable economic toll on the area, the number decreased to thirty-five.[2] The bars at this time were sparsely dispersed throughout downtown and were mostly places for local residents. There were ethnic bars (mainly Ukrainian and Puerto Rican), Bowery bars like Milano's for homeless men, old working-class bars that had been open for many years, and new bars that accommodated the arriving population of artists and musicians. Along with licensed establishments, downtown had a number of unregulated, illegal ethnic social clubs and after-hours bars, parties in galleries and performance spaces, and public drinking on the streets, in abandoned properties, and in vacant lots. Overall, street life at night often meant criminal activity involving drugs, prostitution, and violence. Although there were some instances of residents complaining about particular night-time establishments during this period, especially in cases of drugs and violence, formal nightlife did not present much of a concern for them, many of whom went to the local bars.

How, then, did we get to this point in 2007, when residents display open hostility towards an SLA official? The simple answer is that a great number of bars opened as the Lower East Side, East Village, and Bowery gentrified. As figure 2 shows, the number of bars more than doubled from thirty-five in 1985 to seventy-six in 1995, doubled again to 144 in 2000, and increased to 177 in 2005. The increase in bars corresponds with several other patterns in these

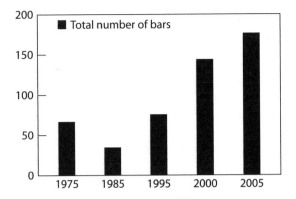

FIGURE 2   Total number of bars in downtown Manhattan, 1975–2005. Data taken from *Cole Directory*, New York County, 1975, 1985, 1995, 2000, 2005.

neighborhoods: declining rates of crime and public drug activity, the renovation of old tenement buildings and the construction of new luxury housing, new law enforcement initiatives, and the expansion of New York University, all of which combined to lure new residents, visitors, business owners, and investors to downtown Manhattan. These new bars increasingly attract consumers from outside the area, and when they do feature a local clientele, it usually consists of young residents who recently moved there. The bar proliferation trends continued throughout the decade. As of 2008 there were 692 establishments with an on-premise liquor license—that is, any place where an alcoholic beverage may be purchased and consumed—within the 1.8 square mile area of downtown Manhattan that I focus on, which includes bars, restaurants, clubs, lounges, cafés, and hotels.[3]

Bars also form highly dense concentrations in neighborhoods with a high level of residential density. According to City-Data.com, on online source for American city profiles, in 2005 the three main zip codes that encompass these neighborhoods had the second (10003), seventh (10009), and ninth (10002) most alcohol drinking places out of every county in the United States.[4] The zip code with the most, in Austin, Texas, is 1.7 square miles in area and has a population of 3,855, or 2,267 people per square mile. The zip code with the second most, in the East Village, is 0.6 square miles in area and has a population of 53,673, or 89,455 people per square mile.[5] Ecologically, bars are widely distributed. Figure 3 breaks down the numbers from the years depicted in figure 2 by location. As it shows, there is a nearly even distribution of bars on larger commercial avenues that already have regular vehicular and pedestrian traffic as there are on smaller residential streets that have little traffic and

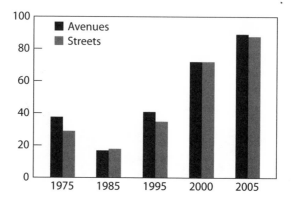

FIGURE 3 Total number of bars in downtown Manhattan, by streets and avenues, 1975–2005. Data taken from *Cole Directory*, New York County, 1975, 1985, 1995, 2000, 2005.

comparatively few businesses. There is at least one bar or restaurant on the majority of streets and on most blocks north of Canal Street. Larger thoroughfares, particularly the western ones that are closer to subway lines, tend to have regular daytime activity and varied forms of shopping during the week. Some streets, however, are rather quiet during the day, either because they are mostly residential or because many of their bars are closed. Other than chic clothing boutiques, cafés, salons, and art galleries interspersed among inexpensive bodegas and utilitarian shops like Laundromats, many of these streets have few businesses and little foot traffic. The steel security shutters protecting bar storefronts create an ominous look, and even make them feel abandoned during the day. For some streets, delivery trucks from alcohol distributors who come in the early afternoon represent the most significant daytime activity. On these streets it is only at night—during the week, but especially on weekends—that the sidewalks and streets are truly alive, populated, bathed in light, and filled with action. The neighborhood follows a rhythm of activity that increases as the day and week come to their ends.

Nightlife scene growth followed a pattern that mirrors the neighborhood's gentrification. Through his rent gap theory, referring to "the disparity between the potential ground rent level and the actual ground rent capitalized under the present land use," Neil Smith shows how the gentrification of the East Village gradually proceeded east.[6] Capital reinvestment pushed the "frontier line" closer towards the long row of public housing projects that represents the district's eastern- and southernmost border on Avenue D and along the East River. New bars first proliferated along the frontier line, which moved eastward. They opened on the major western thoroughfares of Third, Second, and First Avenues and on the western sections of small, popular streets such as St. Mark's Place. For instance, the number of bars on Second and First Avenue in 1985 was four and three, respectively. In 1990, the number of bars on each was seven and five, twelve and seven in 1995, and seventeen and fourteen in 2000. In the 1990s and 2000s, new bars gradually joined or replaced the existing ethnic and artist bars that were already scattered in the eastern section of Alphabet City—Avenues A, B, and C.[7] In 1985 there were three bars on Avenue A, one on Avenue B, and none on Avenue C. By 1990 there were seven, one, and none; seven, three, and none in 1995; and eighteen, ten, and three by 2000. By 2005, Avenue C had eleven bars on it. It was also during the 1990s that new bars began to open south of Houston Street in great numbers, which serves as a key border for many residents between the East Village and the Lower East Side. While bars are well diffused throughout downtown Manhattan, there are several areas—Ludlow and Orchard Streets between Houston and Delancey Streets, St. Mark's Place, Avenue A between Houston and Eleventh Streets, Avenue B between Houston and Seventh Streets—with especially dense concentrations. And even blocks with a small number of bars or none at all can have a noticeable amount of nightlife activity because revelers use them as pathways to get from bar to bar.

But Smith's model excludes the commercial element of gentrification and assumes it represents an outgrowth of residential reinvestment. In reality, bars and nightlife scenes in downtown Manhattan required more than pioneering residents and capital to grow. To understand how nightlife scenes developed in downtown Manhattan, we need to expand the scope of nightlife development from activities at the neighborhood level to those at the level of local government. Instead of being a passive government agency that handles licensing, the SLA played an important role in encouraging liquor license proliferation as a revenue-generating strategy for New York State. Since nearly half of the state's liquor licenses are in the New York City metropolitan area (and thereby a significant amount of its liquor license revenue), and since people were starting to invest in downtown neighborhoods, places like the Lower East Side, East Village, and Bowery became prime areas for the growth of nightlife. Furthermore, Smith and other gentrification scholars who understand gentrifiers as a unified, like-minded group characterize them as supporters of commercial gentrification, such as the opening of new stores that suit their needs.[8] Again, these neighborhoods present a different picture. While many once supported them, the gentrifiers who arrived at the start of gentrification lead today's fight against bars and nightlife. Unlike some aspects of gentrification, such as wealthier newcomers or "as of right" construction projects, New York State residents have a degree of direct political recourse to prevent bar proliferation. Once bars started opening in great numbers, downtown's early gentrifiers formed and joined community groups, organized block and tenant associations, and became well-versed in the Alcoholic Beverage Control (ABC) Law, which the SLA serves and enforces, to fight their proliferation.

But bars opened in great numbers in the late 1990s and throughout the 2000s despite these protests. Residents like Samantha, from the opening vignette, began feeling quite discouraged and powerless in the face of the commercial side of gentrification. They perceived that the pro-nightlife liquor-license policy of the SLA stacked the deck against them. As nightlife establishments continued to proliferate, these daytime communities constructed a role for themselves as victims of the actions of interloping bar owners and an entrepreneurial local government. The actions of the SLA form a basis not only for understanding the growth of nightlife in downtown Manhattan but also for revealing how residents' attitudes towards the bar issue originated. By looking at the state policies and discourse that helped grow the nightlife scenes in downtown Manhattan, and at residents' reactions to them as threats, we can see how the seeds for action and the construction of an ideology of community were sown.

THE ORIGINS OF NIGHTLIFE SCENES

Policies for Nightlife Development

Individual entrepreneurs in search of hip locations help grow nightlife scenes. But they still depend to a great extent on the basic principles of urban growth. Zoning plays a significant role in the development of nightlife in New York City. Land use policy in downtown Manhattan permits a considerable amount of commercial activity, such as on the larger avenues that are zoned for retail establishments. However, two unique zoning codes in downtown Manhattan permit bars to open on smaller, residential side streets, to the utmost chagrin of residents. The first is a residential zoning code that covers most of the East Village and allows nonconforming uses in storefronts. Ordinarily, residentially zoned streets do not allow businesses, unless they have "grandfather" status from 1961, the year of New York City's last zoning resolution. A space loses this status if there is a discontinuance of use of more than two years. The East Village's particular residential zoning code, however, permits nonconforming uses—that is, retail establishments such as bars on a residentially zoned street—for anyone who can show that the storefront had nonconforming uses at any point in the building's history.[9] Tenement buildings in the East Village are on average a century old, and people from the many waves of immigrant groups who occupied them frequently opened their own shops in their storefronts. It has therefore not been difficult for landlords and owners to find a nonconforming use at some point in the building's history so that a bar can open.

The second unique code covers the Lower East Side, and permits high-density commercial developments. City officials purposefully changed the 1961 zoning resolution to accommodate the high-rise developments they planned for the area in conjunction with an eight-lane expressway that would have bisected all of Lower Manhattan. The brainchild of New York City's highly controversial "master builder" Robert Moses, the Lower Manhattan Expressway would have connected the Holland Tunnel to the Manhattan Bridge and, in the process, would have essentially demolished immigrant neighborhoods like Little Italy and the Lower East Side, disrupted life in middle-class Greenwich Village, and likely prevented SoHo from becoming, first, an artists enclave and, then, a globally recognized neighborhood with some of the highest real estate prices in New York City.[10] Moses envisioned the expressway to be the northern border to a Lower Manhattan district that would have been an enclosed fortress for commerce and business. Because of significant opposition by local activists, including Jane Jacobs, the expressway was never built; the special zoning in the neighborhood, however, remained.[11] This zoning code provided the legal right for bars to open as well as for high-rise towers to develop in a highly residential area—although neither occurred until the late 1990s and 2000s, when the neighborhood gentrified. Bowery, meanwhile, contains multiple zoning codes that allow for a range of commercial and high-rise developments. Overall, land use policies provide a foundation for commercial establishments to exist in most of downtown Manhattan. But its nightlife scenes required further political activity to develop.

David Harvey demonstrates how city governments have undergone a transformation from managerialism, or a focus on urban welfare and the provision and maintenance of services for its residents, such as infrastructure and public amenities, to entrepreneurialism, or an active role in fostering economic development and capital investment in a global context of interurban competition: "urban governments [have] to be much more innovative and entrepreneurial, willing to explore all kinds of avenues through which to alleviate their distressed condition and thereby secure a better future for their populations."[12] "Urban entrepreneurialism" refers to the policies and actions that city leaders have used since the final decades of the twentieth century to directly encourage business interests and growth. This shift includes both the scaling back of public agencies, services, and projects that characterized city government activity during the modern industrial era and a transfer and/or sharing of control over such services and project to private actors. Examples of this are business improvement districts (BIDs) and their influence over public spaces such as streets and parks, to attract further investment and consumption in an area.[13]

City governments have always been interested in developing and promoting their cities. However, as Miriam Greenberg notes, after the "urban crisis" of the 1960s, American urban leaders began to use new cultural strategies to create marketable images of key places in their cities.[14] Focusing on New York City in the late 1960s and 1970s, Greenberg shows how political, media, business, and real estate leaders devised and widely disseminated a new brand for the city that replaced its image of danger, filth, and chaos with one of safety, cleanliness, and order. Culminating with the "I ♥ NY" campaign, city leaders identified and focused on New York's attractive areas for rehabilitation and promotion and neglected those that did not fit their desired image. These "urban branding" strategies aspired to promote the city as a fun place for safe leisure and consumption. As Harvey states:

> Consumer attractions (sports stadia, convention and shopping centers, marinas, exotic eating places) and entertainment (the organization of urban spectacles on a temporary or permanent basis) have all become much more prominent facets of strategies of urban regeneration. Above all, the city has to appear as an innovative, exciting, creative, and safe place to live or to visit, to play and consume in.[15]

John Hannigan shows how "urban entertainment destinations," or highly branded and themed developments for amusement and consumption, range widely from city to city in terms of scale and complexity but still follow a similar model and feature a similar set of actors: corporate lenders, real estate developers, gaming and entertainment companies, retail operators, and public agencies.[16] These public-private partnerships exemplify the "entertainment machines" that many observers argue have become a key component in urban growth in the postindustrial era.[17]

Gentrification fits within the urban entrepreneurialism framework in the sense that city governments enact policies that encourage the process, such as rezoning, tax abatements for large developments, and the formation of BIDs. City leaders encourage gentrification in order to expand a neighborhood's tax base, help reduce crime, and broaden its appeal for investors, new residents, and visitors, all of which thereby broaden their city's appeal. This conceptualization of gentrification as a state initiative is also known as "supply-side" gentrification, or the notion that macro actors such as the real estate industry and local state drive the process.[18] But there are also examples of "demand-side" gentrification that are more consumer-driven. In these cases, gentrifiers themselves and their particular motivations determine whether or not a neighborhood gentrifies. Sharon Zukin and her research team contrast the state-led gentrification of Harlem, through its designation as an empowerment zone, with the market-led gentrification of the Brooklyn neighborhood of Williamsburg, through its appeal to young artists who gradually moved into the neighborhood. They find that in both examples, new retail entrepreneurs (i.e., owners of boutiques, restaurants, and bars) were important symbols and catalysts of gentrification, but different factors of either supply or demand mediated their presence in their neighborhoods.[19]

However, neighborhoods do not gentrify solely because of one force or the other. It was not either-or but a combination of market and government, or demand- and supply-side, initiatives that helped the nightlife scenes in downtown neighborhoods grow. The actors were unlike the formal public-private partnerships that launch branding campaigns and develop large-scale urban entertainment destinations. There was not a mastermind with a plan or strategy, a governing body in charge, or a set of legal provisions made specifically for it. Instead, public and private actors—that is, the SLA and bar owners—worked to each other's benefit, but they did so separately with little communication between them. By following a pro-growth discourse, the SLA played an integral role in facilitating new entrepreneurs who wanted to open bars in gentrifying neighborhoods like the Lower East Side, East Village, and Bowery. The story of the SLA shows us the role that local governments play in turning urban neighborhoods into places for fun and consumption.

Liquor Licensing and Economic Growth

Ratified in 1933, the Twenty-First Amendment to the United States Constitution ended national Prohibition and established the modern era of nightlife regulation. The amendment gives each state the right to either continue prohibiting the manufacturing, distribution, and sale of alcohol, or to regulate it themselves. Each state became either a "control state," in which government-run stores sell alcohol, making the state the wholesaler or retailer, or a "licensing state," in which the state grants business owners the right to sell alcohol.[20] Most, like New York, became licensing states. In such states, the law usually allows a high degree of local regulatory autonomy and discretion, with core categories and policies (e.g., venue closing times, application processes) varying significantly within each licensing state. For example, many states allow municipalities, counties, and towns to pass their own local laws, even including whether to permit the sale of alcohol (i.e., "dry counties").

The SLA regulates the manufacture and wholesale and retail distribution of all alcoholic products in New York State. Based in Albany, with offices in New York City and Buffalo, the administrative body of the SLA enforces the ABC Law, which the state legislature drafted after Prohibition ended. Three members lead the SLA—a chairperson and two commissioners—each of whom the governor appoints and the State Senate approves. They handle all liquor-licensing matters under the ABC Law.[21]

The New York State Legislature has updated and revised the ABC Law over the years to accommodate new issues and needs, but it still retains elements from its post-Prohibition period. Today it resembles an arcane, complicated, patchwork law with sections that are difficult to navigate and interpret. It is analogous to keeping the basic structure of the Ford Model T and adding such inventions as power steering and automatic transmission at later dates, resulting in a clunky machine. In 1993 the state legislature amended the law by placing restrictions on the geographic concentration of retail establishments for on-premises alcohol consumption—places such as bars, restaurants, and clubs. Known as the "500-foot rule," it applies to all cities, towns, or villages with a population of 20,000 or more and prohibits the issuance of a full operating, on-premises liquor license in an area where there are already three or more full operating liquor licenses within 500 feet of the proposed establishment.[22] Before the legislature passed this rule, any number of licensed establishments such as bars, restaurants, and clubs could open in commercial spaces anywhere in New York State where the local zoning code allowed them. And according to the ABC Law, the SLA cannot deny a liquor license application unless it has good cause (e.g., an applicant's financial situation). The law placed the onus on applicants to have everything in their applications in order, and, if they did, the SLA had to approve them regardless of how many other bars were in the area. The 500-foot rule changed this onus.

The 500-foot rule is also known as the "Padavan Law," named after State Senator Frank Padavan, who drafted it. Padavan's senate district was in Bayside, Queens—a mostly residential area, relatively remote from Manhattan, with a few major commercial avenues. In the late 1980s and early 1990s several nighttime establishments opened on some of these avenues in the senator's district. A few of them were poorly run, with reputations for crime and violence. But the concentration of many establishments and the conditions they created also raised quality-of-life issues for people in the nearby neighborhood. This problem of nightlife close to residential areas was not unique to Padavan's district. Other areas in the state also shared these concerns. As Joseph, a longtime legal counsel to Senator Padavan and writer of the 500-foot law, remembers:

Interestingly, it wasn't just a parochial kind of thing that the Senator said, "We're going to stop this." We had [State] Senators and Assemblypeople from Long Island that had the same issues, [and] we were joined by people in the city who saw the same thing happening in Manhattan. [They] had the same exact issues, that [there was a] proliferation of bars close to neighborhoods, and it was a nuisance, plain and simple. You know, there were bars upon bars upon bars.

Residents in gentrifying Manhattan neighborhoods such as Chelsea, SoHo, and the Upper East Side began to complain as new nightclubs and bars opened in or around their buildings during this period. But Padavan only acted officially after the shooting death of an off-duty police officer on one of the nightlife-saturated avenues in his district. He felt that the proliferation and concentration of nightlife establishments in his district created a criminogenic environment that was too much for the local police to handle and interfered with residential life. Padavan got several other elected officials to agree with him.

The initial legislation for these issues prohibited more bars from opening in locations where at least three other bars were already open. But this austere legal action raised a conflict with the SLA's authority to issue liquor licenses by threatening to remove its discretion. Furthermore, other legislators recognized the harm of limiting the potential for the growth of nightlife scenes by passing such a prohibitory legislation. Licensed establishments create jobs and add tax revenue to the state. They therefore amended the original version of the law to include three exceptions. The first, a grandfather clause, excludes establishments that were licensed before November 1, 1993, the date the new rule took effect. The second excludes establishments that renew their license. These two exceptions maintain nightlife concentration levels in neighborhoods as they exist, provided licensees renew their licenses or transfer them to someone else, both of which often occur. The third exception allows for the proliferation of liquor licenses under certain circumstances. It has been the most contentious aspect of the rule and has played a direct role in the growth of nightlife scenes in the state. As the law reads:

> The [State Liquor] Authority may issue a retail license for on-premises consumption for a premises which shall be within five hundred feet of three or more existing premises licensed and operating . . . if, after consultation with the municipality or Community Board, *it determines that granting such license would be in the public interest.* Before it may issue any such license, the authority shall conduct a hearing, upon notice to the applicant and the municipality or Community Board [emphasis added].

The subjective concept of "public interest" makes this clause highly elastic. When, exactly, is the sale of alcohol in the public's "interest"? Who is the "public"—regular customers, visitors, the city, other businesses, or residents—whose "interest" it serves? Members and administrators of the SLA often use the following hypothetical example when explaining the rationale behind their decision-making over what falls within the public interest. As Toas, the SLA's CEO, explains to me,

> Is there a need in a particular community for a particular type of establishment? Let's say you have a particular, a growing immigrant community, where there really isn't any establishment there that caters to whatever native foods are there, or native drinks, and you might have that type of situation may be in the public interest because that's something that that particular area of a public wants.

This unique situation may lead the SLA to determine that the criteria for the public interest exception have been met.

But in reality such special cases of new immigrant groups and ethnic liquors are rare. Most often the 500-foot rule takes effect when an applicant wishes to add to the existing amount of nightlife in an area, which forms or grows a scene. Opening an establishment near competition seems to go against the basic business strategy of dispersal, or the notion that businesses seek to rationally maximize market share by opening at a distance from competition. But scenes, or clusters of urban amenities for a collection of lifestyles and different forms of consumption, benefit businesses by creating an image for the place as a destination.[23] Businesses survive despite direct competition by differentiating themselves by price and variety of goods and services.[24] In these cases, the SLA relies on other criteria to determine when an additional license would serve the public interest. The rule itself does not define either "public" or "interest," but it does provide a certain degree of guidance that is clear in some areas but vague in others:

> The [State Liquor A]uthority may consider any or all of the following in determining whether public convenience and advantage and the public interest will be promoted by the granting of licenses and permits for the sale of alcoholic beverages at a particular unlicensed location:
>
> (a) The number, classes and character of licenses in proximity to the location and in the particular municipality or subdivision thereof.
> (b) Evidence that all necessary licenses and permits have been obtained from the state and all other governing bodies.

(c) Effect of the grant of the license on vehicular traffic and parking in proximity to the location.

(d) The existing noise level at the location and any increase in noise level that would be generated by the proposed premises.

(e) The history of liquor violations and reported criminal activity at the proposed premises.

(f) Any other factors specified by law or regulation that are relevant to determine the public convenience and advantage and public interest of the community.

Thus, the ABC Law guides the SLA to consider the character of the neighborhood's existing nightlife (a) and the potential impacts that a licensed establishment would have on a local area's quality of life (c and d) and on location-specific activity (e) in deciding if licensing an establishment is in the public interest. Only one condition (f) mentions "community," and it is in a manner that problematically equates "community" with "public." This condition, however, is most vague in the sense that it states that the SLA may consider "any other factors" pertaining to law or regulation to make a determination on public convenience or the interest of the community.

The key to the 500-foot rule is that it shifts the burden of licensing from the applicant to the SLA. Prior to the rule's passing and in cases where it does not apply, the ABC Law advocates that the SLA members grant a license for applicants who meet the legal criteria for it. The applicant bears the burden of meeting these criteria, since by law the SLA cannot deny a license without cause. In cases involving the 500-foot rule, however, the law dictates that SLA members deny the license because of existing concentration levels. It places the burden on *them* to determine whether or not adding another license serves the public interest. In this way, the elastic public-interest clause becomes a potential tool for facilitating the growth of scenes.

Along with the information provided by applicants on its liquor license applications and the background checks that it conducts, the SLA must base all its licensing decisions, including its definition of "public interest," on several sources, in accordance with the ABC Law. Local community boards, which the ABC Law recognizes to represent areas in New York City and whose opinions the SLA is required to consider, serve as one such source. Along with community board decisions, the 500-foot rule requires additional procedures. The SLA must conduct a hearing before an administrative law judge of the SLA at one of their offices to help determine whether granting a license for an establishment would serve the public interest. At these hearings the judge asks applicants a series of questions about their establishments, their methods of operation, and the surrounding area. The hearing gives any interested party, such as residents or existing competition, an opportunity to question or protest the granting of a liquor license. In addition to community boards and the hearing, residents may also voice their concerns directly to the SLA in writing. The judge then passes this information on to the SLA members. However, community opposition—from community boards, other community groups, or individual residents—does not mean that the SLA will deny a license. SLA members treat these actors' voices as merely advisory. Licensing decisions ultimately come at the discretion of SLA members.

From the 500-foot rule's onset, the SLA began understanding nightlife establishments as economic benefits and interpreting the law in their favor. In postindustrial cities, bars and nightlife scenes have a *qualitative effect* of transforming the image of a marginal area into a popular one by bringing new consumption activities and crowds of revelers. They also have a significant *quantitative effect* in terms of their economic impact, and the SLA played a key role in facilitating their proliferation. From the moment the state first passed the rule, the SLA found exceptions to it by determining that the public interest was being served because of the economic development that licensed establishments and nightlife provided for local areas. The SLA's entrepreneurial interpretation was part of a larger state agenda. The SLA's 1996 annual report states that one of the agency's goals was to "reduce regulatory burdens which hinder economic growth for the industry." Similarly, according to an introductory letter to the governor written by the SLA chairman that accompanied the agency's 2000 annual report (and copied word for word in each subsequent letter until 2005),

> This Annual Report clearly portrays the State Liquor Authority as an agency dynamically involved in the resurging private sector economic development. Information, licensing activities, and support services are readily available to the full spectrum of the state's entrepreneurial interests . . . culminating in our vital retail trades.

In its licensing decisions the SLA regularly cited such reasons as "increasing the tax base," "providing employment," and "improving the neighborhood"—all signifiers of economic growth—as justifications for making exceptions to the 500-foot rule and granting licenses in areas that already had a high concentration of licensed establishments.[25] Although the SLA allows for community considerations in making licensing decisions, it routinely defined "public interest" in narrower economic terms.

Economic justifications, of course, do not apply just to bars but to any type of new business that occupies a commercial storefront, pays taxes, and hires employees. But bars are unique because they are licensed establishments, and the SLA, with its annual fees for liquor licenses as well as civil penalties and fines from licensees who are found guilty of violations, is the second biggest source of revenue of any agency in New York State.[26] Bars also support beer, wine, and spirits wholesalers, distributors, and manufacturers and their heavily taxed alcoholic products. Margarita Lopez, the aforementioned longtime resident, community activist, and former city council representative for the East Village in the late 1990s and 2000s, explains how the local government officials understand this relationship:

> Alcohol is a commodity that is a very particular commodity. It's very important for government. . . . Government has chosen to get a lot of taxation out of alcohol and tobacco, and that taxation that the government gets is very important for services that governments pays for. And that's where the complexity of alcohol [and] bars is—right there. Government makes so much money with the taxation of alcohol that if government would go to reduce the amount of liquor licenses that they issue, government will have a deficit of billions of dollars.

The excise taxes on tobacco and alcohol that Lopez refers to are commonly referred to as "sin taxes" because they are levied on vices—a politically safe policy because of the generally harmful nature of the products. Although states often use excise taxes to curtail unhealthy behavior by focusing on supply, as in the case of escalating cigarette prices, they also use them to balance budgets. And bars and restaurants also pay among the highest rents of any small, independently owned businesses and can garner real estate interest in an area. Such economic incentives complicate the idea of the "public interest" and present local political leaders with important decisions to make on how to handle urban growth.

As the SLA acted on this interpretation, New York City residents started fighting back. The legality of the SLA's decisions to license establishments in locations that violate the 500-foot rule to promote economic development despite significant community opposition has been questioned several times before the appellate New York State Supreme Court. These cases all represent examples of lawsuits brought against the SLA by residents who opposed its decision. They exemplify that the SLA intended its decisions to promote urban growth. The first case of its kind, *SoHo Community Council v. New York State Liquor Authority*, in 1997, featured a community group in the increasingly wealthy Manhattan neighborhood SoHo, who had already opposed a liquor license before their community board, suing the SLA for its decision to approve it. The community group claimed that the SLA's one-sentence explanation for approving the license (because "liquor licenses are in the 'public interest' because they generate employment and tax revenues") was "arbitrary and capricious and an abuse of discretion." State Senator Frank Padavan wrote a letter in opposition to the license, claiming that the SLA's determination "contravene[d] not only the intent but the very law itself as passed in 1993." The court ruled in the group's favor, the SLA's decision was overturned, and the location did not get a license.

In another case, *Waldman v. New York State Liquor Authority*, in 2001, the court ruling identified the licensing burden on the SLA in cases involving the 500-foot rule: "due to the proximity of other licensed premises, the Authority was subject to a statutory mandate to deny appellant's application for a license . . . unless it found that granting the license would be in the public interest." It then stated the SLA's reason for declaring an establishment to be in the public interest: "The Authority has considered that the applicant will operate these premises as a bona fide restaurant featuring Cuban cuisine. Accordingly, the Authority find that approval will be in the public interest." Based on this explanation the court found that "this perfunctory recitation fails to comply with the requirement that the Authority state its reasons for concluding that it would be in the public interest. Obviously, something more is needed." In this case the court determined that the SLA did not lawfully meet its licensing burden.

A final case, *Flatiron Community Association v. New York State Liquor Authority*, in 2004, also dealt with whether the SLA's decision to grant a license was "arbitrary and capricious" or "rationally based" and also identified the SLA's mandate "to explain why overwhelming community opposition to proposed club was overbalanced by value or utility of a new nightclub." The court documented that at the required community board hearing, thirteen people—including residents, elected officials, and a traffic expert—spoke and presented evidence in opposition to the granting of this license for a nightclub at a location that had twenty-one licensed establishments within 500 feet of it. They cited "violence, fighting, crime, noise, litter, public urination, and vomiting" associated with the area's existing nightlife. In support of the license, the proposed nightclub's applicant provided two affidavits assuring their low impact on quality of life. The SLA granted the license and justified that "the issuance of the within liquor license furthers public convenience and advantage and promotes public interest" by quoting directly from one of the applicant's affidavits while ignoring the evidence produced by residents. The court ruled:

> The Authority made no evaluation of the merit, or lack of merit[,] of the evidence introduced by petitioners and failed to indicate why it chose to

accept, without reservation, all of the assertions made by respondents with respect to the club's impact on traffic flow, parking, noise, and the potential for criminal activities.

The ruling concluded that the SLA's decision was "arbitrary and capricious" because it did not satisfactorily meet its mandate to determine public interest in the face of local opposition.

These civil court cases demonstrate how residents react to the SLA's actions to promote urban growth. They pit two competing discourses on the interpretation of the public interest and the proper use of neighborhood spaces against each other. The urban growth discourse, represented by the actions and justifications of the SLA, focuses on nightlife development as an economic benefit. The community discourse, represented by the protests, disapprovals, and lawsuits of residents, focuses on the prevention of quality-of-life disturbances and the alteration of local cultural environments through nightlife expansion. Although these cases involving the 500-foot rule set legal precedents for local actors to fight the SLA's decisions, they are only brought before the appellate courts because of lawsuits that residents and community groups initiate.[27] Since such cases are costly, time-consuming, and difficult for residents to organize, they rarely occur. Usually community groups and residents do not challenge the SLA's economically based 500-foot-rule decisions.

The nightlife scenes of downtown Manhattan benefited from the SLA's actions. In 1993, when the 500-foot rule was passed, there were sixty-four bars in downtown Manhattan. This amount represented an 83 percent increase from 1985, when there were thirty-five, and a 31 percent increase from 1990, when there were forty-nine. In terms of concentration levels, in 1990 only ten blocks in downtown Manhattan had more than one bar on them, and in 1993 thirteen did. These increases occurred at the same time as the influx of new residents to downtown and increasing economic investment in the area. But they are relatively modest when compared with later figures, as gentrification and investment in the neighborhoods intensified and the SLA began interpreting the 500-foot rule to encourage growth. In downtown Manhattan there were seventy-five total bars in 1995, 142 in 2000, and 175 in 2005—a 17 percent, 122 percent, and 173 percent increase from 1993, respectively. Concentration levels also rose. There were eighteen blocks with more than one bar on them in 1995, forty-two in 2000, and sixty-eight in 2005—a 38 percent, 223 percent, and 423 percent increase from the number of blocks with more than one bar in 1993 (thirteen), respectively.

A specific and revealing example is a three-block, 1,320-foot-long section of Ludlow Street between Houston and Delancey Streets that has one of the highest concentrations of nightlife establishments and nightlife activity on the Lower East Side. Only three bars were open on these three blocks in 1993. In 2000 there were nine, and in 2005 there were eight. There are currently seventeen licensed establishments (including restaurants) on these three blocks, as well as eleven additional licensed establishments on the neighboring four blocks of Stanton and Rivington Streets between Essex and Orchard Streets.[28] In short, according to the ABC Law, it would have been impossible for this section of Ludlow Street and any other area on the Lower East Side or throughout downtown to feature nightlife growth at these levels unless the SLA decided it served the public interest.

In addition, the SLA interpreted another anti-nightlife concentration rule in the ABC Law in favor of nightlife growth. Map 2 presents liquor licenses in Manhattan Community District 3. Along with licensed establishments—places with either full liquor licenses or licenses to serve just beer and wine—the map shows both schools and places of worship. A precedent for the 500-foot rule and an original part of the ABC Law, the "200-foot rule" prohibits the issuance of a license for both the on-premises consumption of liquor and the retail sale of liquor or wine for off-premises consumption (i.e., a liquor or wine store) that is within 200 feet of a building that is used exclusively as a school, church, synagogue, or other place of worship. Both rules prohibit bars and restaurants that sell liquor, but not those that sell beer and wine. As the map's 200-foot buffer circles show, there are several examples on the Lower East Side of licensed establishments that are in violation of the 200-foot rule. The concentrations of licensed establishments reveal that there are far more licensed establishments that are in violation of the 500-foot rule. The key is that these decisions in 500- and 200-foot-rule cases, based on a discourse of economic growth, came despite opposition from downtown's daytime actors of the community board and residents.

THE ORIGINS OF PROTEST

Over time, residents gradually sensed that their community was under threat, and they identified the SLA and bar owners as complicit perpetrators in its destruction. They saw themselves as victims of the SLA's decisions. These notions developed out of the shortcomings of their early activism. Once bars started opening in great numbers, residents of downtown neighborhoods took action by resorting to the local body responsible for liquor licensing, their community board. New York City is divided up into fifty-nine community districts and each is represented by a community board. Community boards

MAP 2   Map of Community District 3 liquor licenses.

were written into the New York City Charter in 1975 as the most local unit of city government. They developed after a long period in the city's history of controversial planning (such as the works of Robert Moses) and were intended to look after their localities by scrutinizing government action. Community boards consist of fifty volunteer members, appointed by the borough president from an applicant pool, and are run by a paid district manager, who serves as an administrator, coordinator, and advocate for the district, as well as a small paid staff.[29] Generally lifelong residents, longtime residents, business owners, or newcomers who wish to establish roots in the community join community boards. They volunteer a significant amount of their time out of concern for the well-being and future of their neighborhoods. The boards serve as liaisons between local neighborhoods—for residents, businesses, and community groups—and government agencies and elected officials. They serve an advisory function in local government and have no real political power of their own, but they can still be highly influential actors and provide an important forum for local issues.[30]

Each community board addresses the specific concerns of its district. It forms different committees to deal with issues that can range from public safety, traffic, and planning for a large development to liquor licensing. Some government actions, such as the Uniform Land Use Review Procedure (ULURP) process that deals with land use matters, require local input before agencies make their decisions. The ABC Law specifies that an applicant for a liquor license must first apply and appear before the local community board before applying to the SLA. The community board then makes a decision on the license and sends it to the SLA as a recommendation. The board may decide to deny a license or approve it with stipulations that represent an agreement between the owners and the community over how they will generally run their business (e.g., hours and methods of operation, backyard use, and private security requirements). The SLA then makes a licensing decision based on these recommendations and may incorporate the community board's stipulations into the terms of the license, thus making them legally binding. This process makes the community board the most immediate legal recourse for residents in dealing with a liquor license. However, the SLA has the ultimate decision over licensing matters and does not have to follow the recommendations of community boards, as the court cases discussed earlier demonstrate.

Manhattan Community Board 3 (CB3) represents the Lower East Side, the East Village, and the east side of Bowery. CB3's many committees and task forces meet once a month to discuss and vote on pertinent issues. These meetings are all open to the public and often feature lively debates and commentary on a wide range of issues, from city planning proposals to the riding of bicycles on sidewalks, by a range of groups in the neighborhood. The full community board then meets at the end of each month (also a public meeting) to discuss and vote on their decisions. This final decision gets sent to the appropriate government agency, such as the SLA. Although board members sometimes discuss and contest an item on the committee's agenda during the full board meeting, usually the full board votes to approve of the committees' decisions.

CB3 formed a special committee for liquor licensing in 1992, when it created the SLA Task Force. Before this, liquor licensing matters fell under the board's Economic Development Committee.[31] At this time, nightlife was only emerging as an issue and was not a central priority for most residents or for CB3. In the late 1980s and early 1990s, tensions between the city and East Village residents resulted in riots, evictions, and the controlling of properties such as buildings, vacant lots, and public spaces (such as Tompkins Square Park) by the city and police.[32] Smith refers to this era as the time when city officials began "taking back" the neighborhood for "respectable" classes of people.[33] CB3's agenda reflected these events, and its main priorities dealt with issues of housing and land use—which always have and continue to be among its central concerns.[34] Christopher Mele documents this period as the time when residents, both early gentrifiers and existing low-income residents, set aside their different social backgrounds and fought against city leaders and real estate interests.[35] Their struggles stemmed from the gentrification processes and increasing popularity that were having transformative effects on the neighborhood's image and threatening to displace them. Meanwhile, crime, drugs, and conditions of blight were still major problems downtown. However, the fact that CB3 formed a liquor-licensing task force demonstrates that nightlife was becoming an issue at this important time in the district's recent history. It represented residents' first attempt to have a say in the direction of formal nightlife activity. And the more they got involved, the more frustrated they became and powerless they felt to make progress in protecting their neighborhood from gentrifying further.

Liquor license applications fall into several categories. They can be new applications for licenses at unlicensed locations, renewals for current owners wishing to keep their establishments licensed, transfers of licenses at existing locations (i.e., an owner selling a bar to a new owner), alterations for changes to existing establishments (e.g., the expansion of a bar or addition of a new license), and license upgrades (e.g., when a bar with a license to sell just beer and wine wants also to sell liquor). As figures 4 and 5 both show, the amount of liquor license activity at CB3 increased gradually throughout the 1990s. CB3 voted on 110 applications in 1993, 152 in 1995, and 135 in 1997.[36] It then reached a peak of 242 applications at the end of the decade in 1999—more than double the number in 1993, the year the 500-foot rule was passed.[37] The average number of items that CB3

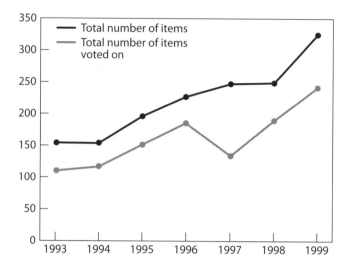

FIGURE 4 Total CB3 liquor license application activity, 1993–1999.

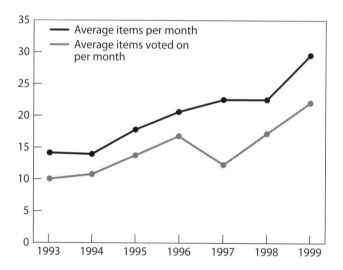

FIGURE 5 Average monthly CB3 liquor license application activity, 1993–1999.

voted on per month also increased steadily during this period from 10 in 1993 to 22 in 1999. Most importantly, as figure 6 shows, applications for new licenses at unlicensed locations also went up during this period with 34 in 1993, 53 in 1995, 57 in 1997, and 77 in 1999—again, more than double the number of applications in 1993.[38] Liquor license transfers—an indicator of owner turnover—were a bit more modest in terms of absolute numbers but also increased substantially

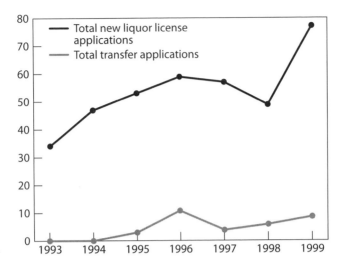

FIGURE 6   Total new and transfer applications, 1993–1999.

during this period from zero in 1993 to 9 in 1999.[39] We can infer from matching CB3 voting decisions with records on nightlife expansion that the SLA approved licenses falling under the 500-foot rule despite community opposition and was unresponsive to community concerns.

Even before the 500-foot rule was passed, CB3 had been complaining to the SLA about the diminished quality of life. It denied licenses for locations that had a "density of bars," particularly on Ludlow Street and Avenue A—two streets whose zoning codes allow commercial establishments—as well as a few on smaller residential streets. In an early case in December 1993 for a new liquor license for a bar on a small residential street, CB3 "Recommended to disapprove because there are nine bars in area and there never was a bar at this site before." It was important for residents that a bar did not open in a previously unlicensed location because of the precedent it set for the physical space and its rent. They knew that a commercial storefront that was built out as a bar would elevate its rent level and make it difficult for another type of business to open there. The SLA nevertheless approved this liquor license for a place called the Boiler Room.

As CB3 received more applications and became more familiar with the 500-foot rule and the ABC Law, it began to use more direct and elaborate language in denying licenses, referencing the law when it could. For instance, in April 1995, CB3 voted to deny a new liquor license for a location on Ludlow Street because of the "500 foot restriction." The Luna Lounge, a bar and rock club, opened there later in the year. CB3 often used such terms as "lack of community support," "disruptive history," and "oversaturation of this type of establishment in area" in their denials and often received support from the police, who attested to the overwhelming amount of disorderly behavior that existed on certain streets and intersections as a result of increased nightlife density. CB3 wanted to explicitly convey their interpretation of the public interest to the SLA and support it with as much evidence as possible. Elena, an early gentrifier and former CB3 member who played an active role in liquor licensing during this period, recalls: "[It was] a learning process. . . . We initiated lots of forms and requirements. Some CB members became Internet sleuths to uncover [the] true business history of applicants, [and] some members became experts in SLA law." While at first they were unfamiliar with the liquor-licensing process and arcane ABC Law, residents became more and more knowledgeable about both, which they hoped would benefit their protests. Another example is an application in April 1999 for a new liquor license on Orchard Street, one block west of Ludlow. At the time there were twenty licenses within 500 feet of the proposed location. Several residents attended the committee's meeting and "stated opposition . . . because too many licenses exist in area, applicant promises restaurant but advertises for a club, crime and noise from existing clubs are problems . . . [and the] precinct is already overwhelmed." However, their efforts to deny applications with detailed explanations were ineffective. The SLA approved the license and the Slipper Room, a bar with burlesque shows, soon opened.

In response to 500-foot-rule violations, CB3 passed liquor license "moratoriums" on streets that were already "oversaturated" with nightlife. Now called "resolution areas," moratoriums were a strict licensing policy against bar proliferation that CB3 originated. The board made the statement that the addition of more licenses on certain streets would be a violation of the 500-foot rule and not be in the community's interest due to existing quality-of-life problems. Residents' groups such as block associations requested the moratoriums. They were the culmination of several years of protesting bars and denying liquor licenses for places that opened anyway. The first moratorium was proposed in June 1996 by the Save Avenue A Committee, a local group of residents that formed to combat nightlife problems. As they state:

> CB3 asks the SLA to impose a one-year moratorium on all new, on-premises, liquor, tavern, or wine and beer licenses, on Avenue A between Houston Street and St. Mark's Place. Exceptions would be made for approved restaurants containing a constructed kitchen inspected by CB3 members. We ask that same location transfers be included in this moratorium and that new location transfers be severely scrutinized.[40]

By passing the moratoriums, CB3 was telling the SLA that the latter had violated the 500-foot rule and that the board was not going to approve anymore licenses in saturated areas. Note that the Save Avenue A Committee was willing to make exceptions for applicants who could demonstrate that they were legitimate restaurants, which they considered to have less of an impact on quality of life than bars. This strategy marks an attempt by residents to influence the type of establishment that could open in a legally zoned commercial storefront. It also demonstrates that residents, many of whom once partook in the local nightlife, were not prohibitionist teetotalers. Ludlow Street and St. Mark's Place joined Avenue A in passing moratoriums in the mid-1990s, and over time residents from around downtown neighborhoods formed or organized block associations to pass their own.[41] As with the denials, the SLA did not take the moratorium on Avenue A or any other street into consideration in its licensing decisions. Still, it became CB3 policy to send a consistent message to the SLA. It also wanted to deter prospective owners from opening bars on certain streets as well as to deter landlords from renting their commercial spaces to bars. Residents wanted to instill in both groups the fear that they would not obtain a license because of the community's disapproval and protests, thus costing them money in business profits and rents.

Residents intended to strictly prevent further bar proliferation with these actions. But they did not have the desired effect. The first five years of the new century continued the upward trend of liquor license activity that began in the 1990s. As figure 7 shows, from 2000 to 2005, CB3 voted on an average of thirty-two liquor license applications per month, with an average of forty-nine per month in 2003 alone.[42] Figure 8 demonstrates this considerable voting activity in actual numbers with an all-time high of 538 applications voted on in 2003.[43] And as figure 9 shows, the number of new liquor license and transfer applications also increased tremendously during this period, with the former reaching an all-time high of 136 in 2002 and the latter reaching thirty-seven in 2003, the highest for a year at the time. This period marked a culmination in downtown Manhattan, when a large number of new entrepreneurs opened new bars and solidified its status as a nightlife destination.

The granting of liquor licenses at specific locations also reveals the limitations of the moratoriums. For example, Tim owns a fast-food restaurant and a neighboring cocktail bar, which is only accessible through a phone booth in the restaurant, on the highly commercial St. Mark's Place, in the East Village (the name of his bar is PDT, which stands for "Please Don't Tell"). He began this enterprise modestly. In May 2003, Tim applied for a liquor license to sell beer along with burgers and fries. CB3 voted "To deny due to oversaturation, community opposition, the existing moratorium, as well as [the applicant's]

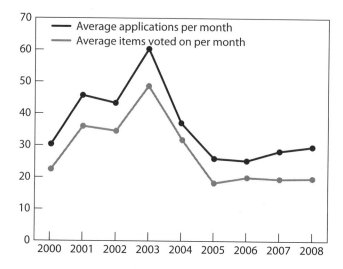

FIGURE 7   Average monthly CB3 liquor license application activity, 2000–2008.

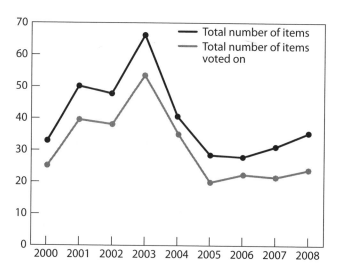

FIGURE 8   Total CB3 liquor license application activity, 2000–2008.

nonappearance." In spite of this denial, the SLA approved the license. Then, less than a year later in February 2004, the owner again applied to CB3 for an upgrade of his license so that he could also serve liquor. Tim wanted to expand into the commercial space adjacent to the fast-food restaurant where the cocktail bar is currently located. "We had the space, but we didn't know

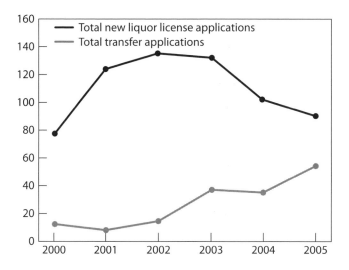

FIGURE 9 Total new and transfer applications, 2000–2005.

what to do with it."[44] But CB3's decision did not change: "To deny because nothing has changed since this Community Board denied application for a beer/wine license at this location in [May] 2003, there are 14 existing liquor licenses on this one block and the community would not positively benefit from an upgrade in this license." Still, the SLA also approved the upgrade. Emma, a lifelong East Village resident and member of St. Mark's Place's block association, says, "I don't know how they got that license. We kept denying it." After considering a few options, Tim eventually partnered with a well-known cocktail bartender and turned the space into a cocktail bar in 2007.

Over time, smaller residential streets began to have not only more bars on them but 500-foot-rule cases. There were two examples of this in September 2003. The first was a new license for a rock club on Suffolk Street, which did not have any bars open at the time but was surrounded by licensed establishments on nearby Rivington, Stanton, Norfolk, and Houston Streets. There were many residents present to protest and CB3 voted to

deny due to nonappearance and because the street is dominated by residential housing and anchored by two educational institutions, the Marta Valle High School and the Clemente Soto Velez Cultural Center, the proposed club is out of character with the existing residential and educational atmosphere of the immediate neighborhood, the area is already oversaturated with clubs, to wit Meow Mix, ABC No Rio, Belly, Noizguild, and Schillers, *there is no pressing social need or economic benefit for an additional bar or club* [emphasis added].

The SLA approved this license despite the denial and despite the fact that the applicant did not even show up at the CB meeting. The music club Rothko eventually opened. The second example is a bar that was opened by a young new owner named Sam. In this month he submitted a transfer application to CB3 to take over an existing licensed location on Sixth Street that was highly disliked by its neighbors. CB3 voted to

> deny because present applicant intends to operate as a lounge and there was an extensive history of past complaints because prior occupant was a lounge, because of applicant's failure to work out agreement with the block association regarding its operation and, further, because of existing moratorium on street as a result of said past complaints at this and adjacent locations.

CB3 and Sixth Street residents felt that this was their opportunity to get rid of a problem location by denying a transfer application for what they felt would be a similar type of establishment. There were also several problem bars open on this block of Sixth Street at the time, and many more on the nearby avenues. Nevertheless, the SLA approved Sam's transfer.[45]

Along with economically driven 500-foot-rule decisions, the SLA also acted in other ways that expanded nightlife and harmed the quality of life for residents. For instance, CB3 identified several cases of the SLA granting a license before the board submitted its recommendation. In February 1993 it wrote a "strong" letter to the SLA stating that "Licenses should not be issued before applications are reviewed and presented to the full Community Board." Since this early letter CB3 has raised this issue with the SLA on several occasions, particularly in this November 2000 item:

> Whereas the full liquor license has already been granted, and whereas the applicant asked to be tabled for one month at the October SLA meeting, a letter to be sent to the SLA noting the above, and noting that SLA once again granted an op license without hearing from CB3 or allowing for any community input.

In this example, the SLA hastily approved a license for an applicant who requested more time before going before the community board. Similarly, there were also cases of applicants completely bypassing CB3 and applying directly to the SLA. For example, CB3 wrote two identical letters in October 2000 to establishments whose owners never approached them. The purpose of each letter was "To write to the owners of this *mystery establishment* asking them to appear in November and tell the committee how they got a license without community approval; to write to the SLA informing them of the same" (emphasis added). There is no indication that either owner appeared or that the SLA took any action (one of the bars eventually closed several years later and the location is currently unlicensed; another remained open and became another bar in 2004, which eventually closed).

With the support of the police, CB3 constantly sent letters to the SLA complaining about specific establishments and requesting that the agency investigate the possibility of revoking a license because of misrepresentation, quality-of-life issues, criminal activity, and the potential endangerment of public safety. But the SLA did not use this information to conduct investigations on or penalize problematic locations. An example of this occurred in October 1999 when CB3 sent the following letter to the SLA:

> Asking them to investigate Oasis [Lounge] for possible license revocation due to the following: 1) Never came before CB3 to get a license, nor have they come in front of us at renewal time; 2) Possible material misstatements on SLA application; misrepresentation as being a restaurant; 3) Arrest of owner on 2 felony forgery charges, also charged with resisting arrest; 4) Unlighted exit sign, no secondary means of egress, curtains hanging in front of door, door never closed when bar is operating; 5) Numerous noise complaints; 6) Failure to meet with CB3 and other neighborhood organizations despite repeated requests to do so; 7) lying to and failure to comply with requests from 9th Precinct; 8) Summonses for misdemeanor assault and underage drinking by patrons.

These concerns of "material misstatements" and "misrepresentation" refer to a "bait and switch" tactic that residents claimed many bar owners used. Bait and switch entailed stating one method of operation on an application in order to obtain approval and then switching to another upon being granted the license. For instance, an owner would apply as a restaurant in order to appease residents—who looked more favorably upon restaurants, which close earlier and are considered to be less noisy—and to circumvent the community board's moratorium on the street, and then become a bar. This tactic infuriated residents and seriously compromised their relationship with owners. But for many years they were frustrated with the SLA for permitting what they saw as deceitful practices. And in this case, not only did the owners apply as a restaurant and then became a bar, they also never appeared before the community board.

The history of this particular location is also revealing. Before becoming problematic, the Oasis Lounge was a place called Zenue, which CB3 complained about in a letter to the SLA in September 1997. Within two years it became Oasis Lounge without appearing before CB3, which denied its renewal and requested license revocation in May 1999. It then denied a transfer of the license in September 2000. The SLA approved them anyway and the space became Openair, a specialized bar for DJs, and then Morrisey Park, a bar with fake wood paneling, a lodge theme, cheap beer, and a cocktail menu (its neighbors regularly complained about both bars). It is now a wine bar with an open facade called Ten Degrees. Such locations are the reason that residents remain active in preventing the opening of bars in new locations. Residents are aware that once a space has been built out as a bar and reaches a bar's rent levels, it is unlikely to turn into something else. Residents risk being stuck with poor quality of life and an altered commercial landscape for a long time.

For many years CB3 has opposed the cutting of funding for SLA enforcement resources from the state's budget and favored increasing it. The SLA's enforcement bureau is very small. It has only seven investigators for the New York metropolitan area, to oversee approximately 35,000 liquor licenses, or 40 percent of the state's total.[46] It therefore depends highly on the investigative abilities of local actors such as community boards and residents, the police, and other state agencies with greater knowledge of neighborhood conditions to make informed decisions on licensing and to enforce problems. The SLA, however, makes its decisions without taking the information supplied by local actors, including the NYPD, into account. Both of the downtown precincts were active with CB3. The police attended meetings, informed CB3 of any quality-of-life or criminal problems they were having with establishments, supported liquor license denials and revocations with letters and testimony, and advocated the passing of moratoriums to prevent the street traffic problems they were handling.

But in the end, none of these efforts resulted in fewer bars, improved quality of life, or even less application activity at CB3. There were 221 total liquor license applications heard by CB3 in 2006, 214 in 2007, and 237 in 2008. Applications for new licenses remained high with 97 in 2006, 91 in 2007, and 103 in 2008—the first year of the recession and the most applications in a single year since 2003—and the number of renewals for places with complaints increased (24 in 2006, 35 in both 2007 and 2008). While these numbers are lower than in the peak period of 1999 to 2004, they indicate that entrepreneurs still have a high interest in downtown Manhattan and continue to open bars.

The actions of the SLA and bar owners have bred feelings of distrust and frustration in residents towards the actors and processes that they consider responsible for nightlife expansion. Without using the term, they identify the SLA's decisions as acts of urban entrepreneurialism that promote the growth of the nightlife scene over their concerns for their community. Based on their experiences at community board meetings, they have created images for both the SLA and bar owners as complicit perpetrators in the destruction of their neighborhood. Still, despite their inability to prevent what they understand to be the state's anti-community entrepreneurialism and despite their feelings of powerlessness, residents continue to attend meetings and fight bars today. Less clear has been why they do so.

CHAPTER 3

WEAVING A NOSTALGIA NARRATIVE

I am aware that it is childish, but sometimes, leaning against the spick-and-span new bar, I am overcome by nostalgia for the gutter.

—JOSEPH MITCHELL[1]

BOB HAS LIVED IN THE EAST VILLAGE SINCE 1972. Stocky and bearded with his curly, frizzy, and thinning hair tied in a small ponytail, he stands near the corner of East Seventh Street and Avenue A, up the street from his apartment, every weekend night and most weeknights, like clockwork, until the early hours of the morning. As I conducted my nighttime fieldwork in bars and on the streets, I knew at some point during the night I could walk over to the corner and usually find Bob there, holding court in front of Ray's Candy Store—a relic of a fast-food joint that opened around when Bob first moved to the neighborhood. A polymath and critic in subjects of politics, architecture, literature, film, and history, Bob spends his nights on the corner engrossed in two activities. The first is his bull sessions with friends and acquaintances. These longtime residents often stop by for varying amounts of time to chat, and sometimes to share "war stories" about their experiences in the neighborhood. But the most common participants in Bob's corner world are people who, in earlier times, would have exclusively populated these streets day and night: homeless people, artists, drug addicts, veterans, squatters, and radicals. This gritty cast of characters always changes, as some of them sometimes find themselves in jail, in a hospital, or somewhere else in the neighborhood or city on a drug binge. Since everyone knows he will be there, Bob rarely stands alone at night. With most people he listens more than he speaks, and he enjoys the random, free-flowing conversations with his fellow stalwarts and remaining characters of downtown. His second activity almost seems to contradict the first. Bob stands on this corner because it is one of the most lively and well-trafficked in the neighborhood, including for new nightlife revelers.

Bob has long had an interest in photography. Today he photographs and writes a blog about the East Village, which he began in 2006 as a chronicle of Jim Power's housing ordeal. Known around the neighborhood as the "Mosaic Man," Jim Power is a Vietnam War veteran and local artist who made his name

by making mosaics on civic hardware such as lampposts and abandoned buildings in the 1980s, some of which remain today.[2] He squatted in a property nick-
named "the Cave" on St. Mark's Place with other artists until a developer kicked
them out (along with his dog and art materials). Bob, who had been photographing downtown neighborhoods for decades and knew Jim from around
the East Village, decided to document Jim's struggles in blog form. He soon
after expanded it into a larger project on how the neighborhood had changed
and was still changing, and of what had been left behind or continued hiding
in plain sight. Like Weegee, the mysterious and eccentric photojournalist on
the Lower East Side from the 1930s and 1940s, Bob embeds himself among his
subjects and aims for realistic portrayals.[3] He spends much of the night taking
still and action pictures of the people he sees and knows, the gritty characters, and the young revelers, all of whom he encounters while standing on the
corner. While the old and new occasionally interact, they usually ignore each
other. Bob understands the interaction to be far more one-sided. He says that
the neighborhood has changed so much that the corner's characters, who once
gave the East Village a distinct image as a place for alternative cultures and
spaces, are now like "ghosts who people pass but don't see."[4] In his blog posts he
combines photos with comments, weaving commentary on the neighborhood's
gentrification with his description of the situation. In his typical calm voice and
steady pace, Bob explains:

> I try to put things together in such a way that you really are not going to get
> what I'm doing unless you both look at the pictures and read it. Generally,
> people assume that, "Oh, I can read it," and know the story, or "I can just
> look at the picture," and know the story. You can look at the pictures in
> *Scientific American*, and you don't have to read it. It's a very simplistic sort
> of magazine. Newspaper stories, they put a picture in, and they re-say what
> they're already saying. I don't do that. And I do it to make people participate
> more so it penetrates a little more deeply and it involves more neural activity
> and they might remember it more.

On a Friday night Bob and I are standing outside Ray's with a few regular
characters: Chris Flash, an activist journalist and publisher of the underground
anarchist newspaper *The Shadow*; Biker Bill, a gruff, heavily tattooed Vietnam
veteran; and L.E.S. Jewels, a heroin addict with several facial tattoos (some
representing the number of times he has overdosed) who has regular run-ins
with the police. Of the four, Jewels maintains the strongest daytime presence
in the neighborhood. He is often among the group of homeless people and

FIGURE 10   Jim "Mosaic Man" Power (to the left of the lamppost), with "experts" making repairs to one of his mosaics. Photograph by Bob Arihood, 2009, courtesy of the Estate of Robert Arihood.

drug addicts who hang out in Tompkins Square Park, directly across the street from Ray's. With pressure from the police, his group competes with new users, namely young families and wealthy residents, over the use of the park's spaces. They usually confine themselves to certain sections or benches closest to Avenue A. At night, Jewels, the local homeless population, and other characters disappear amid the swirl of activity.

Scores of laughing revelers, younger and better kempt than Bob's regular group, steadily pass by. Sometimes the ghosts become visible. "Goddamn yuppie bastards," says Chris to no one in particular as he scans the sidewalk. "I really do hate these fucking yuppies." Biker Bill, who often stares and catcalls at the women dressed up for a night out who pass by, grunts in agreement. "Hey cutie!" and "Hello lovely!" are his common phrases, while the young ladies usually ignore him. Tonight, one reveler says to her friend as they pass us, "Every night, same people," in reference Bill and the others. A scene then takes place in front of the group: two young men are helping a young woman as she stumbles off the curb after they leave a bar. One man flags a cab, while the other holds her up and explains that she is too drunk and they have to go home. The one standing by the cab grows impatient as she refuses to get in. Observing the commotion, Chris and Coney Island Mike, another street character who has arrived, get closer to them. Coney Island Mike asks, "Hey, you guys going to Brooklyn?"

"Yeah," says the man holding up the girl, barely glancing at him.

"Then here, go to Brooklyn," Mike says as he opens the cab door for them.

Chris then starts shouting, "The yuppies are going to Brooklyn! The yuppies are going to Brooklyn!"

They both start singing the song "No Sleep Till Brooklyn," by the Beastie Boys. The young revelers ignore them while the two men continue trying to convince the girl to go home. They eventually succeed and all get into the cab.

The more I hung out with Bob the more curious I became about why someone who laments how gentrification destroyed the sense of community in the neighborhood chooses to stand in the heart of its nightlife scene, one of the smoking guns. I ask Bob why he continues to hang out in front of Ray's.

FIGURE 11 A scene of passing revelers and longtime neighborhood characters outside Ray's Candy Store on Avenue A. Photograph by Bob Arihood, 2009, courtesy of the Estate of Robert Arihood.

"I used to stand here in the old days," he explains, "and Ray had forty-ounce Budweiser, illegal.[5] And I'd smoke cigarettes, drink beer, talk to the hookers, because the hookers would come from the school over on Eleventh and Twelfth between Third Avenue and Second Avenue. That block was a big hooker block; that was the main school. And they'd all do a job, come over here, and they'd always walk diagonally through the intersection, because it was a direct route. And they owned the street anyway. And you always knew it was a hooker because she'd walk diagonally across there [he points to the opposite corner, where revelers are standing outside of a bar]. And they'd go down and buy their drugs, down at the Laundromat, and then they'd come back here for a chocolate shake or something, get the taste out of their mouth.[6] And I'd talk to them, you know, they'd ask for a cigarette, and I could find out what was going on over there, I could find out from the squatters that came through here what's going on over there, the cops come in here, the junkies would be in there, the narcotics cops would be in there, the drug dealer would be in there, the hookers would all be in there, and they'd all be *right in there* [pointing at Ray's]. And it was neutral territory. That was Switzerland. And they could all go in there and I'd stand out here and watch and talk to them.

"This is the way news was gathered. And I don't pretend to be a journalist and I don't really have any desire to be a journalist or a newspaper person, though I have worked for them at different times, but this is the way you get stories. And knowing your subject. It was all here. And then when they started cleaning crime up, that disappeared, and I had to go to this [corner] to find out what was going on. And then this [crime] quieted down maybe early 2000s, this really, really dropped off. But this is a special spot. I don't know how to really characterize it to give people the real understanding of what *this* was. And this was not the only place like this—these kind of places were all over the fuckin' city. In neighborhoods, people knew what was going on. If you had a police force that kept everything under control, these weren't bad neighborhoods at all. But then *they* started moving in."

Later in the night a man in his forties named Lawrence greets Bob. Lawrence knows Bob from when he moved into the East Village, in 1986. He is carrying groceries and heading home, but he stops to chat. Bob introduces us, and I ask Lawrence about his early memories in the neighborhood.

"I saw someone get stabbed in the park on the day I moved in," he replies, pointing towards Tompkins Square Park, across the street. "I thought the two guys on top of him were just punching him, but the guy didn't get up and I saw a lot of blood. Then later I saw the two guys giggling on the ground in the park."

Bob and Lawrence then spend some time catching up. During a lull in their conversation, Lawrence looks around at the nightlife activity, shakes his head, and says, "What the fuck happened with this neighborhood?" Bob does not break his gaze from the sidewalk action. Lawrence pauses briefly, shrugs, and says, "Well, beats getting your throat cut for $7."

"Yeah, I suppose," says Bob.

———

A common theme in my interviews and conversations with residents like Bob was their past experience in downtown neighborhoods when they were slums. I always asked them "What was downtown like when you first moved here?" and they immediately talked about its conditions of crime, open drug activity, homelessness, violence, prostitution, abandonment, decrepitude, and overall feel of menace and danger. They would also often work these vivid descriptions into their answers to other questions, such as those that dealt with their neighborhood or their street in the present, and tell me specific stories of events they witnessed and characters they knew. But I was intrigued by the tone they struck when they discussed their early experiences in the neighborhood and the way that they framed them in our conversations. None of them outright condoned the negative activities or conditions that they routinely saw. They merely described them matter-of-factly. But a clear sense of loss of the place and people they knew filled their voices. They even hinted that they preferred their neighborhood the old way, in a slum-like state, in which they established their own sense of community. Residents regularly made such statements as they behaved in ways that countered downtown's new nightlife activity, such as Bob's nighttime sessions, as well as film screenings, art exhibits, and formal protests. Some residents were giddy when they talked about the adventures they had while living downtown. Many expressed sympathy for their neighborhood's downtrodden population and its victims of violence, poverty, and disease and pointed to the larger structural policies that affected them, such as deindustrialization and a lack of downtown investment. But they also often presented these figures and the surrounding environment as exciting and authentic urban backdrops for their vibrant and creative community.

What these residents have in common is that they are all "early gentrifiers," or those gentrifiers who moved to the neighborhood during its early gentrification and remain there today.[7] Today downtown Manhattan's early gentrifiers hold a distinct position between the lifelong and longtime low-income, working-class residents and the new residents and visitors who inhabit significantly different neighborhoods. On the one hand, early gentrifiers have lived in their neighborhood long enough to have experienced its period as a disinvested, low-income slum (the 1970s until the early 1990s, depending on the specific area).[8] In that time, they have established strong roots and senses of community in their neighborhood. Early gentrifiers possess a high degree of place attachment based on personal experiences, relationships, and social networks.[9] They see themselves as "old-timers" and legitimate representatives of the community, even though they voluntarily moved to the neighborhood as young adults. On the other hand, early gentrifiers generally possess greater amounts of educational and economic—not to mention cultural and social—capital and hold higher-status occupations in comparison with low-income residents. As a result, early gentrifiers are in a more favorable position than lifelong low-income residents to deal with the harms of gentrification, such as an escalated standard of living. This social position gives these early gentrifiers a unique perspective on both the past and the contemporary neighborhood that rests on their own experiences. They have a clear material interest in protesting and fighting gentrification, since many of them live in rent-regulated apartments (either rent-controlled or rent-stabilized), which places limits on how high rents can go and allows low- to middle-income people to remain in gentrifying neighborhoods. Many have experienced pressure to move out from their landlords, who can earn a lot more money on units once they hit the open market. But new nightlife seemed to trigger an especially strong reaction in these residents—an emotional connection with downtown—that went beyond material concerns.

To disentangle the complex web of emotional memory and longing for the special conditions from a lost era while also wanting the harms that stemmed from them reduced, some residents emphasized the positive aspects of life in their neighborhood, such as its cultural scenes, artistic freedoms, and diversity. This claim, of course, faces a recursive dilemma, since the positive and negative aspects of downtown Manhattan cannot be totally separated and observed on their own. Early gentrifiers lived within a unique urban context during which both conditions existed simultaneously. The 1970s and 1980s in downtown Manhattan marked a "transitional moment," or a time of balance between the "emerging and the residual," when the ashes of the old and the seeds of the new coexisted, intersected, and intertwined.[10] Early gentrifiers moved into neighborhoods that were dealing with the harsh pains of urban rebirth. Their experiences during this period had a profound impact on them that lasts to today.

I realized that the tales and statements that Bob and other early gentrifiers were telling me were filled with the complexities of nostalgia. Nostalgia represents a "collective memory," or a powerful social construction of the past in the present, specifically under conditions of impending loss.[11] The nostalgic tales focus on the past, but they tell us far more about the residents' lives today. While people often quickly dismiss nostalgia as an overly romantic and passing emotion, it is in fact strongly connected with one's identity and sense of community.[12] These residents were using a "nostalgia narrative," or an imagined story of the past that deliberately selects certain elements from personal history while excluding others to construct a version that is more favorable than the reality, to counter the contrasting images of their neighborhood and community that a new, powerful force such as a nightlife scene produces.[13] While nostalgia seems to be a common aspect of how established groups of old-timers remember their pasts, nostalgia narratives are more complete and fully realized stories that place people at the center of their own tale. They also require triggers in the present to form, or the sense—real or imagined—that something signifying the past that helps construct their identity in the present is under threat.[14] These triggers represent threats to an ex post facto understanding of place and identity. Contemporary events and processes transform taken-for-granted aspects of historical reality into significant, even indispensable, foundations of the past and present. Most importantly, nostalgia narratives have the power to construct new identities and ideologies that serve as bases for collective action.

Gentrification, particularly as it was represented and aided by nightlife scenes, triggered feelings of nostalgia in downtown Manhattan's early gentrifiers, who saw new bars, revelers, and activities as threats to the social and cultural environments, the sense of community, and the attachment to place that they remembered. Other aspects of gentrification, such as escalating rents, certainly trigger similar feelings. But this commercial dimension dramatically encapsulates several of them. Most importantly, new bars cause early gentrifiers to feel that these newcomers threaten to socially displace them, or to strip their authority, social power, and ability to make decisions and control their own place in their neighborhood. As nightlife establishments and activities continued to proliferate throughout the 2000s, these residents actually witnessed the social and cultural displacement of their community as new bars opened where familiar businesses existed and revelers dominated street life at night.[15] Their nostalgia narrative consists of their personal experiences within their neighborhood, specifically with its gritty past and its ethnic and cultural diversity, and portrays them as integral aspects of an authentic community. At times, particularly when they mention stories of crime and violence, their narrative does not seem to idealize the past, as rose-tinted nostalgia narratives tend to do. However, they weave these negative tales with their own positive experiences in their neighborhood and with its people. Despite internal contradictions, they use this narrative to construct a local identity for themselves as their neighborhood's symbolic "owners" and to legitimate their ideology of community.[16] This community ideology contrasts with newer residents and visiting nightlife revelers, whom they identify as homogeneous (and homogenizing), transient and uncreative consumers, and "inauthentic." The powerlessness that they feel from their inability to successfully fight the encroaching nightlife feeds their perception that their social authority in the neighborhood is under threat, which in turn reinforces their self-identity as symbolic owners.

"OWNING" A NEIGHBORHOOD

Recalling Lived Experiences

An important aspect of early gentrifiers' nostalgia narrative and basis for their identity as symbolic owners is their experience of their neighborhood at the time of their arrival. They particularly constructed place attachments amid downtown Manhattan's negative conditions, including abandonment, neglect, and arson. Doreen is a photographer in her early sixties. Originally from Germany, she came to the United States in 1966. After ten years living and working near the more upscale area of midtown, she moved to the East Village. Drawn to the gritty neighborhood and the murals that were painted on the sides of buildings, she turned away from her work in chic fashion photography. "The whole neighborhood reminded me of Berlin after the war," she says. "It looked like it had been bombed. It was a war zone, it was a bloody war zone." This period was when the city neglected these downtown neighborhoods, landlords purposefully destroyed buildings, and not many businesses were open. For residents during this time, damage and destruction characterized the setting of their everyday lives. Early gentrifiers identify with having been in an extreme situation together. Virgil, a fifty-three-year-old community activist who moved to the East Village in the mid-1970s, explains this sentiment:

> It used to be that this was an abandoned part of the city. The landlords, they were absent landlords, developers did not look at this neighborhood, the city did not care about the neighborhood, it was left to the people that lived here. The people that lived here appropriated it to themselves. They treated it as if it belonged to them.

Structural abandonment meant that newcomers experienced the neighborhood as "theirs," despite legal rights to the contrary and the presence of existing residents.

In facing these negative conditions, many people became politically active and took to community organizing. Along with the local art and music scene, these efforts were a way that they established roots in the area. Physical conditions often necessitated such activity. Madeline, a community activist in her late fifties, explains the work they had to do:

> Every other building was empty, or the ones that were occupied were abandoned by the owner of the building. And the tenants that were there stayed behind, lived with this mess, and it was a moment in which a lot of community organizing occurred in order for people to survive, basically.

Residents formed tenant, block, and community associations in order to address the problems caused by neglect. Without assistance from landlords or reliable maintenance workers, residents were forced to handle their own basic services such as heat, water, and electricity. The city government acquired hundreds of properties in downtown Manhattan in the 1970s through tax arrears and foreclosures, but at the time the buildings had little resale value and the neighborhoods had little hope for redevelopment.[17] The city's fiscal crisis also prevented officials from funding rehabilitation or upkeep. Instead, they formed legal arrangements with tenants to maintain the properties. Under a "homesteading" system, the city government allowed residents to remain in buildings rent-free, provided they worked for its maintenance. While most homesteaders were low-income Puerto Ricans, many were newcomers to downtown who invested "sweat equity" instead of money.[18] There were also various squatter groups who moved into abandoned buildings without any formal agreements and risked eviction at any time. But squatters occupied and rehabilitated buildings that would have likely remained in states of disrepair. Finally, gentrifiers collaborated with existing Puerto Rican residents to develop community gardens in the rubble-strewn lots where buildings formerly stood.[19] For residents, this work not only helped beautify their neglected and blighted neighborhood but also fostered their place attachment amid negative spatial conditions.

Today the early gentrifiers feel that their community activism efforts prevented downtown's total decline. They weave their commitment to the slum into their narrative and their new local identity. Doreen, who was a homesteader, states:

> Because of this kind of pioneering work we did, any of this can exist. Because if the city had had their way, this was slated to be basically connected via the East River Park to Wall Street and it would be a residential area for Wall Street brokers. None of us would be here.[20]

By "any of this," Doreen is referring to the built environment itself and the fact that her neighborhood exists at all, not its gentrification. And by "us," she of course refers to pioneers like her, not newcomers. But she also understands "pioneering" differently from its common academic usage. Many scholars consider early gentrifiers like Doreen to be "pioneers" in the gentrification process, that is, a group that does not mind harsh conditions or impoverished neighborhoods (and sometimes seek them out) and who either signal to real estate and business interests that a neighborhood is suitable for redevelopment or plan on gaining from their own investments.[21] But as Doreen demonstrates, residents understand their role and use the concept of "pioneering" in a different manner. They hardly see themselves as useful speculators for capitalist interests or adventurers going into the wilderness. To them, they are pioneers in the sense that they cultivated and cared for spaces that most people did not.[22]

Non-homesteaders and non-squatters also include downtown's negative conditions in their narrative and use them to construct an ownership identity. It was their experience of living among unwanted spaces—apartments, buildings, and lots—and in a dangerous public environment that fostered feelings of proprietorship despite a lack of actual ownership. Daniel is a thirty-eight-year-old activist, neighborhood historian, and walking-tour guide, who was born in the East Village. He lived in the neighborhood until spring 2008, when he could no longer afford the rent, and moved to Brooklyn.[23] But he still works in the neighborhood and is active in local issues. He recalls, "It was always like we owned the area, that the neighborhood actually policed itself, took care of itself, and [the police] never paid any attention if something was happening. And now all of a sudden the city starts taking it back." Here, Daniel also demonstrates that residents lack culpability when it comes to gentrification, with the city "all of a sudden . . . taking it back" from them. As he and Doreen both imply, early gentrifiers feel the neighborhood was theirs because of the work they did amid abandonment. Based on this experience, residents identify as "pioneers" in the sense that they established their own long-lasting social roots in the neighborhood that they feel should be recognized today.

This nostalgia narrative that underscores symbolic ownership omits several key historical facts. First, it does not include the city's fiscal crisis and ongoing shifts in capital away from urban downtowns during the 1970s. It is more likely that these two conditions, rather than the reparative actions of local residents, tremendously prevented development from taking place. Indeed, these neighborhoods have a long history of being targeted and threatened by developers. But such economic conditions as those produced by the Depression and World War II and such economic shifts as suburbanization played more significant roles in thwarting developers' efforts than residents' protests, as important as these were.[24] Second, it ignores the role that the work of early gentrifiers plays in gentrification, such as by making their neighborhood attractive with improved conditions and new amenities. As is the case with other types of gentrifiers, downtown Manhattan's early gentrifiers do not mention the unintended consequences of their efforts. But through their work, gentrifiers often imperil the conditions they wish to see preserved.[25] Finally, their narrative does not include the existing presence of low-income residents who had already been dealing with the stark realities of life in underserved and underresourced neighborhoods. However, they weave these individuals into the narrative in other ways.

The Authentic Neighborhood: Diversity and Creativity

Along with physical conditions, early gentrifiers also incorporate their neighborhood's social and cultural conditions into their nostalgia narrative. They weave their personal experiences with existing residents, local characters, and local places together with their own contributions to its creativity to claim that the neighborhood of this time, its cultures, and its communities were "authentic." This claim forms a significant part of their new local identity as symbolic owners. In the case of David Grazian's Chicago blues clubs, consumers use popular images of race, namely the hypersexualized folktales of poor black musicians, to confer authenticity and to select from an array of blues venue options.[26] Japonica Brown-Saracino's gentrifier "social preservationists," meanwhile, identify such attributes as independence, tradition, and a close relationship to place as key components for authentic community of the "old-timers" in their neighborhoods and towns.[27] But downtown Manhattan's early gentrifiers do not confer an authentic status solely on other groups. They mostly reserve notions of authenticity and authentic community for themselves and their own lives in the neighborhood. Existing groups are important to early gentrifiers in their narratives in the sense that they were part of their experiences in the neighborhood or resemble their understanding of it as a unique and diverse place. In conferring authenticity on their downtown neighborhood, they particularly focus on the diversity of its people and activities and the amount of creativity that took place.

Early gentrifiers frequently describe their neighborhood's population during their early years as diverse. But it is rarely the reason why they initially chose to live there. The most common explanation for why early gentrifiers came to the Lower East Side was its affordability. David is an early gentrifier who later became bar owner. Now in his early forties, he moved to the Lower East Side in 1984 to attend college at New York University (NYU), located a few blocks west. Quite simply, he says, he chose to live in the neighborhood because it was close to school and affordable:

> Moved over here because I could afford it, in school. I came to NYU on a lark, passed up a scholarship elsewhere, got [to New York City] and realized I was not in Oklahoma anymore and things were much more expensive. In Oklahoma you could rent an apartment for like $80 a month back then. Here [on the Lower East Side], I ended up getting a share for $250. Even then that was a bargain. So I was over on Stanton Street, and it just became my neighborhood.

As mentioned earlier in the chapter, for many early gentrifiers who fight bars, downtown Manhattan is still affordable because they live in apartments that are rent regulated. But these facts are not part of early gentrifiers' nostalgia narrative, nor do they see themselves as part of a demographic trend of more whites moving in that has led to a decline in racial and ethnic diversity. Looking back on early days in the neighborhood, diversity was not just more important than affordability but also integral to what made it unique. Virgil lauds diversity as one of the East Village's significant attributes:

> People love this neighborhood for being a mixed neighborhood. Even when it was a ghetto it was unlike other ghettos. It was unlike the South Bronx, it was unlike parts of Brooklyn, Bushwick, wherever, and it was unlike Harlem, because it had, my block, was about one-third black, one-third white, one-third Latino. At the time there weren't any East Asians on the block, but in

other parts of the neighborhood there were. And people of *all* colors appreciated that fact about the neighborhood, even though in large areas of life, of the life world, they were segregated.

Virgil bases his description of the neighborhood on what he remembers about his block. Many early gentrifiers share his notion of their neighborhood as diverse. When we compare their statements with U.S. Census data from the time, the neighborhood as well as their own census tracts were indeed very diverse and became less so over time. Even though affordability was its key draw for them, diversity is what they encountered and what made living there unique and irreplaceable. Although they often lament the lack of diversity among new residents and visiting revelers, they are unable to recognize their own role in attracting more white residents and visitors to downtown.

Along with its highly varied ethnic composition, early gentrifiers also point to the large number of downtown "characters." They cite their experiences with these people as an important part of what made the area authentic. Many of these figures were artists, eccentrics, or members of various marginal groups or were homeless (by circumstance or personal choice) or mentally ill, artists, eccentrics, or members of various marginal groups. In this sense, as public characters they were more like Duneier's homeless African-American book vendors than like Jacobs's friendly white ethnic grocers.[28] They were "broken windows" in a neighborhood filled with them, who, in the nostalgia narrative, gave their neighborhood charm and made it unique.[29] Given its social isolation and formal neglect during this period, downtown was a place where such people were accepted and where public spaces were accessible to a wide array of groups for their own uses. Despite the negative conditions that surrounded their lives, early gentrifiers often speak fondly of these characters, who lent unpredictability to daily life. For the most part, early gentrifiers describe characters such as the homeless in terms that demonstrate social distance. David remembers his neighborhood by using highly adventurous terms:

> When I came to this neighborhood, it was like you were going to look around and find Colonel Kurtz somewhere. I mean, you were up the river. This was the most singular place in the United States of America. It felt like you were at the edge of the earth. As a bit of an action junkie, I can't tell you how exciting it was. I'm in this place where anything in the world can happen to me tomorrow.

Other residents saw the Lower East Side in general as an ideal setting for such characters.

Early gentrifiers also use their neighborhood's public characters to portray their experiences in the neighborhood as authentic. One day while at a café on the Lower East Side, Virgil tells me about the importance of local people in his portrayal of the neighborhood as authentic:

> We're losing the cultural character of the neighborhood. Instead of having these local places, the neighborhood has completely changed. Instead of having folks who hang out on the sidewalks, you have these nonlocal folks coming in and hanging out in front of the bars. You just don't have the same character of the Lower East Side anymore. When you talk about the authentic experience, who's to say what the authentic experience is? It's gone! You can't find those real folks anymore.

Here Virgil particularly uses the word "real" to describe locality and its importance in characterizing authenticity. I ask him for an example of a local character to determine what he means by "real."

> "There was this guy, Marty, who would play basketball in the morning and then he would, he actually taught a lot of the people basketball, because he came here to be in this kind of environment. Then he would hold court in the park. He had students, they would come to him and he'd teach literature, he'd teach art, history, philosophy, even though he didn't know anything about philosophy. He would hold court, and then he would go back to his place with his 'patients,' whom he could psychoanalyze. This is such a characteristic thing, that this guy would just do this kind of stuff, and he would take money for it too. You'd have to pay him something. And he was highly respected here. People all over knew Marty, 'Oh yeah, Marty!'"
>
> "He was like the 'mayor'?"
>
> "Yeah, they called him the philosopher. He was the philosopher, but he was also the basketball player, and the psychoanalyst, and just a very prominent, important person."
>
> "What happened to him?"
>
> "He jumped off the Williamsburg Bridge."

Overall these statements provide greater nuance to the notion that "pioneers" work to rid the neighborhood of existing negative conditions such as homelessness, presumably to avoid clashing with their own middle-class values or to boost their own investments.[30] While many early gentrifiers took part in this effort, others see the area's characters as intertwined with their personal experiences and therefore remember them in a positive light. But these characters existed because of the harsh realities of life in a disinvested slum, such as substance abuse and mental illness, all taking place in public space. Downtown's public characters may have had substance-abuse problems and personal issues, and early gentrifiers may not have always socialized with them, but their presence in these neighborhoods became a source of place attachment and an identifiable feature of everyday life. Although they originated from destructive processes of deindustrialization and reduced public services, these characters were familiar and normal to residents, who have turned their interactions with them into meaningful social identities. In other words, we see the ashes of decline and seeds of renewal coinciding, on the streets and in daily life, at this key transitional moment in downtown's history.

In many cases, and as in Milano's, they encountered these characters and conditions in bars, where early gentrifiers hung out. Doreen, the photographer, recalls:

> "Those crummy bars really still had been neighborhood places. You know the one on Fifth Street? Fifth and A?"
>
> "Sophie's?"
>
> "Yeah, that, I used to live on that block. That was comical, because I used to go in there with my baby, with my child when he was very little, and have a beer. No big deal."
>
> "That was your local spot?"
>
> "Yeah, totally."
>
> "Who used to go there?"
>
> "Lots of artists, lots of bums, a lot of heavy-drinking bums. Because beer was cheap, and people were always somebody buying them beer, and so on."

Episodes of residents encountering homeless people in bars contrast sharply with the social relations of today's nightlife scenes, in which the local homeless people and the young revelers congregate separately with only occasional interactions, as depicted at the start of this chapter. Early gentrifiers drank in the existing bars that accepted them. They understood these bars to be unique, authentic aspects of their neighborhood, and they relish their experiences in them. As David remembers:

> The Vasmay Lounge, when that [place] was the Vasmay Lounge, it was like the Puerto Rican Milano's back in the day. I lived on Stanton Street, I was right there, I had to walk to NYU. Back then, of course, Houston Street just looked awful. It was smelly, there was all the noodle places, and it just smelled like shit with crack vials everywhere and it really stunk.

So one day I'm walking by, it was right around July Fourth, or maybe Puerto Rican Day, and Mr. Vasquez—there were two guys that owned it, but only one of them was still alive by the time I got here in the '80s—he's outside cooking chickens on the grill. And that's the singularity I'm talking about, you know? It's a bar and he's outside cooking chickens! And he knows everybody in the neighborhood. They're coming down there, eats chicken with them too, playing dominoes. Here I am, this stupid white kid coming by, "Hey hey! Come have a chicken."

That's it! I had a couple beers, and he liked me. He kind of took me under his wing, taught me things, showed me things. So I'd go down there on my way to school.

In short, early gentrifiers protest new bars using an understanding of authentic community that is in part based on their past experiences within bars.

David describes Vasmay Lounge as like a "Puerto Rican Milano's," the last of the Bowery bars. Milano's represents a key example of the authentic community that early gentrifiers encountered and that David "preserved."[31] We will learn more about his early entrepreneurial activities in the following chapter, but based on his experience as a bar owner, and more importantly his own experiences in the neighborhood's local bars, David set out to personally preserve the places from his youth that represented his understanding of the authentic Lower East Side. First, he reopened Vasmay, the bar near his first apartment:

So Vasmay, Mr. Vasquez eventually killed himself. He had cancer. But Vasmay got bought up and then eventually became Meow Mix and everything. I was helping them out to keep them alive because they were my friends. I liked Meow Mix. I lived across the street by then and I'd go in and hang out. Finally, it wasn't happening, so they wanted to sell me the place with the money they were making. So I decided to make it Vasmay Lounge again.

David knew that the neighborhood had changed a lot since his early days and that the bar would never be the same as it was. But there was another bar from his youth that was still open. On his daily travels, after leaving Vasmay Lounge,

. . . about halfway to school, there was Milano's. I'd go in Milano's, and I remember the first time I went in Milano's. They had this old, grumpy bartender, Dennis.[32] He was a great guy. And this goes to singularity—we walk in there, this is probably about '85 or '86, so we go in there, and being college kids, we asked, "What kind of beer do you have?" And he says, "I got Schlitz." So we looked at him, and being college kids, we said, "Is it any good?" And he looks at us and says, "It made Pennsylvania famous, didn't it?" So we had a Schlitz, and back then they had frosted mugs, and we sat down and all the old guys started telling stories, and it was romantic. So that was my trail, all the way through college.

Through his real estate connections that he acquired as a longtime bar owner in the neighborhood, David heard that Denis wanted to sell the bar.

> "Then, all of a sudden I saw this opportunity to buy Milano's, which was going to go to some club kid asshole. So now I have that old trail again."
> "It's almost like a goal of yours is to preserve the neighborhood."
> "Yeah." [He pauses briefly, pulls a somber face, and continues in an emotional tone.] "That's what we named that company, it was 'Preserve Milano's.' I haven't changed anything there. I bought that to preserve it, because God forbid some asshole puts a DJ in there. I'd have to shoot him. That bar, you go in there and there's a real exchange of ideas. I mean, some of the people might be crazy, but it's got that thing. Vasmay, I had to bring it all back and sort of re-create it, which was really impossible because I don't have a C of O [certificate of occupancy] now for the downstairs, which he did, so I can't put the pool table back down there. But it's pretty authentic old-school."

In terms of practices of social preservation, David's act served to maintain a level of authenticity in the neighborhood.[33] He is, of course, a unique case. Most early gentrifiers have been unable to actually preserve the authentic places from their early days in their neighborhood. For David, preserving authenticity required economic capital to invest in the business as well as social capital to learn about its sale. For most of his cohort, such authentic characters and places, as well as the negativity surrounding them, gradually disappear and get replaced by new people and bars.

By moving into commercial storefronts, bars also physically replace many of the commercial establishments that provided the space for early gentrifiers to develop a sense of social and communal ties. Virgil describes:

> The rising commercial rents pushing out all of the mom-and-pops, all of the old stores that were here, all the local services. They aren't all gone yet, and the process is itself a complex process because the rising commercial rents and the upscale residents are actually bringing in some local services, but I think we're on a track which is going to lead to a net loss in local services.

"Mom-and-pop" shops, or independently run stores with owners whom everyone knows, evoke warm feelings of community and trust in a neighborhood,
and early gentrifiers often contrast them with new bars. Patti, a musician in her
early forties, focuses on the cultural institutions that she says were "kicked out,
replaced. I mean, we also lost like six avant-garde little theaters and clubs from
below Houston, which most of them became bars. One, the whole building was
wrecked, where Collective Unconscious was, so we don't know if a bar will end
up there."[34] The loss of both existing commercial establishments and early commercial establishments triggered feelings of nostalgia. For downtown's early
gentrifiers, these places were "theirs" and were important parts of the authentic
community that they created.

Early gentrifiers also describe downtown as a creative place, with well-
documented art, music, and nightlife scenes.[35] They understand these cultural scenes to have been more creative than commercial, which factors
significantly in their consideration of their neighborhood as authentic. As
Daniel recalls:

> [it was] very diverse; it was pretty incredible. Those artists actually lived
> in the neighborhood and participated in the communities here and got
> together and had meetings in the coffee shops and played at night and all
> went out together after and lived here and worked here and all that kind of
> stuff here.

Downtown fits early gentrifiers' understanding of authentically creative communities because it was a place where artists both lived and worked.[36] Inexpensive rents provided affordable living and working spaces for artists and
musicians.[37] Apartments were also in close proximity to affordable commercial storefronts for galleries and performance spaces. Residents also feel that
the abandoned built environment contributed to the type of art that people
made. Daniel states, "There used to be just abandoned buildings and, like, we'd
have a party at 27 East Sixth Street, you know, be there at 7. Or it would be
an impromptu art gallery for the evening, and then a party in the evening."
The lack of regulation by the city and police and the overall neglect of public
spaces gave residents a sense of freedom in their artistic pursuits. Public art—
such as Jim "Mosaic Man" Power's mosaics, as well as murals depicting harsh
local conditions or memorializing the deceased, graffiti displaying political
statements, and theatrical and musical performances—thrived in spaces that
residents appropriated as their own. They used walls as canvases and vacant
lots as stages, and they fondly recall how the area fostered unique forms of
creative expression.

For many early gentrifiers, their neighborhood, its conditions, and its people inspired them to create art. Bob, for instance, from this chapter's introduction, represents such a figure. He had long been curious about the East Village and sought to document its conditions. Another is Doreen, who, as mentioned earlier, was originally a fashion photographer drawn to downtown neighborhoods for their people and murals. She hung out in and photographed the neighborhood more and began including these pictures in her exhibits. One day she invited me to a gallery space where an exhibition of her work documenting the neighborhood was being set up. Doreen recalls her decision to dissociate from the chic fashion world:

> I used to put stuff from the Lower East Side into the same program.[38] And I had parties, so my art director friends from Madison Avenue came to hang out with the crowd from here. And they loved it and they danced like wild and they tried to get the girls. And then, when they came to my office, guess what they said? They said, "Why are you hanging out with all these Spics and Niggers?" Just like that. So I had no choice but to turn on my heel and go.

She became entrenched in the East Village and was inspired to document what she saw around her.

> I got up close, really, really up close. I was hiding. That's the only time I was hiding, when I did the night activity in the shooting galleries that were everywhere. And I photographed police raids where the police abused the drug addicts, stole everything off of them, stashed the drugs away, used the drugs, you know, whatever. Horrible, horrible, horrible.

While highly varied in terms of genre and style, the artists and artistic works from this period share a common origin in the urban detritus of a neglected downtown. In this sense, early gentrifiers argue that the singular cultural production of their neighborhood was intertwined with its social conditions and built environment, which emphasizes its irreplaceability. Most importantly, early gentrifiers (even those who were not active in the art and music scenes) feel that new residents and visitors do not recognize the relationship between art and space, or the diversity and creativity that make downtown unique. Instead, they see the places where they congregate (bars) and the activity they engage in within them (alcohol consumption) as inappropriate and inauthentic uses of their neighborhood.

THE PROBLEMS WITH NOSTALGIA NARRATIVES

The influx of new bars, nightlife activities, and visiting revelers triggered early gentrifiers' sense of loss and the construction of their nostalgia narrative. Early gentrifiers claim that nightlife has displaced much of the social and cultural environment that they remember and threatens to displace what remains and decrease their social power. The presence of new bars and revelers symbolizes that their neighborhood, which once drew a small and self-selected array of visitors, has been opened up to a wide swath of outsiders. They feel that bars accelerate the process of gentrification by attracting "upscale" people as well as outsiders to downtown Manhattan. Seeing and hearing new bars and revelers on a daily basis constantly reinforce the victimhood role that they have constructed and their perception that the neighborhood might not be "theirs" much longer.

The fact that early gentrifiers have been unable to exert any social authority in their neighborhood by preventing bar proliferation represents an important contradiction in, and simultaneously a purpose for, the nostalgia narrative and a new local identity as symbolic owners, both of which purports that they are important actors in downtown Manhattan. Early gentrifiers use the narrative and their new local identity to define themselves against "nonlocal" nightlife revelers and combat the new images of their neighborhood as a destination for consumption and fun. They claim that the newer group possesses specific shortcomings that disrupt their sociocultural environment and damage the expectations that residents have for their own future in the neighborhood. As Bob states, "Today I feel that at times that there's no part of this [the neighborhood] I belong to. And I'm white, and I've gone to college—University of Chicago, Purdue University—and I went through it. I'm a white person, a WASP, and they're too fucking white for me." In a way the situation in downtown Manhattan exemplifies the classic "invasion-succession" model of neighborhood change that members of the Chicago school developed.[39] However, in this case the conflicts are not between established groups and incoming immigrants, and the wave of succession has no clear, identifiable conclusion. The conflicts in downtown Manhattan neighborhoods are also not the reverse process of when middle-class groups move into and revitalized low-income neighborhoods (i.e., gentrification).[40] Newcomers and visitors who may be similar to them in terms of race, ethnicity, and social class—white, college-educated, middle-class—do not share their experiences in the neighborhood. Rather, they compromise downtown Manhattan's diversity and creativity, and therefore its authenticity.

Early gentrifiers characterize newcomers and revelers in two ways, both of which reveal much about and contradict their nostalgia narrative and new local identity. First, they see them as a transient population that does not care about or respect the existing sociocultural environment that they constructed. The early gentrifiers' notion of "transience" contrasts with their conception of their own "permanence," which dovetails with their sense of symbolic proprietorship and affects how they understand the social character of the new population. Most importantly, early gentrifiers argue that these newcomers are not younger versions of themselves. They see young people in their neighborhood as different, but not simply because they are a new cohort in the neighborhood or members of a younger generation. As a transient population, newcomers and revelers—whom early gentrifiers often conflate—do not respect the communities that they established or the neighborhood's diversity and creativity. By contrast, early gentrifiers see themselves as permanent, with roots that are under threat of being torn out. But since they voluntarily moved into the neighborhood, they had to develop their permanent status. In their nostalgia narrative they therefore interpret the existing population's actions as a form of "acceptance."

Beth is fifty-six and moved to the Lower East Side in 1981 to live with her sister, who owned an art gallery in the neighborhood. A writer, Beth got an editorial job in publishing before becoming a teacher. When she describes her early days in the neighborhood, she contrasts it with its current condition:

> I don't like it now. It's just not a neighborhood for me anymore. It definitely was, and I felt we [she and her sister] were the interlopers back then. It still was very Puerto Rican at the time, but they took us in. . . . We thought it wouldn't ever change, the way SoHo had.[41] Partly because of the real estate, you know, the apartments being so small, the storefronts being so small. But then it did.

Beth expresses the common sentiment among early gentrifiers that the neighborhood is no longer "for" them. And like other early gentrifiers, she admits she felt like an interloper when she first moved in. Early gentrifiers recognized that their neighborhood's existing residents were from a different ethnic group, social class, and generation than theirs, and many of them describe how these residents often treated them coldly. Edward recalls his Polish neighbors, "Oh, for the first two years—at least—they wouldn't talk to me at all. But after a while they started saying hello to me. I guess they realized I wasn't going anywhere." At some point in their narrative, early gentrifiers claim or allude to being accepted by the existing populations.

But they see newcomers as qualitatively different from themselves. Beth contrasts her experience with that of newcomers:

> The neighborhood now, from what I see, are younger, wealthier people who, it's their first apartment in New York, maybe, and, well, it was for me, too, but it then remained my apartment. It's their first apartment [too, but] there's a lot more turnover. People aren't staying long. . . . They're not staying long to raise families there the way that [we] did.

Early gentrifiers characterize newcomers by their high turnover in apartments, escalated standard of living, and different lifestyles, which they regularly associate with nightlife consumption. Based on the newcomers' transience and behavior towards them, early gentrifiers conclude that they do not care about the community and sociocultural environment that they constructed. Edward describes new people in his building, "New people, they don't say hello to me. They're too busy with their own lives to get to know anyone." In other words, early gentrifiers do not "accept" newcomers. But their own notion of neighborhood "acceptance," which they depict in their nostalgia narrative, is problematic when we consider that it is a condition based on time. By labeling them as transient, early gentrifiers deny newcomers the possibility of acceptance. This reality largely results because they do not see them as interlopers but as threats.

Early gentrifiers apply this same description of transience to nightlife revelers, which contrasts with their own rootedness in the neighborhood's nightlife scene. As Daniel describes people who go out to bars:

> It's totally different; it's weird. And again, I think that's part of that transient population. Now, the entertainment is mostly geared towards outsiders coming to enjoy it. It's sort of a derogatory term these days, but "bridge and tunnel," whatever it's called, that seems to be more where it is.[42] I guess the main thing behind that is the artists can't afford to live here anymore. That's one of the main reasons. So it's become more of an attraction.

As he expressed earlier, Daniel fondly recalls the time when artists were able to live, work, and play in downtown Manhattan, which contributes to his understanding of its authenticity. He used to hang out in its existing bars as well as in the community-oriented first wave of bars that opened in the neighborhood. Early gentrifiers often describe these bars as places that were for locals. But he feels that the people he sees in the nightlife scene today do not contribute to or possess the same sense of community. He characterizes revelers as members of an anonymous crowd whose motivation in the neighborhood is consumption rather than community-building. Early gentrifiers consider downtown Manhattan's new nightlife scenes to be "attractions" akin to the "urban entertainment destinations" of Bourbon Street in New Orleans and the Las Vegas Strip ("Disneyland for adults" is also a common epithet).[43] For them downtown Manhattan has become a destination for all youth to enjoy without appreciation for its established social and cultural worlds.

Early gentrifiers are especially quick to label revelers as college students because of their youth, the nature of college students in general as a population that is always in flux, and their perception of college students as a rowdy and irresponsible group prone to wanton amusement and consumption. NYU plays an important role in this and is a major target of hostility. Although mainly located in Greenwich Village, NYU since the 1990s has gradually advanced east by buying buildings and constructing several new dormitories. Historically cheaper rents than in Greenwich Village made the Lower East Side and East Village and Bowery area places where NYU students lived and hung out for many decades prior to the school's institutional expansion. But longtime residents feel that new dormitories, gentrification, and nightlife proliferation have greatly increased the number of students living in downtown buildings, walking its streets, and drinking in its bars. Eva, a community activist who moved to the Lower East Side in the mid-1970s and now works for the New York City Housing Authority, describes:

> You will hear a lot of people in the Village, East or West, either one, that are not too friendly with NYU. . . . [Because] where [there are students] from the universities, guess what else is in there? Bars. That population that is brought by NYU is the population then that will become the customers of those places, because wherever you see universities you will have around, like, bohemic kind of communities. These bars tend to be bohemian-looking and attracting students of the university.

Eva's comment echoes the feeling of many early gentrifiers. She places blame on "bohemian-looking" bars and "bohemic kind of communities" for attracting transient college students who they claim merely consume. But she does not acknowledge that NYU's gradual progress into the neighborhood only occurred in areas that were already gentrifying. While residents blame NYU for bringing a transient population, they do not see themselves as responsible for contributing to the conditions that made the area attractive to the university for expansion.

This characterization of revelers as transient and averse to the communities they are "invading" raises several issues that contradict the nostalgia narrative.

For instance, many of the people whom early gentrifiers fondly recall as public characters had tenuous connections to the neighborhood, such as the squatters and homeless whose fate rested with state authorities. Many of their fellow early gentrifiers have also moved out of their neighborhood. Second, they also ignore the fact that nightlife revelers are often residents themselves or regular visitors with social ties to the area. Beth, for instance, despite seeing herself as an interloper, contrasted her initial experience on the Lower East Side with newcomers by claiming that she remained in her first apartment. But many early gentrifiers like her were transient as well; only a select group remains many decades later to represent the large number of people who moved to the neighborhood during its early gentrification. Third, downtown Manhattan had long been a place of interest for visitors from around and outside of the city. While early gentrifiers portray some of these individuals as active contributors to its sociocultural environment, such as those who were involved in the art and music scenes, many were in reality passive and transient consumers attracted to the downtown scene as an edgy, alternative destination.[44]

Finally, several early gentrifiers who complain about bars and revelers and are highly critical of the university's institutional encroachment into their neighborhood were once revelers and even NYU students themselves. They distinguish their own movement into their neighborhood from that of contemporary students by pointing out that NYU did not have an institutional presence in downtown Manhattan when they came and that their own impact was minimal. Steven moved to New York City to attend NYU in the mid-1980s and lived in the East Village because it was "more affordable" than Greenwich Village. "I know, I went to NYU," he says, acknowledging his potential culpability. "But it was different when I went there. They didn't steamroll over tenants like they do now. And we [NYU students] were respectful of the people who were here." Like other early gentrifiers, NYU alumni feel that they deserve credit for their neighborhood's success because they are the ones who stayed and established roots. But they do not actually know the extent to which NYU or any other college students currently participate in disruptive nightlife behavior. They also do not know whether or not NYU students will remain in the neighborhood and contribute to the community, such as by supporting community gardens or getting involved in local issues such as housing and historic preservation. In short, by labeling newcomers and nightlife revelers as transient, early gentrifiers construct a new local identity based on their own permanence, which includes a form of "acceptance" by the existing population and an abiding respect for the community. But they also reveal several problems with their own nostalgia narrative, which imagines an authentic community that underpins this identity.

The second way in which early gentrifiers characterize revelers is as inauthentic people who come to their neighborhood and use it improperly. They contrast the behavior of revelers with their own experiences in their neighborhood and their own uses of its spaces, in particular its streets and commercial establishments. For instance, although the surrounding social environment is teeming with activity, for Bob they are not the interesting interactions that he remembers. Like other early gentrifiers, he contrasts the people of the contemporary nightlife scene with those of the past:

> You know, this used to have a lot more nightlife. You could come out here any fucking night of the week, and the bars were packed, people were doing stuff. Today, people come home, they watch their flat panel TV, they don't go to the bars. The bars are empty during the week. You have the weekend crowds, and of course that's why the bars encourage crowds, they encourage underage drinking, because they have to make their money on the weekend.

Here Bob points out new activities and rhythms that nightlife has brought to the East Village. It has broken up a nightly round of activity that featured people "doing stuff" and replaced it with a weekly routinized pattern of infrequent interactions at specific times, while the nightlife community that they recall teemed with activity. Early gentrifiers pepper their nostalgia narrative with tales of their experiences with the neighborhood's nightlife. They recognize the apparent contradiction between their anti-nightlife rhetoric and pro-nightlife past and are quick to defend themselves by categorizing their behavior as a representation of the neighborhood's creativity. When I asked Caitlin, who is in her late forties and moved to the Lower East Side in the early 1980s, if she used to go out to bars in the neighborhood, she grinned sheepishly and replied, "Yeah, I did. But there was just something different about the bars then. They seemed," she paused, "more real." After I pressed her for more detail, she explained, "There was creative stuff happening in them, and we weren't bothering anyone." Like those early gentrifiers who are NYU alumni, those residents who participated in the nightlife scene claim that their behavior not only was integrated into the authentic character of the neighborhood but did not disrupt any of the existing social worlds. By contrast, many early gentrifiers characterize the contemporary activity in bars solely as acts of consumption, not creativity. Earlier David described Milano's as a place that has "a real exchange of ideas." He expands on this in discussing bars today:

> I don't think there's a bar culture anymore with young people. I think it's changed. We all knew each other, and it was a real meeting place for young people. I mean, these were real watering holes, you know. People went there

and ideas were exchanged. . . . I see young people in bars [today], they don't know each other. And now, it's not neighborhood people drinking in these bars that much. That's not culture, that's just trying to get laid.

Proper "bar culture," in the early days of gentrification, consisted of "real" places where "ideas were exchanged" among new residents. New nightlife has displaced this culture and replaced it with uncreative forms of consumption.

However, this perspective is not informed by actual observation or participation (except for people like Bob, who maintains his role as observer of nightlife from the sidewalk). Early gentrifiers regularly admit that they do not go to the new bars and are not actually familiar with their bar culture. Patti, the musician, regularly played in the neighborhood's bars and clubs back when they mostly booked local talent. But today she neither visits nor performs in the new local bars.

> I don't go to all these places. I mean, I have to live with them. I walk by them and I see a lot of the negatives, because that's what goes on in the street. But it's interesting, I often feel like if I hung out in them I'd probably see more, some of the positives that must exist in them, but mostly I'm contending with the vomit on my doorstep when I come out and the guy under my windows, or the group of people, very, usually, upscale-looking people standing on the street at 3, 4 a.m. drunk and yelling at the top of their lungs.

Here Patti focuses on the external activity in the nightlife scene and admits to not knowing about bars' internal activity. Like other early gentrifiers, she also acknowledges her own ignorance of contemporary bar culture and speculates that there must be some positive elements to it. Even David, whose above quote claims a firsthand knowledge of what young nightlife revelers do in bars, concludes a lengthy critique of contemporary bar culture by saying, "Of course, I never really go out drinking anymore either." Not going to new bars represents one of the several ways in which early gentrifiers are socially distant from newcomers and visiting nightlife revelers. In doing so, they unwittingly concede that the neighborhood is no longer entirely "theirs."

FAINT VOICES OF EXISTING RESIDENTS

Le Souk is a North African/Middle Eastern–themed restaurant on Avenue B, near East Fourth Street, in the Alphabet City section of the East Village. Along with fare like meze plates and tagines, it also offers hookah smoking and belly dancers as entertainment. As evening gives way to night, Le Souk loses its restaurant atmosphere and becomes more like a nightclub, with loud music, dancing, and bouncer-patrolled, velvet-roped queues along the sidewalk. In its years on the block, it has drawn the ire of its surrounding neighbors. One evening, the owners confront the neighbors at a CB3 committee meeting, where they must appear to renew their liquor license.

Along with the regular issues of crowds and noise, Le Souk has had forty-four complaints of criminal activity filed against it in the previous year, which is the most CB3 has received, especially for an establishment of its size. Most of them are larcenies, resulting from stolen bags and wallets. The early gentrifiers who live near Le Souk have been protesting it for many years, and a dozen are here tonight to fight its license renewal. Phil, who has lived in his apartment for thirty years and is a member of the Fourth Street Block Association, says, "When [its patrons are] out on the street it's just like mayhem. We've said it all, over the last five, six years, we've said it all. It's just a continuing nightmare for us." He says that they asked the owner to downgrade the place, but he refused. "It's the wrong place for a nightclub. It just creates all these problems." Louis, another early gentrifier and member of the block association, takes Phil's attitude further: "What we have is an establishment that has outgrown the neighborhood. They have no respect for the law, no respect for the SLA, and no respect for the neighborhood. It's time for a change, it's time to move on."

But a few people are also at the meeting in support of Le Souk, besides its owners and their attorney. A woman named Lourdes says that her apartment windows abut their backyard, where they have seating in a garden. "I have no problem with the place. I have been in the neighborhood for forty-four years and it has really improved. This area had nothing but drugs and crime. It's places like this [that] have helped to improve things." A young man named Mark then speaks. He says he has been living on Third Street for three years, since he graduated from college. "I moved to the area largely because I enjoy all the establishments that are down here. It can be noisy, but the neighborhood is good. I am a regular at Le Souk and I've never had any of my stuff stolen because I check them. I really like this neighborhood for what it is."

"How long have you lived here?" asks one of the residents here in protest, who either did not hear Mark say so, or who wishes to emphasize a point.

"Three years," he repeats. A few of the early gentrifiers scoff at his answer, and shake their heads.

A young woman named Melis, who was born and raised in the East Village, then says that her quality of life has improved. "I remember when I could not walk around the street at night. I bartend in the neighborhood and now I can walk around. That's 'cause the bouncers at places like Le Souk make me feel comfortable. I'd rather take people throwing up on my door than people breaking in and stealing something. You can't have everything."

Finally, a man named Ray speaks. He says he is trying to unify the block and tenant associations around the neighborhood to give residents a united voice against their mutual problems. Ray focuses tonight on Le Souk and responds to the previous three speakers: "It's false to say that it's a trade-off between having violence and drugs and bars and nightlife. It's ridiculous to say that the neighborhood is safer because of the bars. I think it's just as dangerous because it brings tens of thousands of people into the area who drink and are ready to fight. There are probably also criminal activities against women. If you want the neighborhood to be safer, then open up hardware stores and other sustainable businesses."

Episodes such as this meeting are unique in their rarity. As we will see in forthcoming chapters, bar owners rarely receive support for their bars at meetings, even when they attract revelers from nearby. When they do, the supporters are usually very young, in their twenties, and admit that they enjoy going out in the neighborhood and that bars have had a positive impact on life downtown. Their support confirms the attitudes that early gentrifiers have towards them, which fuels their quick dismissal of what they have to say. Even rarer, though, than seeing support from young revelers is seeing support from Hispanic residents, who are mostly Puerto Rican and Dominican and represent nearly a quarter of the Lower East Side's population (although their numbers are declining). Most of them have lived in the neighborhood their entire lives or since they were very young, when they immigrated with their parents. They tend to have multiple generations of family living near them, and they tend to live farther east in the neighborhood, where gentrification occurred later, or in downtown Manhattan's large stock of public housing projects concentrated along the East River. And like early gentrifiers, Hispanic residents who lived in these neighborhoods before gentrification, before the growth of the nightlife scenes, or in sections that did not experience either until recently have also benefited from residing in rent-subsidized apartments.

This episode represents the only time in my fieldwork when I saw Hispanic residents speak out in favor of bars. Lourdes and Melis remind people that drugs and crime once characterized the neighborhood, and they state that if the choice is between quality-of-life issues and unsafe conditions, they would choose the former. Ray, of course, takes exception to their either-or characterization. Early gentrifiers paradoxically do not advocate for the neighborhood to return to its days as a dangerous frontier, even though they yearn for the sociocultural environment that the conditions of abandonment helped produce. Some elements of the arts scene that developed in downtown Manhattan were multicultural, with contributions from writers, poets, actors, and artists of the Nuyorican cultural movement and the presence of such local cultural institutions as the Nuyorican Poets Café and Clemente Soto Vélez Cultural Center. But it was mostly the works produced by artists and musicians (most of whom were white) who moved to the neighborhood from elsewhere that gained widespread attention and had the most immediate and lasting impact on the neighborhood's gentrification. The Hispanic residents such as Lourdes and Melis whom I spoke to are more likely to praise the neighborhood's improvement than lament the demise of their own cultural scene.

Putting aside these rare words of support for the nightlife scene, Hispanic residents react negatively to gentrification and new bars. Their material interests in their neighborhood—namely rent, shopping resources, and the overall cost of living—are the same as those of early gentrifiers. They make the same quality-of-life complaints when they live near or above bars (new bars have not opened near the biggest public housing projects), and they also recognize that the nightlife scene is not "for" them. But two themes came up in my interviews with Hispanic residents on their attitudes towards gentrification and the nightlife scenes that did not with those with early gentrifiers. First, their explanations for feeling excluded from the nightlife scenes and from protests against bars are based on ethnicity, race, and social class rather than generation or culture. Giancarlo, for instance, is twenty-two years old and grew up in the Baruch Houses, one of several public housing projects along the East River. He then moved uptown, to Spanish Harlem (known historically as "El Barrio" because of its strong Puerto Rican population), where he has family, but he often visits his family and friends on the Lower East Side and sometimes goes out in the neighborhood. I ask him if he feels comfortable going out to bars as a Latino. "I guess if you was into Spanish music you would be able to find a Latino club, but it's mostly on the down-low, after-hours spots, not really a club. Sometimes at a bar, if I walk in and notice I look like a sore thumb, I will leave. But the [Lower East Side] is pretty diverse and you see all types of people. If you got money, it doesn't matter what color your skin is." For Giancarlo, going out on the Lower East Side is a privilege that can be purchased. As nightspots for Hispanic residents shrink in number, ethnicity and race remain as perceived social barriers.

Other Hispanic residents understand the growth of the nightlife scene as undercutting the economic foundation upon which their community was based. Alex was born and raised on Suffolk Street after his parents migrated from Puerto Rico. He comes from a large family, with sixteen aunts and uncles on his father's side and fifteen on his mother's side. Some of them and their children live in Puerto Rico, and some on the Lower East Side, with many traveling back and forth. Alex is proud that he avoided the drug scene that plagued the neighborhood when he was growing up, and he credits his parents for steering him away from that life. He obtained his bachelor's and master's degrees from a local public college and works for the city's Department of Housing Preservation and Development. In 2002, he started a block association in response to the local nightlife scene's growth. While he cites quality-of-life concerns as a reason for protesting bars, the greater impact that the nightlife scene has had on the Hispanic community provides him with greater motivation. Alex explains the origins of his block association:

> Basically, there were a handful of main priorities, which was, what we felt at the time, the displacement of longtime merchants, local bodega stores or local bookstores, local commercial establishments that had been here for so many decades. And roughly around the early 2000s, we started noticing that many property owners were now not renewing leases and either renewing them but charging, two, maybe three times the amount of rent that the longtime merchants were paying. So we saw a huge number of longtime establishments closing their doors because they just couldn't afford the rent.

But concern over the displacement of existing businesses was over more than the cultural transformation of the Lower East Side. As Alex continues:

> In the '80s, '90s, and early 2000s this community was comprised of mostly Latinos and African Americans, and they had been here for many decades. But there was a huge number of illiterate families that came from the Caribbean and other parts of the world and never had the opportunity to pick up the language, the English language, so they were just working-class people— working in factories, sweatshops, bodegas, what have you. So we started seeing a great number of those employments diminish throughout the community because the majority of employment were coming out of bars and restaurants, and not necessarily were those employments being offered to local residents.

As we saw in chapter 2, SLA officials cited economic growth as a reason for granting liquor licenses and for having dense nightlife scenes. Providing employment fell under this justification. But as Alex and other Hispanic residents recognize, new bars in downtown Manhattan, which already alienate consumers based on race, ethnicity, and social class, both threaten existing businesses by escalating rents and do not hire people from existing populations. (Melis, from the above vignette, says she bartends in the neighborhood. But as I learned when speaking with her after the meeting, she works at places that

:xisting Hispanic clienteles.) Businesses such as bodegas and inexpen-
:aurants that cater to Latino cuisines are more than "authentic" symbols
of community; they are integral to local ways of life.

A second theme among Hispanic residents concerns their families—both
actual and extended.[45] Alex has a large family who mostly lived near him when
he grew up. He credits their efforts for his own success. Hispanic residents also
refer to the community as being like a family. Alba is twenty-five years old and
lives in the same apartment she grew up in. Her parents moved in the early
1970s from the Dominican Republic to the Lower East Side, where her father
worked as a carpenter while her mother worked in a factory. She describes her
upbringing in the neighborhood fondly: "It was pretty cool. Since it was almost
everybody of the same race, like, you never got really confused, you didn't see
much strangers. You could go out, and your parents knew exactly where you
were going. . . . It was like one big family." Alba talks about the local stores
that have changed or closed, such as the butcher shop that has become more
expensive and the pool hall for teens that is now a wine bar, and she makes
quality-of-life complaints along with her neighbors (a bar recently opened in
her building's storefront). Her whole family, she says, lived within a four-block
radius of her apartment, which her parents moved out of and left for her. But
over time most of her family and friends have been forced to move out. "Anyone who wasn't living in a co-op had to leave, or they were bought out. I saw
a lot of people get bought out, and most of them ended up in Brooklyn." Like
the early gentrifiers, Alba feels that her neighborhood is "not for her" anymore,
and she no longer feels comfortable there. But for Hispanic residents like Alex
and Alba, the people they grew up with who have since moved out did more
than add diversity and character to the neighborhood. They were family, both
actual and imagined, who provided them with a social support system amid
deprived conditions.

CHAPTER 4

ENTREPRENEURIAL SPIRITS

It always changes. That's the pulse of New York, that's the heartbeat. It's all about change, it's always been change.

—RICHARD, LOWER EAST SIDE BAR OWNER

RESIDENTS OF EAST FIFTH STREET, IN THE EAST VILLAGE, and members of its block association are out in full force this Monday night to deny a liquor license application. I take a seat next to a middle-aged woman, who seems highly anxious. I ask her if she is a resident of East Fifth Street, and she says that she has been for the last twenty years. Her name is Nancy, and this is her first CB3 meeting. She greets and waves to a number of her neighbors as I tell her that I am conducting a project on the neighborhood's nightlife and bars.

"There are too many already!" she says while laughing.

I ask her about the item on the agenda that her and her neighbors are here to protest. The name of the proposed establishment is Mighty Ocelot, and the applicants are applying for an "rw" license, or a license to sell beer and wine. Nancy lives down the street from the proposed establishment.

"There is a bar on either side of the street and this one would be in the middle. I don't think that we need it. People walk by my apartment at 3 a.m. and they're drunk and noisy, and this happens every Thursday to Sunday. It's a lot of 'bridge-and-tunnelers.' I hear them getting in their cars when they are leaving late at night, and they are driving drunk."

"Number 22! Mighty Ocelot!" calls Alex, the committee's chairwoman. The applicant, Sasha, a living legend in the world of finely crafted cocktails, stands up. In his mid-thirties, Sasha is dandyishly dressed in slacks and polished brown shoes, with his hair slicked back. Tall and broad-shouldered with a focused and alert stare, his somewhat imposing physical presence belies a gentle and courteous demeanor. Sasha introduces himself to the committee and the residents in attendance. "My name is Sasha Petraske, and I own Milk and Honey. I would like to also point out my business partner and best friend, TJ, and our mothers who are with us tonight."

After pointing out his partner, who sits nervously with their mothers in the middle aisle, he summarizes the business plan. Mighty Ocelot will mostly be a café that will be open from noon until 2:30 a.m. and will serve coffee, pastries, and cheese. They are asking for a liquor license because they also want to serve wine with cheese. He explains that it does not make any sense to serve wine without food. Anticipating a common problem that residents have with bars, Sasha says that he will live in the building's only upstairs apartment, making him his only direct neighbor. He then describes his other bar in order to bolster his credibility in the eyes of residents.

"I have owned Milk and Honey for seven years. It is known as the quietest bar in New York. We go to *extremes* to get along with our neighbors. [To the residents of East Fifth Street] I contacted the head of your block association, Jerry, who was very nice to me, but said that you will not see my application or meet with me because you don't want a bar. I have letters from my Milk and Honey neighbors—which you haven't seen, since you wouldn't see me—saying that I am a great neighbor to have. I have a reservation policy at Milk and Honey in order to keep people off the street. No one works with neighbors the way I do. I implore you to give me a shot."

The community board committee is familiar with Sasha and Milk and Honey, which is on the Lower East Side. The committee members have never had a complaint against the bar since it opened and have only heard positive responses about how he deals with neighbors and makes efforts to reduce noise. They consider him a model bar owner. They also know from experience that it is often best to work with owners on stipulations that could be written into the license and legally recognized by the SLA. Otherwise, they risk that he may apply to the SLA anyway in spite of their denial. Since they view the SLA as complicit in the destruction of their community, they fear it may approve him, leaving them without legal protection on their own terms.[1] Since Sasha has a good track record as a bar owner in the area and sounds honest and sincere, they feel that it is best for the people of East Fifth Street to work with him and hope he will be an unproblematic, longtime neighbor.

However, fifteen people from East Fifth Street have come to protest the bar (many left the meeting as the hour grew late). Over the past ten years, the number of liquor licenses on this one-block stretch of East Fifth Street has gone from one to five, with many more on nearby Second Avenue, and more to come with the impending opening of the Cooper Square Hotel, just down the street at the corner. These changes have brought a significant amount of nightlife activity to the street and the hotel promises to bring considerably more. Still, Alex tries to set them at ease. "You're not getting a problem and you're not getting someone that will be a problem," she says.

They do not agree. A chorus from East Fifth Street quickly replies, "We're getting another bar!" "We don't want another bar!" "It's still drunk people!"

A resident named Damon then speaks about the place on the street that used to occupy this space and is now closed.

"They set a precedent on this block for being little, elegant, and lovely, but it still operated as a big place, with the same deliveries, the same people outside, and the same booze. This neighborhood is like Bourbon Street and with your steep rent in the building you're going to have to sell stuff, and that means alcohol."

"But my impact will be so incredibly small," replies Sasha.

"A lot of booze needs to be poured and people are going to be drunk," continues Damon, dismissing Sasha's point. "I've heard people say, and not just people in this room, that if you're going to have a bar on your street, he's your guy. But you have to see it from our perspective. It's only bars and restaurants in this neighborhood. We're losing our small variety shops. I own a small business on a side street and I'll probably be gone. Landlords know, when a bar owner comes around, that the stakes go up. This has become a shell of a neighborhood."

Despite disagreeing with the residents' request, the community board respects their wish and denies the license. Sasha thanks the committee, urges everyone to at least come by the café for coffee, and exits the room with his partner and their mothers. They do not apply to the SLA for a license.[2]

—

This episode presents a common confrontation between downtown Manhattan's main daytime and nighttime advocates when it comes to nightlife: residents and bar owners. The CB3 committee often begrudgingly approves new applications with stipulations to the license, but in this case residents demanded denial. I deal with the implications of these contentious community meetings in chapter 6, and present them here to introduce the nightlife scene's bar owners. As I did with many bars that residents protested, I went to Milk and Honey to check it out and to speak with Sasha.

First, I had to deal with the matter of access. True enough, Milk and Honey has a reservation-only policy and an unlisted phone number that changes every few months. In its early days, knowledge of the bar and the coveted phone number only spread through word of mouth; Sasha encouraged customers to give it only to people they trusted not to abuse it or to be a potential problem, such as by being drunk or rowdy. The clientele was thus initially a relatively small network of people who were "in the know." The age of blogs ended the mystery and the number began to be spread around the Internet shortly after it was changed. Still, I decided to get the number the old-fashioned way: from a

FIGURE 12 Milk and Honey's inconspicuous facade. Photograph by the author, 2010.

bartender at East Side Company Bar, another cocktail bar that Sasha owns, with an inconspicuous facade but without a strict entrance policy. After a few drinks and some conversation, East Side's bartender said, with his tongue half in cheek, he "trusted" me enough to give it to me.

I call the number and make a reservation for the next night, a Wednesday, at 9:30 p.m. (Milk and Honey only allows reservations twenty-four hours in advance). I walk down Delancey Street, a wide, high-trafficked thoroughfare on the Lower East Side, and away from some of the densest parts of the neighborhood's nightlife scene. The bar is located off Delancey on Eldridge Street, a small residential street, but you would be hard-pressed to find it. At this hour most of the daytime businesses on the street have their steel shutters down and there are no other bars. Only two places are open: a corner bodega and a tiny Internet café with some Chinese patrons. This section of the Lower East Side is the start of Chinatown, the latest "frontier" for gentrification and the nightlife scene, and other than the occasional Chinese resident or group of revelers passing through, the streets are empty. Milk and Honey contributes to and blends in very well with the desolation.

Following the building numbers, I come to a small storefront with a rusted metal grate in front of the window. On it reads "Tailors and Alterations" with the letters "M & H" between them. The door is an industrial metal grey that appears locked. A red fire bucket with cigarette butts poking out of sand and dirt hangs from the rail for the steel security shutter. They serve as the sole indicators that inside is one of the most famous cocktail bars in the world.

After surveying the street and facade, I realize that no one told me how to get inside. There is a small doorbell next to the door, but I take my phone out to call the bar and let them know I am outside. Just as I do so, the door starts making clicking sounds. At that moment I look up and see a closed-circuit camera above the threshold, staring down at me. I take the clicking as my cue to enter, and upon doing so I am greeted by a dark heavy curtain, and then another. After fumbling through both, I finally get inside.

A tall, thin, bearded man wearing a grey vest and slacks, a shirt and tie, arm garters, and wingtip dress shoes approaches me and asks, "Can I help you, sir?"

"My name is Richard, I have a 9:30 reservation at the bar."

"Yes, right this way, sir."

The bar is very dark and narrow. Jazz music plays and aromas of mint and strawberry fill the air. Candles line the walls and a single dim light fixture hangs above the small, four-seat bar. There are six high-backed booths along the left wall—each one filled—with the bar located between the two sets of three. There is no standing allowed, and they only accept reservations for parties of five or less, which means the maximum occupancy that they allow is thirty-four, even though the bar can fit more than this by law.[3] The host (who is also tonight's waiter) escorts me to the bar and offers to take my coat, which he places on a hanger and hangs along the pressed-tinned wall behind me. The bartender, also wearing grey slacks, a dress shirt, and an ascot, greets me with a smile and shakes my hand.

"How are you doing tonight, sir?"

"I'm doing well, thank you."

"Great. Do you know what you might want to have?"

I just then realize I know very little about cocktails. They were always something my father drank, or something from the movies. I feel a little flushed and intimidated. Everything I have read about this bar says that the bartenders are cocktail experts and that they make exquisite drinks that most people have never heard of before, let alone tasted. The only thing that pops in my head is the classic recipe for a martini, my father's drink of choice.

"I'll have a gin martini, stirred, with an olive," I say, as confidently as possible.

The bartender says, "I wouldn't make it any other way, sir."

FIGURE 13 The backbar at Milk and Honey. Photograph by the author, 2010.

Relieved, I sit back and watch him in action, noticing a TV screen behind the bar with a bird's-eye view of the sidewalk outside the door.

Milk and Honey's bar is precisely set up for making well-crafted cocktails. Nearly everything that the bartender needs to make hundreds of drinks is within an arm's reach, or is a slight pivot and lean away. Freshly cut fruit, herbs, and eggs are kept cold in a bin filled with crushed ice. A hand-operated juice press rests on the counter next to lemons and limes. Freezers hold an assortment of glassware and ice that has been hand-chipped and sawed into rough diamond-shaped chunks from a large solid block. The backbar's shelves are lined with an array of rare, high-quality spirits and liqueurs. And an arsenal of equipment—shakers, spoons, muddlers, jiggers, and strainers—is neatly stacked, waiting to be put to use.

Sammy, the bartender, is originally from Australia. He first learned about cocktails and how to bartend from working in his family's restaurant and at other places in Melbourne. He came to New York City specifically to work at Milk and Honey, which he had heard so much about. Given his skill and breadth of knowledge, I did not give him much of a challenge with my order. He has made a martini countless times, but for cocktail bartenders precision is crucial even for the most routine of drinks. Making a martini is for a cocktail bartender what making an omelet is for a chef: despite its simplicity, it requires skills that are fundamental to the craft. It is important to demonstrate that you can make it consistently. Sammy starts by placing a mixing glass on the bar and then pouring gin into a jigger (a small metal measurer), careful not to exceed the number of ounces. He tips it into the glass, picks up the bottle of dry vermouth, and pauses, realizing he forgot to ask me something.

"How much vermouth would you like? Do you like it more gin-heavy or do you want a lot of vermouth?"

Dry, or French, vermouth is a necessary ingredient in the classic martini. But over the decades it has gradually disappeared from the recipe, and gin and stirring have been replaced by vodka and shaking—hence Sammy's earlier reply that he "wouldn't make it any other way" when I asked for both in this cocktail bar that focuses on the classics. Once again, my limited knowledge of cocktails (and of my own taste) compels me to avoid embarrassment. "I like a lot of vermouth," I say.

"Okay," he replies, and pours a nearly equal amount of vermouth in the jigger as he did gin. Next comes the ice, which he cracks into smaller pieces in his hand with his bar spoon and gently drops in the glass, again using the bar spoon to deaden the splash, filling it to the top. Sammy then rapidly stirs the mixture, moving only his wrist in a fast and fluid motion, for nearly a minute. Lastly, he takes out a frozen cocktail glass, pours out the drink with a julep strainer (exactly reaching just below the brim), and lightly drops in an olive. He places a large, folded paper napkin in front of me and rests the drink on top. As I sip I ask him more questions about his background, working at the bar, and the neighborhood. Later, I order another martini.

Milk and Honey presents quite a different picture from the crowds and noise that typically characterize a nightlife scene. It also differs considerably from the bars like Milano's that historically characterized downtown Manhattan. But upscale cocktail bars and "dives" are among the many types of bars that coexist in some of the city's most vibrant nightlife scenes. Owners see their bars and their role in the neighborhood differently than do early gentrifiers, who dismiss new bars and their revelers for lacking creativity and a sense of community. Instead of destroyers of community, owners think of their bars as its purveyors. They vary, however, in their definition of who and what constitutes the community. The point in time when they opened their bars as well as their motivation for opening in downtown Manhattan influences their interpretation.

Older owners opened bars as "third places," or community gathering spaces.[4] David Grazian argues that these types of nightlife establishments conform to a romantic notion in urban sociology of bars as being inclusive, ignoring the many forms of exclusivity within them.[5] As with other gathering spaces, local bars foster the dual nature of community as both inclusive and exclusive, with strong social boundaries maintaining the distinction between the two. A more accurate description of contemporary urban nightlife, Grazian argues, is that venues reinforce preexisting social bonds within social groups, rather than encourage bridging across social boundaries that divide them.[6] While places for local community gathering still exist in downtown Manhattan, new bar owners often define community in an extra- or trans-territorial sense. In other words, they provide a space for existing communities that originate from outside of their neighborhood.[7] Some owners are forced to define community in such terms because of economic constraints, while others intend that their bars serve as a destination for visitors. While their bars are rooted in the neighborhood, communities with weak local roots define them.

Downtown Manhattan bar owners are all "place entrepreneurs" in the sense that they are local business owners who individually construct an image for their establishments and collectively construct and reinforce an image of their neighborhood as a nightlife destination. New bars in the early stages of gentrification in these neighborhoods were opened by and for newcomers. As Christopher Mele documents, new establishments in the East Village's first wave of gentrification reflected the avant-garde, alternative, and working-class cultures that were prevalent there at the time.[8] Richard Lloyd also reveals how nightlife owners relied on the creativity and "bohemian spirit" of an arts scene to create an aesthetic for their establishments.[9] Bohemianism and the avant-garde are no longer predominant in the nightlife scenes of downtown Manhattan. New place entrepreneurs today operate at a stage of advanced gentrification, which includes not just higher rents but also a scene that attracts visiting revelers. With their own definitions of community, they rely on a wide array of sources and themes to produce a marketable bar culture that could compete in the nightlife scene. A look at how longtime and new downtown Manhattan bar owners define and accommodate the community reveals their perspectives on their neighborhood and the appropriate use of their public spaces.

COMMERCIAL PIONEERS

Early owners opened their bars in order to provide a place for newcomers like them—artists, musicians, and counter- and subcultural groups—to hang out. They represented a "first wave" of commercial "pioneers" in downtown Manhattan.[10] The artistic, musical, and countercultural activity by new residents led to the development of new nightlife scenes. As we have seen, the first new bar owners in downtown Manhattan were opening establishments as early as the mid-1970s—with the club CBGB serving as the most famous example—but most of them opened in the 1980s and early 1990s. The early new owners mainly came from other places, either within or outside of the city, to live downtown. They did not set out to open a bar, but many had experience from working and hanging out in local venues. They were drawn to the downtown scenes as art producers and consumers, curious visitors, or as young urbanites in need of cheap housing. Unlike the celebrity-infused, glamorous, and trendy "uptown" nightlife, downtown nightlife at the time was obscure, gritty, transgressive, and synonymous with creativity and expression. Activities took place nightly in nightlife establishments as well as on streets and sidewalks and in abandoned buildings and vacant lots. Members of and visitors to the downtown scenes appropriated these spaces and within them constructed their own hierarchies based on shared meanings of artistic integrity and senses of style and cool.[11] Many of the new bar owners during this period were people who were drawn to downtown.

One day I meet Herman in his bar before it opens and before he has to pick his son up from school. Herman, who is in his mid-fifties, grew up in a Jewish family in the Bronx and became a fixture in the East Village's punk scene. He has adorned his classic rock 'n' roll-themed bar with framed photographs and posters of local and world-famous rock acts. He named it after himself (his now-legal stage name, not his Jewish surname) with a few business partners in 1999 in an area of the neighborhood that had very few bars at the time. He began hanging out in the East Village in the late 1960s while in his teens. Although they were located in the same city, downtown Manhattan was a world apart from his Bronx neighborhood and offered Herman and other urban youth the creative outlet they desired. As he remembers,

[t]here were two main reasons we came down here. One was you couldn't get Robert Crumb comic books in the Bronx. Number two, the Fillmore East was on Sixth Street and Second Avenue. And the Fillmore East, looking back now, now you might understand why I'm spoiled. I mean it was like, "You want to go see The Who this week? Well, Creedence [Clearwater Revival] is coming next week," like five bucks, in my backyard! So we'd get on a train, a forty-five-minute train ride, and come down to the Village, and like eight of us would get on the train, and we'd go to the Fillmore concerts. And that was my introduction. And I knew then that this was my neighborhood.

As they got older and the neighborhood changed, Herman and his friends participated in the new nightlife that developed. He recalls fondly,

We'd go downtown to CBGB 'til four in the morning, then we'd get a little bite to eat for twenty minutes, a pretzel or whatever, and then there was about six to eight famous, well-known, packed after-hours clubs. It wasn't a little secret like open the peephole. Like, hundreds of people in all of them! Every night of the week! And I'd get home at noon, seven nights a week. Those were the good old days.

Many early gentrifiers in downtown Manhattan—both bar owners and residents—mention the informal and largely unregulated public drinking establishments that they would go to. These places would often be in storefronts that landlords collected rent from, off the books, and people heard about them through social channels and the music and art scenes. As part of "the good old days," their memory of these informal spaces relates to their nostalgia for the authentic community.

Although it was the new countercultural attractions that first brought him to the neighborhood, Herman also hung out in some of the existing local establishments. As it was for many of the nightlife scene's participants, alcohol and drugs were important aspects of Herman's life downtown:

> I was kind of a drug dabbler at the time, before I became a drug addict. I mean, I was well on my way, but at that time there was still some sort of innocence tied to the whole thing. Bowery was a lot of fun when I was a kid. When I couldn't afford to drink or take drugs, I'd go to the Bowery and go to, like, the flophouse bars, because they were cheap to drink there. I used to sit there and get drunk for a few bucks.

For young people like Herman, cheap bars for the homeless Bowery population and ethnic groups exposed them to the existing residents. But instead of slumming and then returning to their neighborhoods, for the most part newcomers began hanging out in their own establishments. In the mid-1970s, Herman joined an influential local punk band and began bartending in some of the new bars that were opening. Although he always hung out in the East Village, Herman did not have a permanent apartment there until 1984. He rented rooms, stayed with friends, slept on couches, and went back and forth between downtown and the Bronx. He got sober in 1983, and moved the next year. After years of bartending and playing music, Herman felt the desire to use his background in the downtown scene to build something in the neighborhood. "I could do something for a few years and then I get itchy," he says, "I want to do bigger, better, more. I want to grow. If you put the ceiling this far above my head, I would be bored to death. It's just not the way I'm built." With his nightlife and music connections, he opened his own bar with the classic rock theme thirty years after he first entrenched himself in the neighborhood. While not as old as the bars he played and worked at, Herman's bar serves as a tribute to the neighborhood's recent musical past, or a private act of social preservation.[12] Today he has a family, still wears a bandana and leather jacket from his punk-rock days, and often performs with his bands.

Commercial pioneers in gentrifying neighborhoods open establishments with a strong desire to provide a communal space and to fulfill the needs of the incoming population. They are considered "social and cultural entrepreneurs" who desire to create a community around their business for people in the neighborhood who share their lifestyles, interests, and tastes.[13] New bar owners in downtown Manhattan had a similar community-oriented motivation. Marta is an artist who moved to the Lower East Side in 1977. After working in bars, she opened one of her own with a few other artists in 1989, to support herself and provide a space for both her own art and that of her friends. As she describes, "[At first, the bar] was very neighborhood-oriented. It was basically all very eclectic, but there was, it was a lot of artists. It was just a different group of people living in our neighborhood because the rents were a lot different then than they are now. We would do what the neighborhood would call for." For early bar owners, "the neighborhood" consisted of the new residents and members of the arts scene. Owners like Marta filled a social gap. They had healthy business during the day, because most newcomers did not have typical "nine-to-five" jobs, as well as at night for the art and music scenes. Herman opened his own bar some years later, as a place to commemorate and preserve the East Village's rock music history, but also to provide a place for new acts to play and a music community to exist. "If it was just about the alcohol and the bar and making money," he says, "I wouldn't be that interested. It makes me money, and it's a business, and yes, that's important to me. But the fact that I'm keeping something alive, it's a little extra, a little extra to be inspired by the business rather than just being a business." Owners who experienced their neighborhood's early gentrification, in particular their art and music scenes, took a community-oriented approach in opening their bars and demonstrate a strong desire to preserve the social and cultural environment that they remember. But this community was aimed at the new residents who were moving into their neighborhood rather than at residents who were already living there.

Being a social and cultural entrepreneur by opening a business during downtown's transitional period meant dealing with the area's existing seedy elements. While new bar owners warmed to their neighborhood because of their gritty characters, they did not want patrons to engage in illicit behaviors in their bars as they did in existing bars. They faced a dilemma: they wanted the people and activities that made downtown Manhattan unique to stay, but they also wanted to keep them out of their bars. Those owners that remained in business chose the latter. Chris, a bar owner in his early forties, grew up in Connecticut. He used to come to the East Village for the music scene in the late 1980s and 1990s. After graduating from college, he moved there in 1993 and started working an office job. Growing disillusioned, he used his restaurant experience from his college days and his knowledge of coffee to open a café on Avenue A in 1995. "At that time, Avenue A still had shuttered storefronts. Even in '95, there were places that landlords were just kind of sitting on. They just didn't want to bother with the storefront or anything." With the "frontier line" making its way east to Avenue A, prospective owners began to see the potential in opening a business in spaces that once housed other uses. After a few years of owning a café, Chris wanted to expand into the bar business. "We took over a heroin bar," he says. "*Tons* of open heroin use [in the area] in those days, and this place didn't hide it too much. I mean, the windows were covered up, but it was *really* blatant. There was a woman openly dealing heroin from a gumball machine in there." But this was not the clientele that Chris had in mind when he thought about opening a bar. He wanted a local hangout like his café for people in the neighborhood, a place that could provide for the community and also provide him with a living. He had to keep out the elements that threatened these goals.[14]

> I was very concerned about the clientele. I was like, I'm all for the gritty East Village, but I'm running a business. I can't have drug activity in there. I actually bartended in the beginning, and I knew all the crazies from [the café], basically. There's a difference between, like, a colorful character and the actual, like, drug dealers and all that stuff. So if somebody wants a drink, that's one thing. But then if they're going to start dealing drugs in there, it's another. So if I was bartending and somebody would be like, 'Oh, man, this place used to be Circus Bar,' 'Well, it's not anymore. We're a different bar now,' and I'd try to make it like really, really clear that it's a new bar and we're not putting up with the old shenanigans kind of thing.

Pioneering businesses began gradually occupying empty storefronts while changing the social character of their streets. They provided new uses for their neighborhood's new users. All of a sudden, public activities that once were commonplace were not allowed. Bars became a source of the "taming" that occurred downtown.

Economic conditions in these neighborhoods made opening a bar a relatively affordable endeavor. As Chris remembers, "Back then it was so easy. You just find a space. There was a hardware store on Thirteenth Street, we bought the lumber on credit cards and hammered it together, and we were open. But you could just never do it that way anymore." One evening while sitting in the third of the multiple bars that he has opened, David, from the previous chapter, tells me about the environment he faced when he first moved to the Lower East Side. Unlike other bar owners mentioned thus far, David was not an artist, nor was he drawn to the neighborhood for its art scene. But he still hung out in the same places as artists, corroborating what many early bar owners and residents assert about the neighborhood having fewer bars that catered to a diverse array of newcomers. He recalls:

> Back then in the young people scene there was so much less, and it was way more diverse, and it was a more exciting scene, but there was only like ten bars that anybody went into. So back then if you were young, you hung out at all, or were involved in the arts or anything like that, you were with everybody else, because there were only a few bars. I hung out with [artists], but I don't have any talent.

After graduating with a degree in political science, David had to "hustle"—"in the good sense of the word," he says—to earn a living. "There were no, like, job jobs when I got out of college," he remembers. "It was a bad time, and I had a politics degree, so what was I going to do?" He would go to auctions for closing factories (of which there were many in the deindustrializing city), purchase the equipment on the cheap, and then sell it wholesale to people in that factory's industry. His entrée into the world of bar ownership stemmed from this experience:

> So I'm at an auction, and I buy everything from this restaurant that's going out of business for like $2, because it's over here in what was then the ghetto, and it's like August and it's 185 degrees and nobody wants to come down here, you know. And at the end of the auction, I'm twenty-four years old, I guess, this guy says to me, "Hey, I'm the landlord. Why take all this stuff out? Why don't you just rent the restaurant from me?" I said, "All right," and that's what's now Hobgoblin [opened in 1991]. My girlfriend [who bartended across the street from the location] and I opened it, and then after we broke up I sold it to her.

Existing businesses still served the aging white ethnic groups and Hispanic residents in downtown Manhattan. But young owners like David were making new investments in a neighborhood that commercial and real estate actors had long been ignoring. A weak economic environment gave them great flexibility to open the types of establishments that they wanted. David reflects:

When I came down here, nobody wanted to invest in this neighborhood. There were crack dealers everywhere, hookers everywhere. And we opened Hobgoblin for like $65,000. I opened Wyatt's [his second bar], even with all the delays, I opened Wyatt's for like eighty grand. I mean, we would open bars for nickels and that includes, like, the deposit, the liquor license. I'm not just talking about construction. Soup to nuts. We were opening bars, there were guys back then who opened bars on credit cards. So I think that kind of hustle made places really singular, because [there] was stuff that was wrong with them but there was so much heart in them, you know?

With low business costs and a concentration of creative people in the neighborhood, bars were started, themed, and decorated inexpensively and with the help of local artists.

Early bar owners faced little competition. They formed a tight group around their shared understanding of community. As inexperienced business owners, they also supported each other amid existing owners who were indifferent to them. David recalls:

When I came into the business, there were maybe twelve, fifteen owners. And Ukrainians, there were maybe six or seven Ukrainian bar owners, but they never talked to non-Ukrainians. Outside of the Ukrainian bars, there were twelve, fifteen owners, tops. We all knew each other, we talked, we went to each other's bars.

For new, young residents like David—who was not an artist but hung out with them, who had difficulty finding a job in his field of study, who had an entrepreneurial spirit, and who had a love for the Lower East Side—opening a bar became an opportunity to earn a living, enjoy the youthful excess of the neighborhood, and provide for the community. David was a hands-on owner who lived and worked in the neighborhood, would occasionally bartend, and knew his regulars, who were all locals.

Early bar owners claim that they opened their bars to provide a social gathering place for the community. But being profitable and financially solvent was also always an important part of their business. Marta says that she wanted to support herself and her art, and Chris did not allow certain elements in his bar that could compromise his business. As they got older, early bar owners developed an even stronger business sense. David continued buying bars while they were affordable, and he built a livelihood operating them. "I'm at a point now, though, where there's nothing else I could do. No one would hire me. I'm forty-one. I haven't done anything other than this for seventeen years." Today he boasts that his businesses continuously earn more in profit from year to year. Without a solid business sense, these owners surely would have failed when their neighborhood began to improve, rents increased, and competition grew— and, indeed, most did. We often think of later waves of commercial establishments being the ones whose owners are more traditionally entrepreneurial and investment-oriented. But the early commercial pioneers, the "social and cultural" entrepreneurs in downtown Manhattan, were certainly economically savvy as well as community-conscious.

Early bar owners feel that in providing a communal space, they played a role in improving their neighborhood and making it safer. Marta opened her bar on a Lower East Side street that did not have any bars and had very few businesses, let alone businesses that were open at night. In a manner that reflects Jane Jacobs's notion of "eyes on the street," she describes her bar as a place that brought safety and protection to the neighborhood.[15] "I know when we first moved here, the neighbors were happy because of the security mechanism," she says. "There was nothing at night. You'd walk home and there was just nothing here. It was a challenge. So when we opened there was light, there were people, there was a place to walk into if there was trouble."[16] In their minds, new bars provided the streets with new public activities and forms of surveillance. The new establishments tamed the wild frontier both spatially and temporally.[17]

But bar owners are not oblivious to the larger impact that they had in downtown Manhattan. Although they dislike the later waves of gentrification that occurred in their neighborhood, they recognize the role they played in causing them. "Nightlife is the reason this neighborhood began [to gentrify]," says Mike, an East Village bar owner. "Gentrification in this neighborhood, nightlife played a large role in starting it." Owners understand and lament that the neighborhood that they helped improve and the communities that they built made people feel safer going there and lured new young entrepreneurs to open bars, which they feel turned their neighborhood from a small insular scene into an open destination. As David says:

> Part of [the gentrification] is the extent of the bars. I think there's so many it makes it look more like a playland than a lost world. I guess I was the vanguard of all this, lo and behold. How the hell did I know? Back then I was the only white guy down there in my neighborhood. Stanton Street? Literally, I was it, I was the only white guy on the block. I was living on Eleventh Street; I was the only white guy on the block. I thought it would always be that way. [And now] I'm amazed at how often new owners will come to me for advice. I never knew that I was the vanguard of something that actually kind of in a way changed things.

This level of self-consciousness is different from the typical story of the early gentrifier. Gentrifiers often deny their own culpability in initiating a neighborhood's gentrification. But bar owners are in a unique position in a neighborhood to understand how it is changing. As business owners, they are aware of the economic conditions of a neighborhood, particularly commercial rents. Since most early downtown Manhattan bar owners lived in their establishment's neighborhood and were hands-on, they were able to gradually watch the shifting demographics and changing activities at the street level. They started to have fewer customers during the day and more in the evenings and on weekends, as fewer of them were artists, writers, musicians, and actors, and more worked typical "nine-to-five" jobs. They also noticed the increasing amount of competition that came into the neighborhood. Their self-reflection does not prevent early bar owners from being critical of newcomers and new developments in the nightlife scene or of residents who complain about nightlife.[18] But it does allow them to see how the work that they did relates to the larger picture of gentrification.

BARS IN THE GENTRIFIED NEIGHBORHOOD

People who opened bars in downtown Manhattan in the 2000s faced a completely different place from what their predecessors faced. Downtown neighborhoods were much safer and cleaner, with many enticements for urban youth with disposable income. But they also maintained their reputation as gritty neighborhoods and sources of downtown cool, which real estate developers and other stakeholders exploited into downtown luxury.[19] As Christopher Mele documents, city leaders and real estate actors in the 1980s and 1990s successfully created a "representation of place" in the East Village that reworked the "images, iconography, and symbols of [its] ethnic minority communities . . . marginalized subcultures and the avant-garde" and mixed them with upscale developments to draw the interest of young, middle-class urbanites.[20] By opening funky local bars that improved conditions on the street and promoted safety, early bar owners helped to cultivate this image and make downtown Manhattan attractive for new residents and businesses, as they admit. New bar owners are often among these new residents who were attracted to the sense of downtown cool. But unlike the early bar owners, they usually are not original members of the downtown art, music, and nightlife scenes. Opening a social gathering and performance space in the neighborhood for members of the artistic community was therefore not the next logical step for new bar owners. They also do not reference grit or underground and alternative cultures in their bars. In other words, they neither design them with grit in mind, nor does grit emerge as a natural consequence of having a small budget.

Despite not having lived downtown during that period, new bar owners still use similar terms of community and authenticity to describe it as early bar owners do. Dave is in his late twenties and moved to New York City in 2003. In college he majored in interior design, but he describes himself as someone who has a special talent for hosting parties and events, which he has done his whole life. He also has always had an interest in spirits. After graduating, he moved to Las Vegas to become a VIP host at a nightclub, which give him many ideas on how to run an establishment. When he came to New York City, he decided to live in the East Village. He explains: "I liked the neighborhood. It's got a feel of authenticity to it. It's got a neighborhood's neighborhood feel, and without pretension, without a lot of bullshit. It just seemed to have all those elements that I really liked." Echoing the early gentrifiers, new bar owners often describe downtown Manhattan neighborhoods as "authentic." Interestingly, they employ a similar definition of what makes them authentic. For the new bar owners, the people in downtown Manhattan are the most important part of what makes it authentic—in particular, their diversity and creativity. Dave elaborates on why he chose the East Village over other neighborhoods when he decided to open a bar:

> It sort of encompassed everything I liked. It has that authenticity; it still felt like New York. I mean, SoHo feels like SoHo, and I would get sort of a very mixed, Euro, model-y, sort of trendy-ish crowd, and you get sort of a mix of that in Chelsea and the West Village. West Village is a great location, but it's just not where I had much experience. It just sort of made sense. Downtown was always what I wanted to do. I would never do anything Midtown-y. And the East Village sort of had the type of people that I liked—artsy, creative people—and wanted to see in an establishment I was a part of.

Dave contrasts the East Village, which "still felt like New York," with upscale "Euro" neighborhoods with popular nightlife scenes like SoHo, Chelsea, and the West Village because of the people who he feels are there and the images that those neighborhoods evoke. These areas are "trendy" and put on airs of pretension; but the East Village is a "neighborhood's neighborhood," without bullshit. Cindy, who opened her bar in 2004, describes the appeal of the Lower East Side for her:

> [This neighborhood] used to be an escape for all the misfits of the world: the homosexuals, and the drag queens, and the punk rockers, and everyone who was ever misunderstood in their small town that didn't have a supportive

culture or subculture. And subcultures need places to gather and to express themselves and to be eccentric. And that is really what the definition of New York has always been. It's been that safe haven, that home to be your true self that you were not allowed to be wherever you came from.

Without always referencing history, new bar owners say they were attracted to downtown Manhattan to open a bar because of this understanding. They wanted to contribute to the social and cultural environment that made its neighborhoods authentic. Most importantly, they wanted to give back to the community and provide a space for people to hang out and communities to develop.

At first glance, this sounds similar to the explanations of early bar owners, who opened places to accommodate their neighborhood's newcomers. Indeed, as Sharon Zukin and her research team note in their research on "boutiques"— clothing stores, but also independently owned bars, cafés, restaurants, and other aesthetically similar stores for gentrifiers and new residents—in Harlem and Williamsburg, new retail owners use a "giving back to the community" discourse to describe their establishments.[21] They find, however, that most of these new social and cultural entrepreneurs neither live among the communities they serve nor come from the same social backgrounds as members of the community (e.g., African-born owners among the African American residents in Harlem). This is true for the new bar owners in downtown Manhattan, many of whom do not live there. And while they differ considerably from the existing low-income white ethnic and Hispanic residents in the neighborhood, the new bar owners often come from similar social backgrounds as the early gentrifiers, older bar owners, and young incoming residents. Key differences between early and new bar owners are the economic conditions that the latter faced, the definitions they give of the communities they serve, and their motivations for opening and designing their bars.

The Economic Realities of Bar Ownership

A few weeks after going to Milk and Honey for the first time, I meet Sasha at a restaurant in the West Village for an interview over lunch. While I have many questions for him on what he thought of the community board meeting, I am also very interested in hearing about his story and the origins of Milk and Honey. Sasha is originally from New York City, having grown up in an artists' community in Greenwich Village. He dropped out of high school to work in a café with the goal of one day owning a place that offered quality specialized products.

I was really enamored with making espresso and cappuccino; it was, like, my biggest thrill in the trade. I worked in numerous cafés, here and in California, with this dream in my head that I was going to open up a café someday, it's going to be really good. And when I came back to New York at the age of twenty-six, twenty-five or twenty-six, I got rehired at the café that I worked at in high school.

Upon returning to New York City, Sasha also became a barback—a bar's version of a bus boy—and eventually worked his way up to bartender at a busy bar near Bowery, to save money to open a café. But his plans took a detour:

> After a while it became really clear that there was no way in hell I was going to save up the amount of money that I needed to open a café. A café's a very risky business if you don't have a [liquor] license; very payroll-heavy. So I changed the idea, and I opened up a bar.

As he says this, I think back to the community board meeting and how Sasha made the case for a liquor license by arguing that wine and cheese are natural companions, a taste argument. After hearing his explanation for why he did not pursue opening a café for his first business, I wonder why he did not make the economic argument to the residents that cafés are financial burdens and difficult to sustain. Despite often making arguments against nightlife and gentrification based on cultural proclivities, residents do not appreciate owners who make cultural arguments such as that wine and cheese should be served together. Sasha could have made the argument that serving alcohol has become an important part of business ownership in downtown Manhattan.

The economic and cultural environment in downtown today makes opening a bar a difficult and complicated endeavor. Such conditions as cheap commercial rents, local and daytime clientele, and communities of artists and musicians are all in the past. In the late 1990s, when Sasha found his space for Milk and Honey in a desolate part of the Lower East Side, he paid $800 a month in rent. He chose the space largely for this reason. It allowed him to sign a lease ahead of schedule and absorb losses as he experimented with his method of operation. The nightlife scene on the Lower East Side was still expanding at that time, and Eldridge Street was on its fringes. In 2007, when Sasha leased the small space on East Fifth Street, in a dense nightlife area in the East Village, for his café, Mighty Ocelot (which later opened as the alcohol-less Mercury Dime), he paid a lot more. "The question is," asks Sasha, rhetorically, "how do you pay $7,000 a month selling $3 coffees?"

As Kevin Fox Gotham shows in his analysis of the French Quarter in New Orleans, neighborhoods experiencing advanced gentrification often attract corporate chains looking to expand into new markets.[22] In New Orleans, Harrah's Casino, Jimmy Buffet's Margaritaville, and Larry Flynt's Hustler Club evoke an image of New Orleans as a touristic place for adult play and unmitigated consumption with an air of seediness that the city's leaders promote. Having the capital to back them up, and locations that operate in areas with lower rents, allow corporations to pay high commercial rents in upscale neighborhoods and deal with potential losses. They gain cachet as a business with a presence in a high-profile neighborhood, while they reinforce the neighborhood's image as a place for certain consumption experiences.

Downtown Manhattan has followed this path to a limited degree as it has become upscale. Since they are in old tenement buildings, most storefronts in the area are not large enough to accommodate such businesses as corporate chain stores. The neighborhoods still have their share of them, from the globally familiar (McDonald's, Starbucks) to those alternative-lifestyle chains that borrow from the sense of downtown cool that downtown Manhattan once generated (Urban Outfitters, American Apparel). They also boast several elite shopping stores, such as the John Varvatos boutique and Freemans Sporting Club, an upscale men's fashion store, which do not need large spaces for their expensive products. The modest storefronts are ideal for small bars and nightlife venues, which remain owned by independent entrepreneurs. Of the inquiries that landlords receive when they advertise a commercial space, a majority are for independently owned bars and restaurants—cash-rich businesses with high markups on their products. Nightlife establishments pay among the highest rents of any privately owned business in downtown Manhattan's relatively small commercial spaces.[23]

As Sasha's café demonstrates, escalating commercial rents has meant that obtaining a liquor license and selling alcohol has become a necessity for the survival of businesses, even places that did not intend to be bars. Melissa is a fashion designer who dreamt of opening a clothing cooperative and boutique. Because of its rich history as a neighborhood where immigrant seamstresses and tailors toiled in tiny tenement apartments and sweatshops, she wanted to open a shop on the Lower East Side. As she states, "I want[ed] to have a place that reflects the history of Orchard Street, when Orchard was a designer place with [push]carts." She opened The Dressing Room, a combined cooperative boutique and bar that offers other special attractions, like film screenings and guest DJs. "I have to [sell alcohol]," she says. "It's so hard to survive in retail. I can't survive with those rents. I can't. That's why I came up with it." Similarly, several of the theaters in downtown Manhattan—some of which have been in operation for many decades—have obtained liquor licenses in order to help pay their rents. While their owners and directors acknowledge the social function alcohol serves for the attendees of their events, they also cite financial constraints as a reason for obtaining a liquor license. As Betty, a theater director in her mid-sixties, says, "We've been open for forty-five years, but we need new ways of generating revenue. It's too hard as a small independent theater in this neighborhood now." The nightlife industry serves an important social function for the contemporary fashion industry and downtown arts scene, and indeed there are many social linkages between them.[24] But providing a space for people in these cultural industries today requires considerable capital, and often a revenue stream from alcohol sales.

Along with the new owners, early bar owners also face these economic realities in operating their establishments. Today, older bars once indigenous to the downtown scene cannot generate sufficient revenue to survive under their old method of operation. As we saw with Milano's, bar owners sometimes had to decide between maintaining their regular clientele and appealing to new customers. Other examples are bars that were once music venues. Downtown Manhattan has several large performance clubs, such as Bowery Ballroom and Mercury Lounge, both of which are part of The Bowery Presents, a New York City–based promotion group that owns and operates venues across the country. They attract well-known national and international acts and use the services of Ticketmaster, the ticketing-agent giant. But small performance spaces for up-and-coming and local artists have all but disappeared from the area. Continental opened in 1991 as a small rock club in the East Village, just north of Bowery, and became an important place for members and bands of the local punk and hardcore rock scenes, several of which achieved a degree of mainstream success. Like the more famous CBGB, which was located down the street, Continental was the product of a transitional moment in the neighborhood. It opened when lower rents and a locally based music community allowed such small venues to survive without well-known acts, promoters, DJs, or ticketing agencies. But after fifteen years, the club had to undergo a dramatic transformation of its own to stay open in the gentrified neighborhood. As the owner explains:

> The club is unworkable for any businessman. There's so much overhead—sound people and booking people, advertising, maintaining and repairing the PA and other equipment. It's expensive, and for every great night there are ten or fifteen slow ones, because the arts scene, especially when it comes to rock 'n' roll, just isn't what it once was. There are still some bands doing it, but even then the crowds just aren't here to support them.[25]

In other words, if the social and cultural entrepreneurs were not business savvy before, they certainly had to be in the new nightlife scenes in order to seize opportunities and stay open. By changing their method of operation to cater to a broader clientele and limit the costs of putting on live musical performances, owners can stay in business, just not as they were. Continental's space is too small to provide both live performances and other amenities for customers. In 2006, its owner stopped offering live music and turned his place into a "dive bar," with fake wood paneling, random items on the wall, signs from cheap beer companies, and extremely inexpensive drinks (e.g., five shots of any spirit for $10). Today it appeals to a young clientele from around the city, many of whom are unaware of its former status as an underground rock club. (NYU also built a dormitory a block away.) It was the local conditions of downtown Manhattan in the 1980s and 1990s that allowed Continental to exist, and it was the changing local nightlife conditions in the 2000s that allowed it to remain open in a different form.

A final pattern in bar ownership that reflects the shifting economic realities in today's nightlife scenes is owners with business backgrounds, which provides them with their own capital, a network of investors, and the knowledge to operate a bar. Jim, for instance, holds an MBA and owns an Irish pub–themed bar. After graduate school he worked for several years in investment banking on Wall Street. After moving to the East Village, he eventually decided he wanted to own a bar. "I knew I didn't want to work in banking forever. I wanted something else," he explains. Jim used his business connections to raise the initial money required to purchase the bar, pay the lease, and renovate ($300,000 in renovations). "I had some money, but I got some friends, people I know, to invest," he says. The theme and decor, however, were based on his own ideas, without any creative interference from investors, who based their investment on his business plan. He opened his bar in 2004, and three years later applied to open another in a different part of the neighborhood (the community board denied the second location, and he decided to not pursue it).

Serving the Community

On top of escalating rents and dwindling music communities, new bar owners have also had to deal with greater competition from the proliferation of bars and with a clientele that largely reserves its public alcohol consumption to nights and weekends. There are more people with disposable income in downtown Manhattan, but these young professionals have many more options for where to go out, and they are mainly limited to certain times of the day and week for their revelry. To accommodate these patrons, most owners schedule their opening hours around the conventional work week for young urbanites by not opening until the evening. Many are fairly empty during weekdays. Some do not even open on unpopular nights for going out, such as Sundays and Mondays, and some open only on the weekends. Not only do bars save money in operating costs, these methods of operation signal that they are seeking a particular clientele that conforms to the standard separation between daytime work and nighttime play. Or, as Frank, a new bar owner, puts it, "You've got to maximize your hours. The days of having customers all day are gone." Today's owners must make conscious efforts to most effectively utilize time and their space.

A popular hangout on the Lower East Side that manages these factors effectively is a place called Pianos. Opened in 2002, Pianos got its name from the space's former business (it sold pianos). It is a two-floor, multientertainment establishment with a clear division of leisure. The ground floor features a DJ booth, a sizable white marble-top bar, and tables along the opposite wall. In the back, through a soundproof door, is the live music room, which has a much smaller service bar, a station for the sound mixer, and a stage. The first floor also has a full kitchen, which serves food from a fairly substantial menu of bar fare until midnight. The second floor is a large and fairly wide-open space with another DJ booth, another bar, more tables, and couches and other cushioned seating. Depending on the arrangement, it could serve as a lounge or a space for dancing or performances. I sit there with Brandon, the bar's manager, one late afternoon, shortly after the bar opened, during happy hour. This section is not yet open and staff members are busy setting it up. "What's funny is that a lot of people that I run into have never been upstairs," he says. "Or they've only come upstairs and they didn't know we had a live room."

Pianos also organizes itself temporally by offering different types of entertainment on different nights of the week (e.g., karaoke on Mondays, game competitions on Tuesdays, standup comedy on Wednesdays) and at different times of the night (e.g., restaurant segueing into a bar crowd, live music segueing into DJs and dancing). Brandon explains its clientele:

We have regulars, we have local people, we have neighborhood people, and we have people that come in for the weekends. They come in to dance, they come in for whatever, they just come to the block and wander bar to bar. And then you have the people that the bands bring, and that's where the real key is. The bumper crowd is the bridge and the tunnel, and the local people. [Right now at this time of day its] people that live and work in the neighborhood, and then at night it's whoever's here for the bands or whatever's going on up here, DJs, that kind of thing. And then the weekends is just the weekends.

Organizing space and time allows Pianos to attract people with a wide variety of tastes, resulting in a clientele that is fragmented. Multiple communities of regular customers who do not know each other, and sets of anonymous customers, all use the bar at various times or in different spaces at the same time. Visiting customers often only go to their desired section of the bar or on their desired night of the week.

"What are you writing?" a young man asks me while taking a drag from his cigarette.

I am standing near the corner of Ludlow and Stanton Streets, just a few yards from Pianos, on an unseasonably warm Friday night in November and taking notes on the police announcement I just witnessed. Like other residential streets on the Lower East Side, Ludlow is one-way and very narrow. It has a dense concentration of bars, which means revelers cross at all points of the street and use it as a shortcut to get from place to place and avoid the congested sidewalk. Taxis regularly stop abruptly to pick up and drop off passengers, which often causes backups on the one-lane street as people stumble in and out (usually while intoxicated), sort out the fare with the driver, and count their change. Tonight it was a taxi-induced jam that led to a waiting police officer to get on his car's loudspeaker and announce, "You're blocking the intersection. Move along." The curious young man saw me noting the incident. I explain to him and his friend that I am conducting a research project on the effects of bars and nightlife in the neighborhood. They think this is cool, if a little strange, and I use their smoke break to ask them some questions.

Michael and Andy are both twenty-five years old and live in Williamsburg, a gentrifying neighborhood in Brooklyn that also has a large nightlife scene.[26] Michael is a freelance graphic designer and Andy is pursuing a master's degree in creative writing while working part-time at a Williamsburg café. Along with going out in their own neighborhood, they also come to the Lower East Side about three nights a week to hang out and drink. "There's a lot going on here," says Michael. "There's always something happening." They have both have been in New York City for a couple of years, since moving here after graduating college, and are very familiar with the hot nightlife scenes.

"What kind of people hang out on the Lower East Side? Are they different from Williamsburg?" I ask.

"Meh, they're all hipsters," says Michael, dismissively.

Andy laughs, "And we're kind of one of them."

"Where are you guys hanging out tonight?"

"Pianos," replies Michael, nodding over to the bar/club closest to us by the corner as he takes another drag from his cigarette. "But we've bounced around a bit."

"Are there any bands you're here to see?"

"No. We're just in there. Well, there's a band on at one we might check out."

They finish smoking, and I go with them into the bar. Tonight the first-floor DJ plays danceable indie rock, a band is playing in the live music room, and the second-floor DJ is playing loud, bass-driven trance music. Each room is packed with a different set of people interested in its offerings. The band Michael and Andy were referring to outside is Wolff, a tuba-and-drum duo that plays every Friday night in Pianos' live music room after the night's other bands have played, with *Planet Earth*, the acclaimed nature documentary series, screening in the background. Their experimental blend of electronically looped tuba lines, incomprehensible effects-laden vocals, and heavy percussion curiously fit tonight's vivid images of nocturnal animals. It is after midnight and Wolff will be going on soon. Michael and Andy decide they are going to stay and see them, even though they have seen them before. I decide to return to the street, and wish them a good night.

Pianos reflects three dimensions of new downtown Manhattan bars. First, it draws some of its clientele from the area, which makes it a local hangout for new, young residents. But at the same time, it is also extra- as well as transterritorial. Pianos is extraterritorial in the sense that revelers travel from around the city to go to it. For these consumers, Pianos and the neighborhood are destinations for nightlife consumption, rather than local gathering places for reinforcing social relationships and networks within the neighborhood. But Pianos also has the feature of live music, which can attract specific communities of revelers depending on who is performing on a given evening. These revelers sometimes form affinity groups around a particular band or genre of music. For them, Pianos is one of several music venues in the area and in the city that they can go to for this particular form of consumption. These "taste communities," or social groups whose members are connected to each other through a common understanding of values that surround particular cultural products, are transterritorial in the sense that the physical locations that sustain their sense of community are geographically dispersed throughout the city.[27] Bars are significant for their dedication to supporting the cultural product that undergirds the taste community, such as a style of music or an alcoholic product like cocktails, craft beers, rare wines, and trendsetting cuisines. Members of taste communities are spread out throughout the city, and owners often open bars or dedicate sections of their bars or nights during the week to attract them.

New bar owners acknowledge that most of their normal customers do not live locally, and that they must attract outsiders for their business to survive, because of high costs and intense competition. But some specifically target outsiders. These owners recognize that downtown Manhattan has adopted an image of "downtown luxury" and appeals to a wealthier clientele than those who came to its bars in the past. Harold opened a boutique hotel on a popular nightlife street on the Lower East Side in 2005. As a longtime landlord in the neighborhood, he recognized the direction it was going in, and knew who he wanted to attract.

> I guess, having been in this neighborhood for as long as [I] had, I kind of sensed that some of the people who stayed in my apartments, a lot of Europeans, people who came from outside New York and kind of saw the Lower East Side as a preferred destination and not just a destination that was driven by affordability—it was actually a place that they wanted to be. For a lot of people, the diversity and the energy down here is more interesting than being in sort of a relatively static environment in midtown; and for those that *get* that, this is a great venue to be in. Candidly, even in the three years [the hotel's] been around, it's changed a great deal. It used to be, I guess it's still edgy, but it's certainly not edgy in the way it was three to five years ago, where it was kind of a bold step to even come down here. Now there's been such an explosion in restaurants and places, and now it's all hotels coming in. It's not quite the same statement to come down here as it was a while ago. By announcing where you're staying, you've already made a statement about who you are by choosing to be here . . . as opposed to more conventional locations, like some place in midtown.

Here Harold summarizes many of the sentiments of new bar owners. He recognizes the importance of diversity and edginess to the Lower East Side's image, particularly in contrast with more traditional areas in the city, like midtown. He is also aware of its status as a destination for visitors, who seek it out for its amenities and not just because it is affordable. To accommodate these revelers, Harold designed the hotel to have substantial nightlife spaces on the ground floor—two lounges, a bar, a restaurant, and a VIP area. They are prominent, with accordion-style French doors that open onto the street and velvet ropes for queues on the sidewalk. The check-in desk is on the second floor, out of visitors' sight. In other words, the nightlife spaces are meant to attract visitors rather than serve as amenities for guests. In fact, people with room reservations must pass the nightlife areas and go upstairs to check in. Harold describes the lounge: "When we opened the place, we wanted to make a statement that this was a place that catered to people who pay $400 a night for a room. We wanted to send a message to everybody that this wasn't a Lower East Side budget destination, it was a destination on its own."

Downtown Manhattan does not have corporately owned bars, but many new owners have experience in the corporate world or use corporate strategies, such as hiring DJs and promoters to handle publicity. Liam, for example, works in finance and opened a bar in the East Village with a business partner in 2004. Owning a bar was always a dream of his. He wanted a place where he could express some of his creative interests, such as electronic dance music and welding, since his corporate job did not grant him an outlet to do so. Like Harold, he planned on distinguishing his bar from existing places in the neighborhood by attracting a more upscale clientele. It did not matter to him whether they lived in the neighborhood. He only wanted customers who desired the type of atmosphere he constructed:

> Our customers are from all over the place. It's more of a destination spot now. We definitely attract a very young professional, twenty-five to thirty-five, typically people that have good jobs. We're not a dive bar, we don't look like a dive bar, we don't feel like a dive bar. But we're also not a high-end club, so we're somewhere in between and that's how we've always catered to. It's like people who are sick of clubs but like the club atmosphere. They like the bottle service, and we'll do bottle service downstairs, we'll do a guest list, it's the whole atmosphere. People dress up to come here. You don't have to, you can come in flip-flops and a T-shirt if you want, but I think people, when they do come dressed up, they don't feel like they're overdressed for the establishment.

Music became an important means for him to attract a clientele. "If you could generate a crowd," says Liam, "if you are a DJ that has a following, that's what we're always looking for." Having the right DJs and music helps a bar create a reputation and an image as a destination for revelers, which means it does not have to rely on local communities for business.

Motivations and Themes

Along with hours of operation and use of space, new bar owners also come up with themes for their bars to attract clientele. John Hannigan describes "urban entertainment destinations" as highly thematized, corporate-run, and large-scale projects with a "top-down" organizational planning structure.[28] Corporate actors create all-encompassing, totalizing environments based on themes that may or may not be consistent with the urban locales within which they are embedded, such as the Hard Rock Café or Planet Hollywood. The nightlife scenes in downtown Manhattan differ from these developments.

They consist of independent owners, most of whom own a single bar, and as a whole they have no dominant theme. Owners choose themes—which are reflected in their bar's decor, drink selection, entertainment offerings, and staff—based on their own personal interests and their vision for the clientele they wish to attract. Pianos, for instance, seeks to attract a broad array of customers, mostly entertainment seekers who enjoy rock and dance music. Its owners designed the decor to create different environments in each room. As Brandon describes:

> The idea was to have separate rooms, where it's different feelings in each room. The original concept was for the main floor to be like a beach house kind of feeling, up here to be like a jungle kind of feeling, and the live room, visually, was supposed to be like nighttime—you know, it's a black room—from the beginning. That's kind of changed and progressed over time. But the concept has always been to have, like, separate, different rooms with different stuff going on.

Overall, owners aim for their bars to become a destination for revelers and gain distinction in a competitive nightlife scene by creating a unique nightlife experience.

In conceiving a theme for Milk and Honey, Sasha partially relied on his original café ideas. "I just couldn't deal with drunk people anymore," he says. "So I had the idea that I would open up my bar and it would be much more like a café—quieter, a place where people could have conversation." Despite limited cocktail knowledge or experience ("I knew not to shake a martini," he says), Sasha opened a bar that specialized in cocktails. I ask him how he came up with this idea and his cocktail style. I receive a history lesson.

> The idea for Milk and Honey comes from a place called the Angel's Share on Ninth Street. It's a Japanese bar that did a very specific kind of service that they do in Japan, which I don't think was originated in Japan. I think pretty much Japanese bartenders, the top ones back in the '20s, they managed to teach their craft to the next generation, as opposed to American bartenders who because of Prohibition just, you know, life being what it is, everything went downhill. So the stuff that was standard in the 1920s—squeezing juice to order, having ice from a big block—all of these things were kind of forgotten in America, because of Prohibition, because of technical innovations like the soda gun, if you want to call that an innovation. So the Japanese kind of kept all this stuff alive, stuff that was largely developed here in New York. And then a guy in the early '90s, I guess, opened up this bar in New York.

And this bar had a somewhat hidden entrance, rules of behavior, big ice, olives on the side of the martini. Milk and Honey is very much an homage to this bar, the Angel's Share.

The model for the thematic concepts behind Angel's Share and Milk and Honey is the Prohibition-era drinking institution of the speakeasy. Speakeasies were secretive by nature and visibly removed from city street life in order to avoid attention of the authorities. They required "connections" and passwords to enter through unmarked doors. Today's speakeasy bars are similar to the unregulated, hidden places that Herman discussed earlier in the sense that you had to be "in the know" to be aware of them and to get in. But these places are not trying to hide from the authorities, nor does being "in the know" entail membership in a community of artists or an alternative subculture. It instead refers to knowledge of the location in the network of spaces within the taste community, or simply knowledge of the establishment as a nightlife destination. Today, the speakeasy and its airs of secrecy and exclusivity are popular historical references for bar owners.

With café experience, a desire to make specialized products, and Angel's Share's model as his sources of inspiration, Sasha found a cheap space on the Lower East Side in 1999. The community board, which had already begun its anti-proliferation activism, initially denied his liquor license application. He reapplied with a petition signed by one hundred of his neighbors (he made petitions in English, Spanish, and Chinese so that all of his neighbors could read it), got approved, and opened Milk and Honey on New Year's Day 2000.

The business was touch and go at first. The bar was not just located outside of the nightlife scene, it was also hidden, and therefore empty. But Sasha used this freedom to experiment. One day, he fortuitously met Dale DeGroff, also known as "King Cocktail," a veteran bartender who during the 1980s revived the bar at New York City's historic Rainbow Room by incorporating pre-Prohibition era cocktail culture into the bar program. Members of the cocktail communities in the United States consider him to be the founding father of the cocktail's renaissance. Sasha recalls their meeting:

In an incredible piece of luck and coincidence, Dale DeGroff—[well,] a friend of his from college—happened to live across the street. He brought him in, and Dale looked around, and he saw what I was trying to do and that we had not made much progress. And he reached into his bag and he took out a copy of the Trader Vic Rum Book from 1948 and said, "Here's a gift," and he gave me a solid fruitwood muddler, which lasted quite a while before it finally died.[29] And he taught me how to make, well, in the first couple of times that he came he taught me how to make a Southside, a Sazerac, and most importantly he told me to put the ice in last, which is the basis for this bartending we do.[30] So from there the notion that there were antique bar books out there that you could get information from was the starting point.

Through research and trial and error, Sasha gradually developed a considerable amount of knowledge on cocktails and spirits. More importantly, he says, he developed a service plan and an efficient system that provides customers with a unique experience, from drinks to interactions with bartenders.

Sasha describes Milk and Honey as a boutique and more like a café than a bar. But the reputation of the bar with the hidden door and the handcrafted cocktails spread, and Milk and Honey became a destination for people from around the city. Some have become regulars and members of New York City's cocktail taste community, while most have been attracted to its novelty. These latter customers are a largely transient group: "We have a *huge* amount of one-time customers," says Sasha. "They come, they like it a lot, they don't like it enough that they're going to go through the hassle more than once a year." Its customers are willing to go to a bar for which you need a reservation, must travel to the neighborhood, and must pay $16 per drink. From Milk and Honey Sasha built a cocktail empire, opening new bars on the Lower East Side and around the city.

Specialized bars like Milk and Honey inspired new bar owners in many ways. Dave, for example, was influenced by how Sasha created a destination based on atmosphere and specialized products.

If you go to Milk and Honey, you walk through that door, and just the experience of getting to that door is a very transporting thing. I love going to Milk and Honey because you walk into some place that's really jarringly different from, completely juxtaposed from that street. You want to be removed and be very much in the environment, in the element. I think that's one thing that most successful places have, that most successful nightlife or bar places have, is that all-encompassing-feel environment, followed through. So that the drinks, the bartenders, the service, and atmosphere—it should all sort of meld seamlessly to provide this sort of night and experience for you. You'll definitely get that if you go to Sasha's places.

Dave interestingly uses similar language as Hannigan does for "urban entertainment destinations" to describe successful bars, namely the "all-encompassing feel" that they create and the unique experiences that they provide for customers. New bar owners have latched onto the notion that their influence extends beyond the downtown's boundaries. Like Pianos, Milk and Honey is extra- as well as transterritorial. On the one hand, young urbanites from around the city have heard about it and seek it out for the novelty of the secret door, personalized service, and specialized products. On the other hand, Milk and Honey is also a serious bar for cocktail enthusiasts from around the city and the world. They seek it out regularly and are members of the cocktail community, which extends beyond the bar's door and beyond the boundaries of the neighborhood, city, and country. It is not uncommon to see cocktail bartenders and enthusiasts visiting Milk and Honey from around the world. After all, Sammy from this chapter's opening vignette heard about it from Australia, and then moved to the United States to work behind its bar. In both cases, the clientele they serve are different from the communities within which they are embedded.

Similarly, when he decided to open a cocktail bar with a business partner, Dave's strategy was to take advantage of being located on the East Village and within a vibrant nightlife scene while keeping separate from it.

> [We] chose this spot for a very specific reason . . . that it was sort of a destination bar with convenience. So it's a destination bar in that it's just off the beaten path; there's nothing really on this street, but it's a very convenient location. There's a bunch of places *around* here, but no reason why people would really walk past our spot. We designed the facade that way, we designed the interior that way, so that it's not sort of jumping out in your face and we would get a very specific type of clientele that was interested in what we're doing and not just popping in for Southern Comfort and beer or something.

Dave's bar is spatially in the thick of the action, but at the conceptual margins of the nightlife scene by his own design: a place you need to seek out, know about in advance, know cultural codes, and be able to afford. Like Milk and Honey's, his "type of clientele" is mainly transient. Some of Dave's customers live in the neighborhood, but most travel from around the city because they know of its reputation as a fairly hidden and highly stylized place with unique drinks. And while some of his customers are interested in the niche product of handcrafted cocktails and are part of the city's larger cocktail community, most come based on this reputation and for the experience of being there and consuming its unique products. The cocktail culture created by figures like Sasha and Dave has also influenced new owners wishing to capitalize on the products themselves. Other bars downtown and around the city hire Sasha and his skilled bartenders as consultants to develop a cocktail menu and train their staff. As people developed a taste for cocktails, new bar owners saw them as necessary to stay competitive with other bars. The specialized cocktail community produces cultural items that new bar owners borrow and use to their own advantage.[31]

Although the new bar owners are not from downtown Manhattan, many make connections between themselves and the area, which often serve as motivations for them to want to open a bar there. For instance, Melissa, the clothing designer, opened her bar-and-clothing-store on Orchard Street because of its historical importance in New York City immigration and clothing manufacturing. Other new bar owners make more personal connections. Although she grew up on Long Island, Sandee developed an affinity for the Lower East Side from a young age. "My grandmother used to, this was a destination for her to come down for fabric and clothing and things, and she lived in Stuyvesant Town and then she moved out to Long Island, but she still would come in."[32] Sandee's grandmother served as a connection between her and the Lower East Side. She also developed an interest in the neighborhood's history, particularly its lore from the nineteenth century, such as that depicted in Herbert Asbury's classic *Gangs of New York*.[33] Sandee uses these characters and stories in her decor. "I'm interested in this woman whose depicted in this painting very scarily. [That's] Hellcat Maggie, so she collected men's ears, she had brass fingernails, shaved her teeth to points. So I like that history, I even have a painting up there of Big Mose and Short Change Charlie." These historical references combine with her interest in bourbon and single-malt scotch to create the bar's name— the Whiskey Ward—and its specialized products. "The way we got the name Whiskey Ward is back at the turn of the century the city was broken up into political wards. The Bowery and this area were the Fourth and Sixth Wards, and combined they called them the Whiskey Wards, so that's how we came up with the name."[34] For new bar owners without a direct link to downtown Manhattan, family connections and historical references provide a connection to a place that eludes their own biographies.

Despite the economic environment and having a nonlocal clientele, new bar owners in downtown Manhattan still use a community discourse to describe their bars. And in spite of attracting a destination-seeking clientele and existing under difficult economic conditions, these young owners maintain an identity as social and cultural entrepreneurs. As a result, new bar owners create a nightlife environment that is marked by transience and anonymity among visiting revelers in search of a consumption experience.

CHAPTER 5

REGULATING NIGHTLIFE SCENES

> Night spots are today overwhelming the street, and are also overwhelming the very life of the area. Into a district excellent at handling and protecting strangers they have concentrated too many strangers, all in too irresponsible a mood, for any conceivable city society to handle naturally.
>
> —JANE JACOBS[1]

LIKE OTHER INDEPENDENT ENTREPRENEURS, bar owners rarely gather together in any considerable numbers. About fifty have done so on a cold December night in 2007, to attend a meeting hosted by the Seventh Precinct. Tucked in the southeastern corner of the Lower East Side near some of its public housing projects and in the shadow of the Williamsburg Bridge, the area right around Manhattan's Seventh Precinct is devoid of bars. But nightlife issues demand a significant amount of the precinct's attention. Lieutenant Joe Del Duca is the Special Operations Lieutenant of the Seventh, a position within the New York Police Department (NYPD) that handles issues unique to a precinct's neighborhood. In his case, bars and nightlife and the quality-of-life issues they generate are a central focus of his special operations, although he would rather handle more serious criminal matters in the neighborhood. Along with contributing to the monthly public community council meetings that all of the city's precincts conduct, for members of the neighborhood to hear police updates and address their concerns, he also runs semiannual meetings on quality-of-life and safety issues solely with bar owners, such as the one tonight.

Lieutenant Del Duca called this meeting to discuss the "Best Practices for Nightlife Establishments" guide, recently released by the NYPD in cooperation with the New York Nightlife Association (NYNA), a lobbying group for nightlife owners, with the bar owners in his precinct. Nearly half of the Seventh's bar owners are here, and Del Duca knows most of them by name. He has visited their bars for either enforcement purposes, such as to address complaints and investigate incidents, or to advise owners on how to reduce the potential for quality-of-life issues and make their bars safer. Many of the bar owners present tonight at least periodically attend the monthly community council meetings as well as the semiannual meetings. They have heard Del Duca and other officers explain the main issues residents have with their bars as well

FIGURE 14 The police and residents often request that bar owners put up signs in their windows or on their facades asking their customers to keep quiet while they are entering and exiting the bar or while they are smoking or talking on their phones outside the bar. Many residents also criticize this measure as ineffective. Photograph by Chantal Martineau, 2011.

as possible solutions to address them many times before. The "Best Practices" guide represents a step towards codifying the private strategies the NYPD has been encouraging bar owners to adopt for many years. The list of guidelines is historic in the sense that New York City nightlife and the police have regularly been at odds with each other. Tonight Lower East Side bar owners will listen to the relevance of these best practices for them.

"Basically," Del Duca begins in his New York accent, "within the past six months to a year, arising from a lot of, from a couple of newsworthy tragic events that surrounded nightclubs, the New York Nightlife Association got together with the police commissioner and the police department and they came up with this guideline. Now, just so you know, I'm sure everybody has it, this is a guideline. It's not the laws, it's a guide. Some of it explains the law on certain areas, but it is a guide, it's not law. But I, just from reading it, there's a lot of stuff in here, I mean, I've been doing this for two years now, I've been Special Ops Lieutenant for two years, and a lot of this stuff, if you've been to my meetings, if you've had meetings with me or I've seen you out in the street, a lot of this stuff I've been saying for two years. A couple of things I want to go over that they highlight, that they stress here, which I feel can benefit this neighborhood."

Before getting to the actual best practices, Del Duca discusses his overarching policy with bar owners: "Something I need to stress to you is that what we're looking for is cooperation. Every business owner should take a social responsibility in the neighborhood that they're in, as far as I'm concerned. And part of that social responsibility is the quality of life in the neighborhood and any criminality that's going on. And it's always a good thing to be friendly with your neighbors. They live here, and they were probably here before you."

He then proceeds to go through the guideline, highlighting the best practices for safety that he feels would benefit owners in his precinct, such as hiring private security, maintaining a list of patrons who have been banned, and using security cameras and ID scanners. Del Duca then returns to the issue of noise in the neighborhood. But as soon as he does, a bar owner changes the subject.

"What about tenant harassment against bars?" he asks.

"What do you mean by 'harassment'?"

"Calling every forty minutes for absolutely no reason. Before I opened the place that I have right now, the apartments above me tried to, they wanted me out before I even opened. So since I opened the bar they've informed me that they want to get me kicked out, so they call every enforcement agency every single day. That's harassment, without anything wrong."

"If those complaints come in there, and believe me, I understand there are some people in the neighborhood that just want to call 311[2] because they want a voice and a lot of them have legitimate complaints, and then there are other ones that are bad apples that are just making life hell for the police department and businesses. I understand that, I've dealt with them. I've written them off, because I feel like they're wasting police department resources. Then again, there are some bars that haven't accepted what the police department has asked them to do, too. Some bars I've written off, from being uncooperative and not accepting any social responsibility, where I don't go there and be peaceful—well, peaceful is a bad word to say, but I don't go there with the mind of giving them a warning. I go there with the mind of doing enforcement."

Lieutenant Del Duca uses the example of the previous month's workload to discuss his policy for dealing with quality-of-life issues and further explains what he expects from bar owners.

"In the last month we had 180 calls for noise on the Lower East Side, just in the last twenty-eight days. And again, the whole noise problem, each situation I take differently, and I take separately. And I think if you ever, at 1 PP [Police Plaza], they use the word 'totality of the circumstances,' which is kind of what

I use when it comes to a lot of this stuff. I take the totality of the circumstances. I take what's happened in the past—is it just one bad night, did someone call anonymously, is there really a problem, is some crazy person across the street just called—I take the totality of the circumstances into account every time I look at each place.

"The way I view this is that every time, now at least 180 times we've had to go and respond to noise complaints, those were 180 times within the past twenty-eight days where my guys weren't looking for people that are robbing somebody, that were drug dealing in the neighborhood, that were looking for people stealing bags. So to me, every time we are on one of these jobs, that takes us away from doing something more serious. Yes, noise is a problem, it's a quality-of-life issue. The way my police career went, I'd rather be finding the people that are robbing people and those type of things. So by you cooperating with noise codes and helping out in that situation, it actually improves your neighborhood. That's the way I look at it, because that'd give the police more time to take care of more serious problems. That's the exact way I look at it. So if I come to you and I say, 'This is a problem. I need you to do this, this, and that,' I expect it to happen, especially when it comes to noise codes, because I'd rather be doing other things, to be perfectly honest with you."

After the meeting adjourns, I catch up with Frank, a new bar owner who spoke often during the evening and asked several questions, as he was leaving to go back to his bar. Frank says he occasionally goes to the monthly community council meetings and always to Lieutenant Del Duca's meetings, mostly to stay in the precinct's good graces.

"They see you as a concerned bar owner, which is what they're looking for."

But Frank does not come away from the meetings completely convinced that by trying to make efforts towards reducing his impact on quality of life, he will be left alone by residents. I ask him if police mediation has improved his relationship with his neighbors. He shakes his head. "You're damned if you do and you're damned if you don't. This guy says, 'Turn down your stuff and it'll make it all right.' Unh-uh. Not here. Not Community Board 3."

NIGHTLIFE REGULATION REFORM IN NEW YORK CITY

In between downtown Manhattan's daytime and nighttime actors are the mediating figures of local politicians and the police. Residents rely on their elected officials and local precincts to help them protest the disruptive growth of nightlife scenes, even when they have become frustrated by the lack of progress. But downtown bar owners have different attitudes towards these groups. They react strongly to what they perceive as threats to their local self-identity as purveyors of community, as place entrepreneurs, and as independent businesspeople. The sources of these threats are both the residents who protest their bars and the city's nightlife policies. A period of nightlife reform began in New York City in 2006. But change did not occur because of pressure from community groups on quality-of-life issues. Rather, it was born out of tragedy.

On February 25, 2006, Imette St. Guillen, a twenty-four-year-old graduate student, was abducted from a bar near the Lower East Side by an unlicensed bouncer with a criminal record at 4 a.m., after her friends left.[3] The next day her bound, raped, and murdered body was found in a desolate area in Brooklyn. This gruesome event and its unfolding investigation made headlines in local papers for several weeks and focused attention on public safety in nightlife. On July 24, 2006, Jennifer Moore, an eighteen-year-old New Jersey resident who was out at a nightclub on a Monday night in Manhattan, was abducted while intoxicated from the side of a highway after separating from her friend. She was taken to a New Jersey motel, raped, and murdered. Her body was found two days later. Along with the brutality of the incident, the local media highlighted the fact that she was underage but was still able to consume alcohol publicly in a premier nightlife district.[4]

The public outcry over these incidents, as well as increases in crime reported in nightlife-dense precincts with large nightlife scenes, pushed nightlife safety into the political spotlight. Local politicians interpreted these events as an "image crisis" that threatened the city's status as a place for safe nightlife.[5] They saw them as signs that nightlife had become too volatile, with too many bad operators, too little oversight, and ineffective enforcement. To keep the city marketable as an entertainment destination, they had to address these problems and make nightlife safe—or at least make it appear to be safe—without compromising its vibrancy. Local politicians adopted a consensus that attempted to balance the concerns of their constituency within their neighborhoods and the economic growth of their districts and the city—a precarious balance since these needs often conflict with each other in cases of nightlife. Just as they are aware of nightlife's harmful community impacts, local politicians are also aware of its importance for New York City's economy. As Louise, the chief of staff to a State Assembly member, says, "It's a very important industry: it brings people into the city, it's certainly a moneymaker, it generates taxes. So it *is* very important. There just has to be the proper balance of things." Courtney, the Manhattan borough president's director of intergovernmental affairs, shares this perspective:

Nightlife is a $9 billion-a-year industry—we can't shut it down. We shouldn't be going towards Prohibition. We can't *not* have nightclubs, we can't *not* have cabarets, and other types of entities for people to come and enjoy themselves, for tourists to come to their huge tourist attractions like some of these clubs, and then the local watering hole, which I think that most of us will say we enjoy, or a fine restaurant where you could have a bottle of wine or something else. But there's got to be a balance. . . . We'd like to see the proliferation [in downtown Manhattan] kind of move around.

As with the question of what is in the "public interest" that State Liquor Authority officials must answer, local politicians have never precisely explained or measured what it means to find a "balance" between keeping nightlife vibrant, ensuring safety, reducing quality-of-life issues, and maintaining local communities. They have been unable either to articulate it through legislation or to clarify it at public meetings or for me in my conversations with them and their staffs. But with a mindset that straddles community and entrepreneurial concerns, local politicians do not address factors such as the quantity of bars and density levels of nightlife scenes when attempting to strike this balance. Instead, they focus on nightlife problems at the individual level of the owner and the establishment. They identify, label, and target "bad operators" and "problem locations" rather than handle dense nightlife scenes. Courtney continues:

I'd say that probably 90 percent of bars and clubs in this town are not offenders. Probably if you reviewed their file [they] have very few infractions, if any. But those *bad operators* that exist and are there, that's what they are, they're *bad operators*. You need to weed them out, punish them.

This perspective asserts that unscrupulous owners, not dense nightlife scenes or droves of revelers, cause nightlife issues. On top of protests from residents, bar owners also have to face scrutiny from public authorities.

Starting in summer 2006, city and state government officials established several initiatives to combat the problem of "bad operators." First, people at the SLA acknowledged that they needed to make changes to the agency's licensing decisions in light of public outcry and political pressure. They had already conveniently made personnel changes in the months preceding St. Guillen's death in response to a public scandal in the state's liquor industry involving the illegal practices of wholesalers. The SLA hired its first CEO in more than a decade, Joshua Toas, to manage the general operations of the agency, and a new chairman, Daniel Boyle, to head it. Boyle had a strong background in law enforcement and replaced a pro-growth chairman who was a friend of the Republican governor George Pataki (the state legislature confirmed Boyle to the appointment just two weeks before St. Guillen's death). With the existing personnel and a mandate to clean up the wholesale industry with strict force if necessary, the SLA was in a position to address these new problems in the retail industry.

Toas explains their approach: "We definitely decided that licensing decisions have a great impact on enforcement problems. So we're doing everything we can to make the proper licensing decisions, to make sure a neighborhood is not overrun with *bad bars*. And when they are, *we put those bars out of business.*"

The SLA issued a moratorium from September 2006 until the end of that year on all full on-premises liquor licenses in 500-foot-rule cases so it could evaluate its licensing policies. Praised by residents and Community Board 3—which had seen the SLA ignore its own 500-foot-rule protests and local moratoriums on liquor licenses—and vilified by the nightlife industry and bar owners, the statewide moratorium dramatically halted thirteen years of pro-growth licensing decisions, at least temporarily. In conjunction with the moratorium, the SLA established the Taskforce for the Review of On-Premises Licensure. The task force brought together representatives from disparate groups—community boards (including CB3), NYNA, local politicians (members of the city council and the state legislature), and, most importantly, the SLA itself—to discuss licensing matters, policy reforms, and possible legislation. Forming the task force was noteworthy, not only because government agencies rarely open themselves up to external actors for critiques on their policies, but also because the SLA had been uncommunicative with these actors during its pro-development period. The group met three times in fall 2006 and released a report of its discussions, with a list of ten recommendations, at the end of that year. The report encouraged greater transparency at the SLA, stronger communication and collaboration between it, the police, and other city government agencies, and a more streamlined application process. The findings in the report demonstrate a consensus between these groups, including NYNA, that a few bad individual operators weaken the reputation of the industry and cause unruly and unsafe conditions.

Stemming from this task force, city government passed several legislative bills in 2007 that targeted individual nightlife owners. The "bouncer bill" requires nightclubs with cabaret licenses (i.e., licenses for dancing) to hire licensed security guards, and a similar bill requires them to have surveillance cameras at the entrances and exits of their establishments. The "independent monitor bill" allows places that are issued violations by city agencies to hire a court-approved independent monitor for a probationary period to ensure legal compliance in lieu of having their licenses revoked. New legislation also helped the police handle more serious nightlife problems. An expanded "nuisance abatement" law gives the police greater powers to shut down problem establishments. Although before this law the police were able to close places that endangered public health and safety—such as those that housed drug sales, prostitution, and gambling—they can now close an establishment if three or more felony charges have been made there in the previous twelve-month period. These charges could range from violent incidents to serving alcohol to minors. A nuisance abatement proceeding can lead to the revocation of a bar's liquor license or to assignment of an aforementioned court-appointed independent monitor to the establishment. Each of these laws carries a financial penalty on owners found in violation. But more importantly, each identifies and brings "bad operators" under the direct regulatory control of government agencies and addresses concerns about public safety. The laws and politicians did not, however, target the dense concentrations of nighttime establishments that had been causing problems for residents in neighborhoods, which would have meant shrinking nightlife scenes.

At the same time as the SLA task force was meeting, the New York City Council held a Nightlife Safety Summit, which also brought together disparate nightlife stakeholders—including the NYPD and the SLA—and resulted in a report with a list of policy and legislative recommendations. Entitled "Safer Nights, Safer City," this report focused on strengthening the regulation of nightlife establishments through legislation, private security, and closer working relationships between bar owners and the police. Along with the aforementioned legislation, the summit also resulted in the formation of a working group between NYPD and NYNA as well as better communication between top officials at the NYPD and the SLA.

Historically, the nightlife industry and the NYPD have had a hostile relationship. Some individual owners, officers, and precincts may have had informal local partnerships, but on the whole the two actors conflicted. Law enforcement officials and bar owners recall that since, for the most part, the nightlife industry did not want to attract attention to itself, owners would not always alert the police when there was an incident at their establishment. They feared they would be fined, compromise their liquor licenses, and become targets for future monitoring if they called the police, even for minor infractions. The police resented this willful inattention that threatened their investigations. And since nighttime establishments were already sources of local problems for precincts, this caused them even greater frustration. But the murders in 2006, and the fact that the SLA's enforcement arm was woefully inadequate (as mentioned in chapter 2, at the time it only had seven investigators for the 30,000 licensed establishments in the New York metropolitan area, which represents 40 percent of the state's total), forced them to collaborate. After a year of meetings, the working group published a pamphlet entitled "Best Practices for Nightlife Establishments" in September 2007, discussed in this chapter's opening vignette. These "best practices" are behavioral guidelines for owners to follow in operating their establishments. They cover private security, employee policies, and proper procedures to take when an incident occurs. While not official law, the best practices hold bar owners accountable for a number of activities within and outside of their establishments. Downtown Manhattan's two police precincts, the Seventh and the Ninth, collaborate with bar owners to address the neighborhood's problems.

The most time-consuming problem for the police in downtown Manhattan is quality-of-life complaints by residents because of nightlife, particularly noise generated by sound systems and customers as well as street noise that passing revelers and cars make. They must address these issues because of their own policing policies. For example, residents complain directly to the police, or they call the city's 311 system. Mayor Michael Bloomberg implemented the 311 system in 2002 as a resource for citizens to obtain information on or to complain about civic and governmental services or public issues. It records and forwards such questions and concerns along to the appropriate city agency or department. City Hall holds the latter accountable for addressing the issue or complaint. The 311 system is linked with the NYPD's Computer Statistics (CompStat) program. CompStat is a statistics-driven monitoring program that geographically tracks coded incidents throughout a precinct's command. And, like the 311 system, City Hall and police headquarters hold the precinct accountable for solving them. Commanding officers receive weekly reports on their precinct's crime and complaint statistics, and central authorities in the NYPD and in city government expect them to address whatever issues they are having and account for the actions they have taken to combat them. Along with quality-of-life complaints, one of the most important nightlife-related crimes in downtown Manhattan is property theft, particularly purses, wallets, bags, coats, laptops, and other items stolen from people in bars. When the items are valuable, the NYPD characterizes these incidents as grand larcenies, which increase major crime statistics and reflect poorly on the precinct. As one detective at the Seventh Precinct says, "It's so important he [the commanding office] treats a stolen bag like a nonlethal shooting." These policies—311 and CompStat—were hardly intended to divert police resources to target crowded, vibrant nightlife scenes. The police certainly prioritize high-profile crimes such as violent incidents and drug activity when such incidents occur. But most of the problems they deal with are not high-profile, and they interpret quality-of-life offenses as drains on their resources and blemishes on their statistical records.

While the city pressures the police to address quality-of-life issues in dense nightlife scenes, the NYPD knows it does not have the resources to combat such problems effectively. The precincts in downtown Manhattan take quality of life seriously and follow the NYPD's protocol to address any issues, but they still do not consider nightlife noise complaints to be as serious as other crimes. As Lieutenant Del Duca explained in the opening vignette, the time they spend on quality-of-life complaints is time they do not spend on more serious criminal activity. Furthermore, the NYPD does not want its officers involved in nightlife matters any more than they already are, best evidenced by its refusal to establish a "paid detail" program for nightlife establishments. Paid detail is a common police security service that serves as a form of overtime for officers. Private businesses such as sports stadiums and retail stores pay to have uniformed off-duty police officers work at their locations and provide additional security. Bar owners, the nightlife industry, and local politicians support such a program, believing that more police officers on the street would reduce quality-of-life issues and deter crime. But the police speak adamantly against it and claim it is illegal.[6] The law they cite originated out of the fear that direct police involvement in nightlife could potentially lead to corruption between them and owners. But they also acknowledge the increased chance of officers getting involved in violent incidents with revelers if more of them walked a beat on a nightlife strip, which would attract negative media attention.

A direct action that the police take to target bad operators is a strike force called the Multi-Agency Response to Community Hotspots (MARCH). The MARCH initiative was implemented in the 1970s to combat quality-of-life problems in Times Square and has since been expanded citywide. It is an interagency enforcement program that sends representatives from several government departments and agencies to "problem locations" in a neighborhood, which, in the case of bars, they usually identify by an excessive amount of 311 complaints. Members from the police and fire departments, as well as the SLA, Department of Environmental Protection, Department of Buildings, Office of Public Safety, and Department of Health show up at a bar unannounced and en masse. They check it for any violations and write fines when applicable, which can be quite costly and can stain a bar's record when the owner renews its liquor license.

At a little past midnight on a midsummer Saturday night, while conducting fieldwork, I notice two police officers walking on Rivington Street toward a parked patrol car with its lights on blocking southbound traffic at a busy intersection. Surrounding it are several parked government vehicles and both plainclothes and uniformed service personnel standing around. One of the officers in the street has a folder under his arm that reads "March Op, 6/28/08." It is a MARCH on Spitzer's Corner, a large, popular corner bar on the Lower East Side that has received many noise and sidewalk crowding complaints from their neighbors.

Only the police and firemen are easily identifiable, but representatives from the State Liquor Authority, Department of Environmental Protection,

Department of Buildings, Office of Public Safety, and Department of Health also participate in this operation. While the SLA is responsible for the bar's license, each agency has some regulatory authority over the establishment. For example, the Department of Environmental Protection is here to conduct a sound reading and determine if the bar is breaking the noise code, and the Department of Buildings is here to see if it has a public assembly permit, which is required for any establishment with occupancy of more than seventy-four people. Any violation will result in a summons and likely a fine. In this case, Spitzer's Corner does not have a public assembly permit, yet an interior sign that the bar has made and posted in the front reads "Maximum occupancy not to exceed 250," and there are clearly more than seventy-four people in the bar.

Although the service vehicles and personnel on the street cause many revelers to stop and see if anything serious is happening, the representatives who enter the bar to inspect it do so as inconspicuously as possible, and the activity inside and outside continue as normal. After nearly an hour, the agency officials write their own summonses for any violations of law that they have found, and the police officer in charge hands them all to tonight's manager. The members of the MARCH operation get back in their vehicles and, in single file with a police van in the lead, they slowly drive away to their next location.[7]

To avoid diverting too many resources to such issues or engaging in direct enforcement, officers in downtown Manhattan precincts prefer private solutions to combat nightlife's public problems, namely by encouraging bar owners to take a "social responsibility" for their neighborhood. This includes implementing private security measures—such as hiring bouncers, using identification scanners, and installing surveillance cameras—to deal with quality-of-life issues, deter crime, and aid in investigations and working out problems with residents on their own.[8] They convey these messages to bar owners in meetings, such as their monthly community council public meetings and special meetings such as the one at the start of this chapter, and on a one-on-one basis. Bar owners who do not "cooperate" risk being "written off" and subjected to intense scrutiny from the precinct.

In spite of these reforms, nightlife thrived in New York City and in neighborhoods like those in downtown Manhattan during this time, with bars opening steadily and liquor license applications continuing to inundate the community board's office. Still, bar owners in the neighborhood interpret the reforms as threats to their businesses. They are baffled that the city would target *them*, particularly given their self-understanding as purveyors of community and valuable assets to the Lower East Side and to the city. Bar owners respond by proclaiming the positive contributions they make to the community and by deflecting blame away from themselves. But just as residents understand bars to be symbolic threats and daily reminders of how their neighborhood has changed, so do owners identify protesting residents and community groups to be the main threat to their local self-identity as place entrepreneurs.

THE VICTIMS OF SUCCESS

"The only people that are actually being blamed for anything *ever* are the bar owners that are in the *ho-spi-ta-li-ty* industry," says Sarah.

A new owner, Sarah opened her bar with a lounge-like atmosphere in the East Village in 2004. A native New Yorker, Sarah cut her teeth in the nightlife industry working in large nightclubs before opening her own velvet-roped place. Like other bar owners, she is aware of the recent efforts by local politicians, the police, and the SLA to regulate nightlife by enacting new laws, shifting policies, and prioritizing quality of life and safety. They know that these actors and the NYPD are targeting them to handle nightlife problems, holding them more accountable for their bars, and pressuring them to comply with the new regulatory agenda. And they must deal with their neighbors, the community board, and other community groups who complain about their bars, bring them to the attention of the police and other state authorities, and potentially compromise their liquor licenses. Finally, owners like Sarah are highly sensitive to the "problem owner" designation that underpins the new nightlife regulation.

"It's not really a level playing field," she continues. "We're not being respected; we're not being appreciated. We're being undervalued, criminalized; we're being pushed out; our business lives are becoming a living hell."

A theme of victimhood pervades the responses of bar owners towards the policies, criticisms, and actions against them. They react to these perceived threats by proclaiming their benefits to their neighborhood and the city, deflecting blame away from themselves, and finding fault with the perspectives and actions of residents. They do not, however, always react uniformly as a group. Old and new bar owners often differ over several matters.

Benefitting the Neighborhood and City

As discussed in chapter 4, older bar owners often assert their status as commercial pioneers in downtown Manhattan. They use their pioneer status and longevity in their neighborhood as defenses against protests from residents and threats from city policies. They often describe the negative conditions that characterized their neighborhood, and the sense of safety that they provided, not to mention the economic benefits they brought to a depressed area. But new owners have also adopted this perspective, even though the area had already gentrified when they opened their bars. They still claim that their establishments contribute to downtown Manhattan's improvement and success and see themselves as key actors in its transformation from dangerous and slum-like to safe and coveted.

Dave, introduced in the previous chapter, opened his cocktail bar, Death & Co., which references a Prohibition-era term that the temperance movement used against imbibers, in early 2007. As mentioned, he chose the location because it was a bit off the neighborhood's main thoroughfares on a side street, which would make his bar a convenient destination. But he and his business partner converted a space that had an existing establishment, an Indian-fusion restaurant. When neighbors heard that a bar was going to open, and one that was dedicated to a specific alcoholic beverage category at that, they came out in large numbers to protest. CB3 denied his application (but the SLA still approved it), and Dave was highly frustrated by the experience, in part because of the important role he feels bars play in the neighborhood.

> You're looking around at all these people that have been here for ten years and you're like, "Listen, remember ten years ago? And look at it now. You know why it's better? Because the fucking restaurants and the bars came in here!" No one was going to come in here. [Bars are] going to open up, that's what's going to slowly make it better. What makes people comfortable to come here, venture here, and eventually start moving in here is going to make it a safe place, and it *is* [safe] now.

As Dave's comment demonstrates, new owners often contrast their presence with residents' descriptions of what the neighborhood was once like. With their self-identity as positive contributors to their neighborhood, new bar owners do not understand residents' inclusion of its negative past in their nostalgia narrative. To owners, bars are among the solutions to critical urban problems.

In addition to self-identifying as benefits to the community, bar owners also understand themselves and their industry as valuable assets to the entire city's economic and cultural well-being. Like politicians, bar owners are highly aware of the importance of nightlife in the contemporary urban economy. They attach themselves to New York City's larger agenda of tourism and entertainment. As Edward, a New York Nightlife Association (NYNA) representative, states, "New York is known as a nightlife place. We modestly refer to ourselves as the nightlife capital of the world. People come here, many times, just to go to the restaurants or just to go to the clubs, and it contributes." Liz, a new bar owner, frames nightlife in a context of global tourism:

I mean, my God, part of travel and tourism is like: Where are you going to eat? Where are you going to hang out? How do you hang out with people? It's part of what you do. In my life, going to Barcelona, London, and Dublin, it's all sort of revolved around that. You go to neighborhoods that have that. That's what gives it character, and charm.

Owners see themselves as part of a long tradition of nightlife in New York City that they take pride in maintaining. Sarah praises New York City's cultural importance:

There are cities in general, and then there's Manhattan. I mean, I'm totally New York-centric. It's all about us. We reverberate and ripple to the rest of the world and they can learn from us. And we are sort of the standard on how things can and should be. It's like a real historical exploration from the beginnings of New York itself because there's always been a very vibrant and raucous nightlife.

Furthermore, owners also see themselves as noble members of the hospitality industry, in the business of providing services for the pleasure and enjoyment of other people. These feelings of self-worth and self-importance contrast with the stigma of being considered a "problem." Personal complaints by community residents, fines imposed by the SLA, police and government monitoring, and continual licensing difficulties cause owners to see the new nightlife regulation as an attack against them and even as a contradiction for a city that supposedly wants to encourage such amenities as nightlife. As Sarah says, "They are biting the hand that feeds them. Shooting themselves in the foot. Putting up a 'Not Welcome' sign at the doorstep of Manhattan. And ultimately, they're going to lose power, if their city sucks."

But bar owners differ over the role that nightlife played in improving downtown Manhattan. The older bar owners use their longer tenancy and experience in their neighborhood to distinguish themselves from their newer counterparts and the self-understanding as benefits to the community that the latter possess. Mike moved to the Lower East Side in the late 1980s and worked as a music promoter. He started working at Brownies, a popular bar and club in the East Village, in 1994, and then bought into it in 1998. In 2002, with a declining music scene in the neighborhood and rising overhead costs, Mike decided he no longer wanted to operate a live venue and changed the place into what he describes as a regular local bar. His early days living downtown inform his understanding of how the area gentrified. Along with nightlife, Mike cites several factors that played an important role in the neighborhood's gentrification, including the economic boom years in the 1990s, the quality-of-life policies under Mayor Rudolph Giuliani, and the expansion of NYU. "This neighborhood didn't change overnight," he says.

> My impression of it is that it has been a cumulative change over time. I mean, there have been times when it's quick, there are periods of like, "Wow, that changed! That changed!" But it happened little by little; it happened piece by piece. There were big moments of change, like redoing the park [Tompkins Square Park] was a pretty big moment, when the gardens started disappearing and they started putting up high rises, when new apartments were going in.

But Mike is critical of newer bar owners who claim downtown Manhattan improved and remains vibrant because of bars. He continues:

> The only people who use that "we made this neighborhood what it is" [argument] are the people that showed up after. I'm not going to go to a community board meeting and say, "If it wasn't for my bar this neighborhood wouldn't have [improved]." I would never. It just doesn't make any sense. The carpetbaggers say that, not the people who were here.

Older bar owners also distinguish themselves from newer ones in terms of how they feel they benefit their neighborhood. As commercial pioneers, old bar owners were among the few nighttime establishments in downtown Manhattan. The area's newcomers welcomed them as much-needed community hangouts that also made the area feel safer. But as an increasing number and variety of bars opened downtown, the old bar owners have joined longtime residents in criticizing the growth of dense nightlife scenes. First, they acknowledge that there are already too many bars. They realize the importance of a dense scene to attract anonymous revelers, but at a certain point the competition becomes too great. "I don't think there should be any more liquor licenses, says Joseph. "I don't want any more liquor licenses. It doesn't help me, it hurts, because it's too much competition."

Older bar owners also take issue with the types of bars that have opened, the unscrupulous practices of new bar owners, and the types of customers they attract. Mike criticizes owners who do not regulate their establishments, saying "You have too many sort of places that don't police themselves the way we do so they're probably more attractive to young drunk people." David identifies with longtime residents when he considers bars with clublike atmospheres, such as those that feature DJs and promoted events, to be detriments to the community and sources of local tensions:

The problem is unlicensed [dance clubs]. You have guys come down here that want to open up nightclubs in storefronts, and you can't take a place like this with neighbors upstairs and make it a nightclub. And most of the guys, when they do it they do it on side streets so there will be less police scrutiny. And that just makes it worse! Because people move to the side street to be quiet. If you look at what happened on Sixth Street between [Avenues] A and B, I understand completely why those people are pissed. I'd be furious. They went from a street with one little tiny gin mill on it, it's been there forever, and they probably loved having there, to a street with five nightclubs and a gin mill. And now they hate everybody [all bar owners] and I understand. Some of them hate me—and I'm on their side, and I understand.

Mike has similar issues with new methods of operation that owners choose, such as using outdoor spaces that generate noise. In particular, he criticizes what he sees is an attitude towards dealing with residents that the new bar owners possess:

I don't use [my backyard]. A lot of people are like, "Why don't you use it?" Because I don't need the complaints from people upstairs. . . . What you have in this neighborhood is a combination of ignorance of owners, lack of planning, and a lack of understanding of what they're getting into. They've got a backyard, and they don't think three minutes ahead of themselves to think, "I'm going to start having large parties out here until two o'clock in the morning on a weeknight and even on Friday and Saturday night." The idea that it's not going to cause issues is a lack of planning on your part. If you're somebody who is in the nightlife industry, if you're in the business, then you know that you're operating in residential neighborhoods and you have to take those things into account. You can't just expect to steamroller over residents.

As longtime fixtures in their neighborhood, old bar owners share certain attitudes towards nightlife in common with other early gentrifiers. Despite certain points of agreement, however, old bar owners conflict with longtime residents, and align with new bar owners, over other complaints made against them.

Deflecting Blame

Bar owners respond to the "problem owner" characterization by deflecting blame away from themselves and towards several other sources. They frame their arguments in a manner that provides alternative explanations for why the nightlife scenes' problems exist, downplays the complaints and accusations made about them, and criticizes the effectiveness of regulatory solutions. Owners criticize public policies and claim that they target problems that are beyond their control, create problems where they did not exist before, and magnify those that already did.

For instance, they take issue with the implementation of the 311 system that monitors complaints and dispatches the police and other government agencies to their bars. For local state officials, the 311 system has efficiently organized a quality-of-life agenda that, among other issues, allows them to target specific problem bars. But owners feel that such a simple and direct recourse for complaining about nightlife encourages too many unjustified complaints. As Sarah explains:

> What the 311 call system did was basically open up the floodgates for all of New Yorkers to have somebody to complain to. And what wound up happening was just like 18,000 calls, I think, were logged in in less than a year just for nightlife alone. So then [residents] start getting politicized in the sense where you have city council people and borough presidents and [state] senators looking to address the needs of their constituency and heed their call.

Owners often claim that residents abuse the 311 system. They feel that a handful of them can make repeated calls throughout the night, which makes problems seem greater than they are. Owners also feel that by providing residents with a simple and direct way to complain, 311 limits their potential to open up communication. As Paul states, "I'd rather they come talk to me if they're having problems with noise. That's why I give all the people in my building my cell phone number. If I'm not [at the bar] they could still call me and I'll take care of it. I tell them, 'Look, don't call 311; call me anytime and we'll talk about it.'" Owners claim that this would be more effective in solving their neighborhood's quality-of-life issues than a system that bypasses direct communication.[9] Furthermore, dealing directly with residents would also help shield them from the regulatory spotlight.

Another policy that owners cite is the 2003 law that banned smoking in bars and restaurants. A public health initiative promoted by the Bloomberg mayoral administration, the smoking ban forces bars to send customers outside onto the sidewalks to smoke. In support of their business interests NYNA campaigned vigorously against the law's passing, but the negative economic impacts to bars and nightlife that they feared did not occur. However, the smoking ban has had a significant impact on quality-of-life in downtown Manhattan. Many owners point to this law that forces revelers to congregate outside on sidewalks as a central cause of noise problems. As Brandon states,

> I'm sure I'm not the first person saying this, but with the cigarette laws changing, it's a no-win situation. It's impossible to fix the situation. The only way that it could get fixed is if they allowed smoking in bars again, which I think they should. . . . But seeing as how that probably won't happen, we're all stuck together.

Politicians concede that elevated noise levels at night were an indirect consequence of this public health measure, and even residents acknowledge that the quality of life worsened after the ban went into effect. However, individual bar owners are caught in a dilemma. On the one hand, they risk incurring fines if they allow smoking in their bars. On the other hand, they are held responsible for the noise that their customers create when they are smoking and talking on the sidewalk. They feel that the law puts them in an impossible situation. As Mike states,

> I can't tell a customer to shut up. There's no law against talking on the sidewalk. There's a law against us allowing stuff, but we don't have the ability to stop it. I can't touch somebody. I can't make them move. I can't do anything, really. I've no enforceability. I can't arrest somebody for disturbing the peace, public intoxication, I can't do any of that. So really, we're responsible for it, but we can't do anything to affect it.

Another example is the political conditions that helped grow downtown Manhattan's nightlife scenes. The first of these are the zoning laws that determine which areas of the city can legally accommodate different types of commercial establishments. As Sarah explains, "We are being unfairly criminalized for what's happening or what has happened as far as the 'proliferation' of bars in the East Village or in Chelsea. I mean, these things happen because of the zoning laws as far as where liquor licenses were approved." Chelsea is another Manhattan neighborhood that has developed into a popular nightlife scene, but with mostly large nightclubs rather than small bars. A former industrial district, Chelsea's empty warehouses and manufacturing zoning make it one of the few places in Manhattan that can legally accommodate large nightclubs, which require a cabaret license that is only allowed in manufacturing zones.[10] Sarah compares the East Village to Chelsea to demonstrate that because of the city's land use policies, bar owners are more or less forced to open in certain neighborhoods. Of course, these policies do not explain why some zoning districts in the city that permit commercial nightlife establishments developed nightlife while others did not. Still, owners cite zoning laws as a source of nightlife problems.

Second, owners also blame nightlife issues on the SLA's entrepreneurialism. They argue that if the SLA had listened to the concerns of the community board during the nightlife scene's growth and properly followed the 500-foot rule then, there would not be such dense concentrations of bars as there are today. Rob recalls when downtown Manhattan had only a few bars and connects their proliferation to the SLA's policies,

> The fact is that the State Liquor Authority just looked the other way as more and more and more licenses were being issued. There's a real gripe about the way the liquor authority allowed the quantity of licenses in this neighborhood to really, really mushroom. I think it's completely valid. It's a totally valid issue; it's a totally valid complaint.

Owners claim that if the SLA had not granted so many licenses then, there would not be the problems that stem from dense concentrations of bars in the district. Interestingly, this is the same complaint that residents make against the SLA. And ironically, this argument undercuts the very existence of many bars in downtown Manhattan. Had the SLA listened to community boards and followed the law, many owners would not have been able to open their bars in the first place and nightlife would not have proliferated. But this logic does not prevent owners from making such an argument in their defense.

Along with these criticisms of public policies, owners also cite problematic conditions of contemporary nightlife culture. This argument echoes residents' complaints and even demonstrates a degree of nostalgia that owners feel. Michelle makes a distinction between her regular customers who live on the Lower East Side and those who come on weekends from outside the neighborhood:

> That's why I loved it when we had a lot of regulars that lived in the neighborhood: it's their neighborhood too; they respect it. [But] you get a lot of these kids that come in on the weekends, they're pissing in somebody's doorwell, they're throwing up, they're leaning against their buzzers, they're screaming at their friends, they're honking their horns. . . . They're from wherever, Idaho, they've never realized that there are cities where people live above where you're hanging out downstairs.

Herman, whose bar serves as a tribute to the East Village's rock music past introduced in the previous chapter, is also critical of new, younger customers and the variety of places that attract them:

> Now we have all these little fucking pockets where people can go smoke a stupid hookah pipe, and they could come into my bar and have a drink and they don't even notice the pictures! They don't know, they don't care, and that's what it's become. It's become a bunch of fucking vacuums in a bunch of bubbles. . . . It used to feel like it was more like a melting pot, of a cultural melting pot in those days, and [now] it feels more like a bunch of different, fragmented, separate [people who] have nothing to do with each other. We walk by each other, nothing to do with each other.

Like longtime residents, owners recognize that nightlife revelers treat downtown neighborhoods as if they existed for their own amusement. They are aware of the forms of public disorder that they cause without regard for who lives there. But they also know that this is the nighttime population in downtown Manhattan and is often the clientele that they must attract to survive as businesses.

Finally, owners also blame the harsh economic realities of owning a bar, particularly landlords who maintain high commercial rents, for nightlife's problems. Michelle lays out the argument:

> You can't blame bar owners for wanting to open a place. You have to sort of put blame on the landlords. They're the ones asking these astronomical prices for commercial spaces. The only people that can afford them are people that sell liquor, because there's such a high markup on liquor. A dress shop is not going to be able to afford the kind of rent that a bar can afford.

This interpretation also aligns with that of residents, who blame landlords for the increasing lack of commercial diversity in downtown Manhattan. To owners, high rents force them to attract large numbers of patrons through noise-generating strategies such as DJs and promoted events, even for those who never intended to operate their bars in these manners.

Liz is in her early thirties and opened her bar in an area that was already nightlife saturated in the East Village in late 2005. An artist who was drawn to the neighborhood because of its legacy as an arts scene, she noticed that the new bars were not catering to artists or artistic endeavors. She wanted to open a place that resembled the downtown arts scene that she had heard of and read about. Liz distinguishes her bar from other new places, "[When I opened] I didn't sort of typify . . . what was [going on]. I continued to do a lot of really artistically aimed things. Lots of screenings, benefits for artists, we use our office window as a gallery space." In other words, Liz, like other new entrepreneurs, aspired to open a bar that would continue her understanding of the neighborhood's legacy, specifically its history as a place for community-oriented nightlife for local artists. She quickly discovered the difficulty in this endeavor:

> The nature of running a bar has actually changed from when I was bartend-ing and working in bars. You didn't have to book DJs all the time, you didn't have to have somebody kind of come in and really bring along twenty peo-ple all the time. It's like, you had a bar and that was it! People came because they had the space and the environment, they wanted to come in and have a drink. . . . I [open] and I'm like, "Wow, there are things I have to do to pull people in. I need to have DJs." . . . Because now they can go to all these other bars that compete, they'll have an open bar, and they just follow the party.

Here Liz summarizes the competitive nature of downtown's nightlife scenes. Unlike Liam from the previous chapter, who intentionally hires DJs to attract a clientele, she discovered the necessity for doing so. Her comment also under-scores the accepted reality that today bars cannot survive with just a small community of regulars. Owners understand that they need to attract random, anonymous customers. Liz continues:

> Now, you need to do [DJs and themed parties], which is exhausting because that's like running a club. I don't want to run a club. I wasn't trying to be the hottest party by any means, but I tried to do something rather casual. I want people to come in and drink and chill out and have dialogue. So you need to have an incentive for people to want to choose your place over someplace else.

These methods produce conditions of noise and disorder in buildings and on the surrounding streets and sidewalks by attracting streams of anonymous cus-tomers and emanating loud music. As a result, Liz has had ongoing issues with her upstairs neighbors, who eventually moved out of their apartment after she underwent significant soundproofing and negotiation with them, and with the residents on her street, who often make formal complaints to the police, the community board, and other city agencies about her bar because of the noise and crowds that it brings. In sum, owners feel that rowdy customers and greedy landlords are beyond their control and go far to explain why problems persist.

Relations with the Police

Both old and new bar owners also criticize the regulatory reforms for overemphasizing them as the main sources of nightlife problems and making unreasonable demands on them as individuals to address them. Many are particularly critical of the police. Mike takes issue with officers coming into his bar to check for violations on weekend nights when he has the most customers:

> If they were to go to Tavern on the Green in the middle of a Friday business lunch time or whenever their big rush is, let's say Saturday day when there's tourists and go in and make everybody stop eating and inspect every dish in the place and do whatever, how do you think that would be received?[11] Would it portray the Tavern on the Green as being a law-abiding place? Would it tarnish the reputation of the place if the cops were constantly going in there?

Bar owners feel that they are sometimes unfairly targeted and even singled out. Kevin opened a bar on the Upper West Side of Manhattan with his brother in 1998. In 2006 they decided to open a similar establishment on the Lower East Side. He was taken aback by their treatment by the police there:

> The real difference, however, has been the local police precinct, which has attacked the downtown location almost from the start. . . . For some reason, [the precinct's commanding officer] seems to want to shut our business down, and we have experienced numerous raids by the MARCH program. . . . This problem has been so costly that we haven't profited from the downtown location. Not only is it costly, but it is very distracting. Our focus of hospitality and improving the business has been replaced with the problem of protecting the establishment from the police.

MARCH inspections do not just mean that owners incur fines. They also disrupt business during prime hours. A related complaint by owners is that too often the police target them at random and cite them for minor issues. As David states:

> The police now are raiding people on a random basis. The whole MARCH raid was supposed to be based for unlicensed cabarets, if you were causing problems, or you were running a nightclub, you know, and now they just raid everybody. I think that's horseshit. I'm not doing anything wrong here. What the fuck I gotta have a guy coming in on Friday night and telling me I've got a fruit fly? That's just bullshit.

Although they acknowledge that something like having fruit flies is a punishable offense, owners feel that they should not warrant police inspections, as David implies.

While owners complain that fines are costly and time-consuming, they see the implications behind such policies as the larger, more important issue, namely that such raids implicate all owners as "problems." This relates to the feeling that they are mistreated and unfairly targeted for nightlife's issues. Mike characterizes his relationship with the police this way:

> What it basically does is it doesn't give anybody like me a reason to want to work with the cops. It doesn't give me a reason to want to feel as if I am welcomed in my community, where I've lived for twenty years. I don't do it because I'm afraid of the cops, because if I'm good or bad they're still going to fuck with me. They've made that abundantly clear. In their minds they're not fucking with me. They're doing their job, which is what they're doing, but there's ways they could do it.

For owners, the new nightlife regulation casts a wide net over the industry and many feel that they are regarded as problematic simply by existing.

Many owners, such as those who regularly attend community council and owners' meetings, make great efforts to cooperate with the police by communicating with them and complying with their regulatory requests. As Brandon recalls:

> When we first opened, whenever there was a problem with the police we'd go down [to the precinct] and say, "All right, so listen, what can we do to fix this? Do you want us to put up the velvet rope thing? Let's do that. Do you want us to keep people away from the front? Let's do that. Do you want us to keep people moving on the sidewalk? Ok, let's make all this stuff happen." It's the best way to do it. Because what are you going to do? Are you going to fight the police? It doesn't make sense. You've got to pick your fights. Don't fight the police.

These owners try to distinguish themselves from other owners as models in the eyes of the police. They try to stand out amid an environment that is hostile to nightlife and in front of actors who are quick to label owners as "problems."

Owners also take issue with the security measures that the police pressure them to implement. They believe these measures are ineffective in solving the quality-of-life problems for which they are blamed and are costly for their establishments. The police see hiring licensed bouncers, for instance, as an important indicator of owners' compliance with the new nightlife regulation.

Michelle states, "I have my doorman out there if [customers] are blocking the sidewalk, 'Come on guys, don't be in a circle, stand single file or whatever.' But come on, people are out to have a good time. They don't want to be told how to stand outside."[12] Some bar owners, such as those who have larger establishments, would hire a bouncer anyway without encouragement from the police. But others, with smaller establishments, never intended to have one, either because of their expense or because of the perception they create of their bars in the eyes of their customers. "It's intimidating," says Michelle, "I mean, I remember even when I got my professional door guy, a lot of my regulars were a little put off by [him]." Owners who intended on having a local, neighborhood bar found themselves changing the culture of their establishment, and in a manner that futilely addresses the problems bouncers are intended to solve. A bouncer signals to regulars that they no longer regulate the bar space, while the anonymous customers signal to them that the bar is no longer theirs.

ON RESIDENTS: OLD, SUBURBAN, AND IRRATIONAL

Owners direct much of their criticism of the threats to their livelihood at residents. They absolve themselves from guilt over nightlife problems by downplaying the complaints and accusations that residents make. Owners characterize residents and the community board—their most vocal opposition—in manners that discredit the validity of the concerns raised. They do this in a number of ways, such as by holding residents' ages against them. A common sentiment, especially among new and young owners, is that as longtime residents have aged they have simply stopped participating in nightlife activities and have settled into a different way of life. Peter explains this generational phenomenon:

> When you go to community board meetings it's clear that there's a transition, and people who are maybe older who have lived here for twenty years, they're in a different mode in their life. And it's difficult because some of these, the new destinations, don't necessarily serve the needs of people that have been here twenty-five years.

Unlike when longtime residents were younger, the nightlife culture in downtown Manhattan has little to offer them, the owners posit. Today they are in a different stage in their lives. As Stephen states, "Now they're in their thirties or forties and they have kids, and it's a problem. It's a quality-of-life issue and that affects them more because they're not utilizing the bars the way they did when they first came down here." Owners consider community board members to be older longtime residents who have autocratic control in their neighborhoods, but do not accurately represent its demographics or the full range of residents' opinions. As Edward notes, "You know, community boards aren't elected, they're appointed. And as a result of that it really isn't a democratic process, necessarily. Some of these people have been on the community boards for years and they're like their own little fiat." This characterization serves to portray residents as out-of-touch old-timers who are simply averse to changes, particularly those changes that do not benefit them.

Owners also claim that residents who complain about nightlife noise are not "city" people and do not have a high tolerance for urban life. This follows from the assumption that residents are originally from quiet suburban environments and are unaccustomed to city conditions such as noise. As Rob says, "Isn't noise a part of living in a place like this? I'm not saying all noise should be accepted, but isn't there a trade-off when you live so bunched together that you're going to hear shit from next-door people?" Their thinking goes that since noise is a natural part of living in a city, then perhaps residents who complain about nightlife because of its noise are not cut out for living in downtown Manhattan. But they are cautious not to make such a claim directly to residents' faces. As Sarah states:

> I mean if [residents] are looking for silence. . . . But you see, the thing is, if I or any [other owner] goes into any community board or any of these gatherings and use[s] the first argument that comes to mind—"Why do you live in Manhattan? You should just move to Brooklyn," or something like that—they'll flip! That's *the* most taboo thing you could say, is, "Why do you live in New York?"

Owners like Sarah question residents' capacity for living in urban environments. Of course, they are not always correct in their assessment of longtime residents as people who come from quiet suburbs. But they understand residents' sensitivity to noise as an indication that they come from suburban communities, where noise is presumably absent.[13] While owners recognize that their bars sometimes genuinely bother residents, they also feel that too often residents do not make reasonable complaints. For example, longtime owners question residents' claims that the neighborhood was quiet in the period before many bars opened. As Marta says, "This street? This street was never quiet and tree-lined. Never. The people who lived here, the drug dealers, they used to be so loud. Twenty-four hours, cars, radio, car radios, really loud, fights, cops and robbers. This was never a quiet neighborhood. I don't know where these people come from." This perspective criticizes those residents who have an overly nostalgic view of downtown.

But through their nostalgia narrative, most longtime residents acknowledge that their neighborhood was loud during their early days, which includes the public drug dealing and guns and violence that made it dangerous. Owners, like Dave, do not understand how residents could make a positive spin on such negative conditions in their interpretation of the downtown's gentrification.

> [Residents] see it as completely opposite. Like, no matter what you do they're not happy. The drugs and violence is here, they want the cops to come in. The cops come in because [of] the restaurants and business owners, and taxes are getting paid here—finally—and then they're not happy because it's too gentrified. It's like, you can't have it both ways. You're going to win with a sketchy neighborhood in a really dangerous area, or you're going to win with a semi-gentrified area. Either services are provided or they're not provided; either there's, like, drugs and violence, or there's actual sustainability going on. People just don't give a shit, it seems like. The people who live here that are throwing such a fucking tantrum about it, I don't know what their justification is or how they justify any of it to themselves. It's completely beyond me.

Dave frames gentrification in an either-or manner, with residents' recollections of their neighborhood's past on one side and the bar-fueled revitalized downtown Manhattan on the other. He is correct in saying that many longtime residents fought against drugs and homelessness and favored increasing police presence in their neighborhood.[14] But he does not recognize that these residents developed an attachment to their neighborhood during its negative period and through the rehabilitation process, which they often led.

Another common interpretation is that many residents are impossible to deal with because of the irrationality of their strong anti-bar stance. This perspective goes so far as to question how reasonable residents can be. Sarah explains: "You get those who are really probably the more eccentric, more vocal, angry people. It's pretty much like their focus in life. A lot of these people have gotten to the point of such irrational anger that it's almost impossible to communicate with them without major mediation involved." This perspective nearly essentializes residents by turning their anti-bar stance into a character trait. They have resigned themselves to the fact that they cannot communicate rationally with residents, who they feel will reflexively oppose them. And as with the suburban claim, bar owners refrain from directly calling residents irrational to their faces.

Owners do not perceive residents who protest them to be a monolithic group. In many cases, they understand and are sympathetic towards those neighbors for whom their bars are a legitimate concern in terms of daily quality of life. Most importantly, they make a distinction between the small number of residents who complain about a bar in their building's commercial storefront and a more specific group of residents who comprise what they call the "anti-bar movement." This latter group consists of residents who may or may not be significantly affected by bars in terms of their quality of life, but in any case make strong extra efforts to combat bars by organizing community groups, attending meetings, and petitioning politicians. As Mike describes these residents:

> It's very clear to a lot of us in the bar industry . . . that there are people who, for a lack of a better way to describe their motives, have nothing else to do, and they see this scourge of young people in the neighborhood and it just bothers them. They just hate it. They don't want them here, so they go over-board in how they log their complaints. They become zealots.

Owners feel that these residents are inspired to act because of larger political motivations, which often leads them to dismiss their complaints and actions out of hand. The following exchange between Marta and me over a conflict between another bar and its neighbors demonstrates this attack:

> "When people moved here, they wanted to move here because they wanted to live where there's action. And those people who complain, I have no idea where they come from. Did you read that article in the [New York] Times last weekend about Heathers?"[15]
>
> "Yes. What did you think about it?"
>
> "I mean, do you feel compassionate for the couple upstairs? I mean, what the fuck, they're paying $1,100 for a sound meter instead of putting a carpet down? It takes a day to put a fucking new floor and a carpet down. No matter how crowded your house is, you move stuff from one side to the other side and put it down. They spend $1,100 on the sound meter. Now doesn't that tell you something? It's the same thing with the Lower East Side Alliance.[16] They're vindictive people."
>
> "Yeah, I spoke with Heather and she's put a lot of money into the soundproofing."
>
> "So did we. We have three ceilings."
>
> "Have you had neighbors complain?"
>
> "It's always the same people."

Marta goes on to describe her neighbors as more irrational complainants than local activists. But she recognizes a distinction between them and berates the actions of the latter in the case of Heathers as a misguided attempt by residents to prove a point.

The basis for owners' interpretation of residents as irrational and overzealous is their personal experiences in dealing with residents directly, such as at community board meetings. These are often the first time that owners meet their neighbors. Earlier I mentioned that Dave, owner of the cocktail bar Death & Co., faced opposition from his neighbors when he wanted to open his bar. He faced even more from them at the community board meeting when he had to renew his liquor license.

The first speaker at the late meeting is a Hispanic man named Johnny, who says he is a resident and the super two buildings away. He explains that because of the bar there is now excessive noise on the street, not to mention cigarette butts and smoke, and that people dump their drinks in the garbage can, all of which makes a big mess for him. Samuel, a middle-aged man, then speaks, saying he is at the meeting on behalf of Rabbi Ackerman at Congregation Meseritz Syngg, a century-old synagogue located down the street from Dave's bar, that he claims may be within 200 feet of it, which would mean its full liquor license is illegal. He says that the rabbi is opposed to bars, to nightlife proliferation in the neighborhood, and to this bar's proximity to the synagogue. Samuel then brings up the bar's facade and a black flag that hangs above the door. "The flag they have is deeply offensive to Jews because it resembles fascism and hate, and our synagogue has Holocaust survivors in it. The front also looks like a train car, like those that were used to carry Jews by Nazi Germany. We are disturbed by the images of death and concerned about what's going to happen over the summer," when even more revelers are out in the neighborhood at night.

A woman named Sylvia, who lives right next door, says that their street had always been quiet and is not the place for a bar. She takes issue with Dave's characterization of Death & Co. as a restaurant, saying, "You can call it a restaurant, but it's not," and reads from numerous Web site reviews that she had printed out that focus on its status as a bar. One, from the *Gothamist* blog on New York City, reads, "You come to Death & Co. to drink, and drink well." Another focuses on the cocktails that the place has: "You need to eat something to keep from tipping over." Sylvia also points out that the place only offers small plates of food and does not serve entrees.

Joe, a longtime resident and musician, has lived in his apartment upstairs from the bar for eighteen years. He has played in many downtown bars over the years and does not want to be seen as anti-nightlife, but he feels that the neighborhood has become saturated with bars. Joe then reads from a very long list of complaints about Death & Co.: the bar had floodlights that shone on their black flag, and he had to call the Department of Buildings to tell them to turn them off, but they are still on in the afternoon; workers there left ladders outside of the bar that people could have used to break into apartments; they were working without a permit during their construction; it is primarily a bar and is much louder than the Indian-fusion restaurant that used to be there; the doorman doesn't disperse crowds, and since people aren't allowed to speak on cell phones inside, there are always people talking on them outside; the noise will get worse in the summer; he has tapes of the noise; it is within 500 feet of more than three other bars; its license stipulates soundproofing, but the noise from the bar "shatters our right to quality of life," and when confronted about this, the owner told him, "You live in New York. Deal with it"; they have a heavy door that rattles objects in upstairs apartments when it closes; he has photos of a motorcycle that was parked on the sidewalk; and, finally, that they do not have a "Please be quiet and respectful to our neighbors" sign that many other bars have up in their windows. He concludes by saying, "Our quality of life has been destroyed by this bar. As a musician, I've played many charity gigs to try to give back to the community. These owners should give back to the community."

Finally, a man named Jacob speaks, reiterating much of what had already been said. He particularly points out the bar's name and boxcar-like facade and calls them "an insult to the history of the neighborhood" as a destination for Jews.

Dave's face ran through several emotions—shock, disbelief, disgust—while the residents complained. The community board then gives him an opportunity to address his neighbors' concerns. Dave explains that he has lowered the music, soundproofed the premises, and muffled some of his speakers. He put padding around the heavy door so it doesn't rattle items in apartments like it used to, and he has security cameras outside to monitor the sidewalk, which recently helped the police catch a graffiti artist. In regard to the facade and flag, Dave says that he is also Jewish and has Holocaust victims in his family. He explains that the bar's name is a Prohibition reference and not meant to evoke death, dark themes, or anything anti-Semitic. He agrees to take down the flag. Still, the community board denies his application.

I got to know Dave over the following months, regularly seeing him at Death & Co. I usually spoke with him about some of the cultural elements of his business and about the city's cocktail community of which he and his bar are a part. When I finally asked him about this community board meeting and his relationship with his neighbors, it became obvious that his emotions had not subsided. ("I figured it'd come up" in one of our conversations, he told me.) His statements reflect the perspective that owners have of residents as irrational and vindictive:

> I went in, totally casual, got blindsided at the meeting. *No* idea. *No* idea! Felt like I got fucking run over. People were taking issues with the flag, calling us a Nazi bar. I was looking around for some rational-mind person to [say], "You know what, this is retarded. This is retarded. You guys are absolutely ridiculous. This is a respectable establishment."

Dave was all the more taken aback because of how he understood himself as a place entrepreneur, and in particular as a good neighbor. But he describes neighbors who opposed his bar as a group who could not be satisfied:

> In the beginning we tried to do everything we could to make sure that we ran a respectable place and respected our neighbors, as much as possible. We agreed to soundproofing, a great deal of money invested in that. Our music is always very low, low-level jazz. We closed off the front so that there would never be any spillover to the street. We take phone numbers so that no one ever waits outside. We never do anything with the backyard. We're doing everything that they wanted, like everything that they want you to say, we're doing, like, "We don't want you to have an open facade, or bay windows." Okay, no bay windows. I don't want that anyway. I want it to be very tucked away, a very quiet little spot, and everything [else] they want you to do. And still, as soon as you do that they say, "Well, you don't have bay windows, what type of restaurant doesn't have bay windows?" I'm like, "But you guys don't want me to have windows. Tell me what to do and I'll do it."

He continues on this theme:

> It's been *hugely, hugely* frustrating, especially for me because I'm not very jaded yet. I'm getting there, which apparently is better. I really took [the opposition] personally, because it's hard not to. When this place opened up it was very much like my baby. I would be here every day. My phone number, my cell phone number, and my e-mail were posted on the facade every day when we were renovating everything. And the people that complained never contacted me, never emailed me. [I said] if you have problems, come down. If you're worried about what it is, come down, I'll walk you through it. It was just so frustrating because I kept trying to reach out and people have such a need for reaction to it that it's really, really unfortunate.

At this point, Dave grew very emotional discussing the actual community board meeting:

> The community board is just the most ridiculous, unpleasant experience that I've ever had to deal with. I was like, "You dragged your fucking kids down here to hold a banner?"[17] And the people that were against us, I was like, "You're using your fucking Judaism against me? This is a personal vendetta, man. This has nothing to do with you being Jewish." It's like, "Fuck you! I'm Jewish too, man, and that's embarrassing." It's just, it was infuriating, man. And people up there are just bashing your name, like, "You don't know me. I've been here every day, I've welcomed you into my place every single day, you don't know me." And there's like nothing you [as an owner] could do. You feel completely, completely hopeless.

In our chat, Dave describes his experiences as a bar owner as at first being perplexed by his neighbors' reactions to his efforts to please them and his contributions to the neighborhood, then being frustrated by the seemingly irrational behaviors of his neighbors, and finally only being able to explain their actions angrily and without much clarity. He is left to conclude that residents must have some sort of personal issue with him. And to him, his neighbors and the community board collectively have the absolute power to determine whether or not he and his bar are problems.

Still, Dave successfully had his liquor license renewed by the SLA despite the community board's denial, and his bar is still in operation. In fact, continued nightlife growth was the norm during most of the late 2000s, even with the state's regulatory reforms. Over time, many of the changes that favored residents and community groups either ended or reversed course, particularly at the SLA, which always retained authority over liquor license decisions. The SLA's moratorium on full liquor licenses in 500-foot-rule cases expired at the end of 2006, not to be renewed. Joshua Toas, the SLA's CEO who helped clean up the agency, regularly communicated with downtown community groups and residents, and gave them hope that bar proliferation might end, resigned in 2008.

In 2009, Governor David Paterson replaced Daniel Boyle, whose law-and-order approach and intense scrutiny of liquor license applications tremendously slowed down the licensing process. The national recession had hit by that time, and New York City and the state both needed the additional revenues that nightlife brings. Boyle came under attack by the nightlife industry and lawmakers for delaying a process that could have been aiding the economy. The previous year, Boyle claimed that Governor Paterson's staff intimidated him into levying a lesser sanction on a high-profile nightlife entrepreneur who was guilty of several major infractions. In addition, the state inspector general's office raided the SLA's Manhattan office to investigate whether agency employees were taking bribes from applicants to expedite liquor license applications. Along with the delays this public bribery scandal did not help Boyle's case, either. Governor Paterson replaced him with Dennis Rosen, an assistant attorney general who helped prosecute the parties involved in the wholesale liquor industry scandal that led to Boyle's appointment, in 2006. Despite his legal background, downtown residents understood Rosen's appointment to be a pendulum shift at the SLA away from scrutinizing bar owners and liquor license applications that the reforms promised and towards the unfettered growth agenda that had characterized the agency in the 1990s and early 2000s. Indeed, at the start of his appointment Rosen stressed that streamlining and expediting the application process so that applications would go through it quicker was one of his major priorities. And without any high-profile violent incidents, nightlife issues faded from the public's memory and the city's political agenda. In short, everything went more or less back to normal, including in downtown Manhattan, where residents and owners continued to conflict.

CHAPTER 6

THE LIMITS OF LOCAL DEMOCRACY

> Telling me that you will deter crime and that you're involved in the community is like telling me you're a nice guy.
>
> **—ALEX, CB3 MEMBER AND LIQUOR LICENSE COMMITTEE CHAIR**

PATTI, A NATIVE NEW YORKER IN HER EARLY FORTIES, is a musician who moved to the Lower East Side in 1984. I first meet her at a community board meeting in 2006. She goes to speak against two bars that are on the agenda. For the first, a license renewal, she says, "I'm against renewing this license because this block has already become saturated, and this is one of the few quiet blocks left. The car traffic is becoming unbearable and there has been honking at four in the morning. This is still a poor neighborhood with working people. You've got to keep it quiet outside."

I get intrigued. It is a rare moment when a longtime downtown resident uses the poorer residents of the neighborhood as an argument against advanced gentrification and the growth of the nightlife scene. The second item, also a renewal, is for a location on the same block. Patti requests to speak and says to the owner, "OK, this place is right under my window. I've been forced into this adversarial relationship with you people. This bar makes it very difficult for me to live. It's not the bar's fault. When you have thirty people outside your bar, there's not much you can do." After the second item, I notice Patti standing in the back of the room, talking to an applicant in his mid-thirties. I stand near them and catch a piece of their conversation.

"Look, all these new bars in the neighborhood and on my street disturbs me," says Patti. "I'm not anti-bar, but I'm fighting for low-cost housing and the area's quality of life. This is a residential neighborhood that at night gets filled with bridge-and-tunnelers, not people who live in the neighborhood. It's not that the bars have violations, it's that the way they naturally act is no way to treat their neighbors."

"Well, if there's a problem then what is the SLA doing?" asks the man.

"The SLA is evil! They just want to make money from all these licenses. Why don't you open on Canal Street. That's more commercial."

"My place is going to be different. I'm . . ."

"No, it's not."

"Well, I live in a Mexican building in Bushwick and I hate certain types of places that have come in."

"Look," says Patti, interrupting him again before he can make his point, "I'm sure you're very nice and have good intentions, but I still don't want your bar. Did you want something?"

I snap out of my note taking when I realize she is talking to me. I tell her I am conducting a research project on the neighborhood. Patti shrugs and continues talking to the bar owner. I sit back down and write some notes on the parts of the conversation I had missed. I got the impression that the man is opening a new place on or near Patti's block that she was going to protest later in the evening. It seemed one of them had already either discussed the SLA or the owner just brought it up. Patti was clearly in control of the conversation, interrupting the man twice and denying his attempt to relate to her the conditions on the Lower East Side. Patti then comes up to me, whispers she has to leave, and hands me a note that reads, "I'm sorry. I thought you were with the press or were an owner or something." She leaves me an e-mail address and says to contact her if I want to chat.

Over the next week we have a spirited and lengthy e-mail exchange in which she confirms several of my thoughts on her conversation with the owner from the previous night and tells me a bit about her community activism. We soon after meet for dinner at a Dominican restaurant near her apartment. Patti grew up in an artists' household in a rundown area of Manhattan, so moving to the Lower East Side was not an extreme step for her. When she arrived, her new neighbors were also artists living in a low-income neighborhood. And as she was a young musician and performance artist, the few bars and clubs for the avant-garde music scene that had opened in the neighborhood were perfect for her and her budding career.

"When I first moved down here, we had one or two bars, and I always played in them. But they did seem to still sort of cater to something that was actually in the neighborhood, you know, and had been here for a long time. But it just, it's so remarkable to see what it became."

"Around when did this happen?"

"Like '97, '98. Around then."

Like other early gentrifiers, Patti acknowledges the new bars that appeared in downtown Manhattan that she went to at the time of her arrival. She also recalls a general time period when the area started to change. More important than specifically when new bars began to open was the time when residents recognized that the new bars were damaging their quality of life and threatening their sense of community. Patti lives in a rent-regulated apartment and works in the office of one of the neighborhood's few remaining small factories to add to her small musician's income and help her pay rent and bills. She has had many issues with her landlord in the past, who she claims harassed her and other longtime tenants when the neighborhood gentrified and apartments could be rented for much higher rates, and she eventually won a rent reduction from the city.

The catch-22 of it is, as this neighborhood becomes a nightlife district, after putting twenty years of my life in here, it's not like I could just pick up and move somewhere else. My apartment's really modest. It's a sixth-floor walk-up. The paint's still peeling. They haven't painted in twenty years, so I've painted it when I can. That's kind of like golden handcuffs 'cause we put so much stock in living there and we couldn't see this coming, that every-body would find this such a desirable neighborhood in quite the way they have and started seeing potential in it.

And meanwhile the whole neighborhood has become a place where we couldn't afford to move! So the whole thing is if I want a better quality of life at this stage in the game, because I'm thirty-eight and maybe I do want a little bit of sleep, I'd have to leave the city and the band that I've had for ten years and that I've worked with. So I started seeing and getting a little sensi-tized and educated about this kind of community upheaval, because I have to say I was totally, like most people, I was totally ignorant about it until you kind of experience it. And it's a very hard thing to understand that they can't stop the tenth bar from opening under your window. So I was saying if I go to these community board meetings and think, "Well, okay, I'm a musician, I'm not anti-bar—I play in bars, you know?—and don't want people to not have a good time, but why isn't this being spread out more through the city? And why are there so many licenses, like forty a month, on the community board agenda? Why is there no mechanism that hears people and is just sen-sitive about it?" And then I started going to the community board meetings and sitting there quietly in the back and just kind of getting more involved in community stuff as I saw it being destroyed.

From her neighbors Patti heard about community board meetings being not just a forum for voicing her concerns and receiving answers to her questions but a place where she could possibly influence what she saw happening in her neighborhood. From this point, Patti became an activist against the forces that she felt were damaging her community. She fought for community gardens and affordable housing, both of which developers were threatening to eliminate, and she especially fought against the bars that attracted revelers. With her neigh-bors, Patti started several grassroots groups devoted specifically to protesting bars. She educated herself on the ABC Law and the community board's policies so they could present the best possible arguments against liquor licenses to the SLA. And she adopted an understanding of the SLA as "evil" and of bar owners as threats despite their outwardly good intentions. But after several years of activism, Patti grew disillusioned with the lack of progress:

> The bar proliferation thing's been so frustrating because we put our faith in this community board process and didn't quite understand that "advisory" *really* meant advisory. Like, we thought, "Wow! That's six [items] before the board, and they rejected this license, and the SLA or somebody must take this in; it must account for something." And it never did, over and over.

As I saw from her conversation with the bar owner applicant, Patti recognized that the actions of the SLA played an important role in thwarting their efforts. She identifies the agency's role as a revenue generator for New York City and the state and labels it as an important force in the destruction of her neighborhood.

> It's kind of been exposed that the SLA has no protocol. They're an unmonitored state agency that brings in something like $60 million a year. They were all appointed by Pataki and none of them, until people started acting up, not one person on the SLA lived in Manhattan, or in New York City![1] They all lived in Westchester. All of them. So they're not even suffering the problems of what they do. I mean, it does sort of boggle the mind that they [were] allowed to rake in this kind of dough and do this. City planning doesn't even have the power to remodel a neighborhood or issue some decree that would allow a neighborhood to be remodeled to this degree, where you're becoming a nighttime economy and you're losing your services.

Along with the SLA and city government, she also reserves a degree of animus for bar owners, who she feels deceive the community. She recalls, for instance, the bait-and-switch tactic:

> We saw the lies. The neighborhood went through a phase where places were lying and saying they were restaurants, . . . they'd install a kitchen for fifty grand or even a hundred grand but they'd never use it. It would be empty, but they would just do it to get the liquor license because it's so lucrative. And all this kind of wiliness that was so incredible.

After several years, Patti does not think she will continue with her local activism much longer. Maintaining a voluntary neighborhood organization among residents, each with their own agendas, suggestions, and schedules, is difficult and time-consuming for her. Neighborhood groups lack institutional support or resources other than the knowledge and skills that each member brings to them. Most importantly, Patti understands nightlife growth as a "stacked deck" against the community. After participating for so long in the liquor license process, she has begun to think that it is impossible to successfully diminish the nightlife scene or, for that matter, any other issue related to advanced gentrification occurring downtown. Her education in community activism and her interpretation of bar proliferation began with her experiences at the community board. Her ongoing participation in the liquor license process eventually caused her to become disenchanted with it and skeptical of any hope in making positive change in downtown Manhattan.

—

Patti exemplifies an arc that many residents have experienced as a result of their protests against the nightlife scene. She shifted from concerned citizen to fiery community activist to, eventually, a person disenchanted and dejected by failure. Not all residents have started community groups as she did. Most are only active when a liquor license issue arises on their street. And some residents use their community ideology in ways besides protesting bars through the liquor-licensing process. However, community board meetings remain important sites where many residents form, shape, and reinforce their community ideology. As we saw with bar owners in chapter 5, residents developed their interpretation of the SLA and bar owners as co-conspirators, as well as their self-understanding as victims in the growth of the nightlife scene, from their experiences interacting with them, which occurred most often at community board meetings.

Patti was one of the first longtime residents whom I observed and interviewed, and in many ways she set the tone for how the following observations and interviews went. Residents' voices during community board meetings and in our conversations ran a spectrum of emotional frustration and tiredness. They ranged from anger at the SLA and bar owners for transforming their neighborhood and damaging their community to sadness for what their community lost to desperation for having seen their efforts go to waste. Before she ended her community activism, I saw Patti regularly at meetings for the next year, and I would chat with her about how things were going and what she had been working on in the community. Her voice contained the same mix of feelings, until she discontinued her involvement altogether.

There are many potential targets for residents' collective action. Nightlife revelers may be the social actors whom residents regularly hear and see on the streets around their buildings. But revelers are anonymous to residents. They often visit from other areas of the city or from outside the city or country. Revelers are also in constant flux, moving from bar to bar, coming in and out of the neighborhood sporadically, shifting their tastes and preferences as fashions change. At least, residents perceive them in these ways. In reality it is quite difficult to target revelers through collective action against the threat of nightlife. Additionally the nightlife issues residents abhor may stem from density rather than from the behaviors of revelers or the actions and inactions of specific bars. But the residents perceive the SLA as an upstate agency with an agenda to develop nightlife scenes. They learned, from years of organized protest, of the agency's silence and inaction. And gentrification, as they admit, is a larger process than the growth of a nightlife scene. Absentee landlords often own buildings, or impersonal, bureaucratic management companies own and control them. Real estate developers may not be local figures, and investors are sometimes unknown or may even live in another country. Residents identify each of these actors as culpable in the failure to resolve the issues satisfactorily, but all are difficult targets for protests.

Bars, on the other hand, are stationary, bound to their storefronts. They are not faceless entities, like branded chain stores or management companies, and elected officials do not appoint them. Specific people own and are accountable for them. As we have seen, owners come sometimes from the residential population and sometimes from other neighborhoods. Either way, state law compels them to meet and deliberate with their neighbors.

Overall it is rare that residents in a gentrified neighborhood are able to confront the people whom they identify as the forces behind its gentrification in a controlled setting. Many gentrification studies depict the actions of gentrifiers towards gentrification. Japonica Brown-Saracino's social preservationists use symbolic (festivals and streetscape), political (protests against developments), and private (support for old-timers' businesses) practices to demonstrate their disapproval of gentrification and support for authentic local groups and cultures. Richard Lloyd shows how Wicker Park artists express their disdain for MTV's *The Real World* by either putting up signs of protest in commercial establishments or denying them permission to film in them.[2] The CB3 liquor license committee meeting gives downtown residents a regular opportunity not just to affirm their local identities and perform their beliefs through protest but also to directly confront existing owners and prospective entrepreneurs, who represent the most tangible targets among the forces of advanced gentrification. It is where the daytime and nighttime actors construct, reinforce, and use their community ideologies in action against each other.

As we have already seen, residents and owners each hold a set of negative perceptions towards the other that is in part based on their community ideology and local and entrepreneurial identities. The community board meeting is a key place where they form these ideologies and identities through practice and interaction. Residents base their construction of local identities as their neighborhood's symbolic owners on their interactional past and nostalgia narratives. This local identity and their interpretation of bar owners get reinforced at the community board liquor license meetings. Residents often have personal memories of owners who misrepresented themselves on their applications, such as professing to open a restaurant and then actually opening a bar, and claimed that they would not create undue burdens on their lives. Even residents without direct experience in dealing with untrustworthy owners learn and become aware of the neighbors' history with them. They therefore go into the meetings already anticipating an application with a business plan that will not match the eventual reality. Residents link owners' statements during meetings to the acts of misrepresentation that past and current owners have made, which reinforce their distrust of them. In addition, residents use the forum to vent their frustrations, which mix anti-gentrification sentiments with quality-of-life concerns, towards other culpable groups, such as the SLA and nightlife revelers. Although they direct their concerns about gentrification towards bar owners, they also acknowledge that the process is greater than the individuals deciding to open bars. Finally, residents use community board meetings to assert their own understanding of community, rebuke owners for theirs, and consequently reinforce their own local identity.

Bar owners, on the other hand, generally have less experience with the community board process than residents do, and they lack their group support. Owners therefore confront their neighbors as independent entrepreneurs rather than as an organized group. Residents see them as members of a group, and they speak of themselves as part of a group and an industry that positively contributes to the neighborhood. But owners do not use their community ideology to act as a group. Despite their popularity among young residents in the area and around the city, people very rarely come to vocalize support for their bars at meetings.[3] In reaction to protests from residents and the liquor license committee members, bar owners become either emotional (e.g., act frustrated, angry, incredulous) or conciliatory so as to assuage residents' concerns. The former reaction occurs more commonly in young owners who are new to the process and to downtown, while the latter occurs more commonly

FIGURE 15 This scene from a community board liquor license committee meeting features a resident presenting a map that she created of bars in her area and a bar owner and his attorney responding to her concerns. They stand on either side of the liquor license committee members. Photograph by the author, 2011.

in experienced owners who have already confronted their neighbors at meetings. Owners who are new to the process sometimes do not hold back their criticisms of residents and express disagreement towards the board members as legitimate representatives of the community. As a result of these experiences and interactions, they form a negative perception of residents that is then reinforced. Although intended as a forum for resolving local issues, the community board meetings reproduce conflicts and tensions between these groups.

THE WORLD OF CB3: RESIDENTS' GROUPS, OWNERS, AND PARTICIPATORY DEMOCRACY

Edward is an attorney with his own practice, concentrating in bars and restaurants and focusing on leases, liquor licenses, and other legal issues that arise for nightlife business owners. He has clients all over the city, but the majority of his work is downtown. Edward has at least one client on Community Board 3's agenda every month. When not talking with his clients about their upcoming meeting, Edward usually sits in the back or to the side of the room and reads his *Daily News* newspaper, glancing up from it to watch when tempers flare. I often chat with him as he waits for the board to call his items. Since Edward deals with many community boards around the city, I ask him one night if CB3 is the strictest.

"Yes, absolutely," he says. "Absolutely! This is the strictest community board. Everybody's [other CBs] got their own preferences, their own differences. Every community board tends to focus on different problems. But this is certainly the strictest, most organized in their preparation, in their forms, in their homework."[4]

Edward says he is honest with his clients about what to expect when they appear before CB3. He encourages them to attend a meeting before their own, to get a feel for what they are getting into, and to communicate with their neighbors before meetings on how they will operate their bars and to find out what their needs are. I wonder if this knowledge about how CB3 operates and how local residents feel about nightlife deters potential owners from wanting to open a bar in downtown Manhattan. He answers:

> Certainly, certainly. Most times a client won't even bother. A client will say, "The heck with it. I don't need the place, I'll find a different location." It goes on on the Lower East Side more than anyplace else. When you walk into a community board meeting that gets the way this one is tonight, people say to themselves, "I'd rather go someplace where I'm welcome."

As discussed in chapter 2, city leaders established community boards in 1975 as district-level local bodies that monitor government activity, alert government officials to problems within their communities, advocate on behalf of the neighborhood, and serve as forums for residents and groups to discuss local matters. Volunteer residents mostly compose community boards, but business owners can also join. City and state law requires that community boards weigh in on certain government decisions as legal steps of the process, such as liquor licensing. But the community boards' decisions remain advisory, and government agencies need not listen to their concerns.

Community boards represent prototypes of urban participatory democracy, in which local actors make key local decisions on their own behalf. Archon Fung and Erik Olin Wright examine several empirical examples of what they call "empowered participatory governance."[5] This model represents how "ordinary people can effectively participate in and influence policies which directly

affect their lives" through deliberation.[6] They argue that empowered participatory governance is based on three principles and has three design features.
The three principles that empowered participatory governance is based on are
that problems are specific and tangible, that the parties involved are ordinary
people and officials who are affected by and close to these problems, and that
solutions to these problems are developed through deliberation. For Fung
and Wright, deliberation is the model's linchpin: "Real-world deliberations
are often characterized by heated conflict, winners, and losers. The important
feature of genuine deliberation is that participants find reasons that they can
accept in collective actions, not necessarily ones that they completely endorse
or find maximally advantageous."[7] The three design features of empowered
participatory governance are local units that are empowered to make public
decisions; formal linkages of responsibility, resource distribution, and communication between these units and larger centralized authorities; and the use
of new state institutions to support and guide these decentralized problem-
solving local units.

Community boards like CB3 achieve the first two principles of Fung and
Wright's model. They focus on specific, practical problems that affect people
living downtown in some way, and they involve ordinary people in the area,
as board members or members of the public, and put them in direct contact
with political officials and state agencies. But they falter on the third principle,
and mostly on each of the design features. As we will see, deliberation as a
result of discussion and compromise does not always succeed in the community board's liquor license meetings. The interaction between residents and bar
owners, who become part of the deliberation process, often results in heated
conflicts, all-or-nothing propositions for maximum gain by each party, and
begrudged compromises. Each group enters the deliberation with its own conception of community, and each deliberation either shapes or reinforces the
images that residents and bar owners construct about the other. In addition,
community boards are not designed to be truly effective bodies of participatory
governance. Empowerment, or a group's ability to decide on its own behalf,
plays an important role in successful forms of local participatory democracy.
Members certainly feel a sense of empowerment as active volunteers in their
neighborhoods, and residents believe they can use it for positive change when
they first start protesting. However, as mentioned, community boards as governance bodies remain advisory. While there are formal connections between
community boards and superordinate centralized authorities such as the SLA
and other state agencies like the Department of City Planning, there are no
obligations for the authorities to adopt the decisions of the community boards'
internal deliberations.

The CB3 liquor license committee meets monthly and consists of approximately ten members, most of whom, like members of CB3 in general, are longtime residents.[8] Their agendas address several licensing issues: license renewal applications for owners who have had complaints about their establishments within the last two years; license transfers, upgrades, and alterations; sidewalk café licenses; and new license applications.[9] The committee intentionally places applications for new licenses at the end of the agenda so that prospective applicants who may be new to the neighborhood and unaware of residents' feelings towards nightlife can witness how it handles existing problems during meetings. At the beginning of each item, the committee gives owners the opportunity to discuss their business plan or to explain the problems that they have been having and the steps they have taken to address them. The committee asks questions about their statements and then opens the floor to residents who have requested to speak.

Committee members are knowledgeable about the liquor-licensing process and the ABC Law. They also know the nightlife scene and the history of many specific establishments quite well. In general, people join CB3 because they want to get involved in their community and in local issues in their neighborhood. Some have specific matters that they want to focus on, such as affordable housing or preserving arts institutions, and they therefore gravitate to those committees. People on the liquor license committee, however, for the most part did not initially seek it out intentionally. Alexandra, who goes by Alex, has chaired CB3's liquor license committee since 1999, a year after she joined the board. She moved to the East Village in 1992 while attending law school, joined her street's block association, and, through a friend who campaigned for the Manhattan borough president, heard about volunteering on community boards. She decided to deepen her involvement in neighborhood matters.

> I hadn't gone to any community board meetings. Then when I joined the community board, I really just asked for only the . . . committees that were the most involved. I joined the committees that were the most involved. I don't think I had any sort of agenda. I think I just thought it would be interesting to see what the community was built up by. Get a sense of what its issues were.

Anti-nightlife activism was starting in downtown Manhattan by the late 1990s, and the liquor license committee became one of CB3's busiest. The position of committee chair brings countless hours of volunteer work: carefully reading through dozens of applications (including maps, petitions, photos, and blueprints), asking the police precinct about any issues or violations at a location, trawling the Internet for information on applicants, and checking CB3's detailed files on existing applications, locations, and owners, as well as visiting the location itself, when necessary. Committee members understand their role as a service and duty to the needs and desires of the district, and not as a form of resistance or activism. "I feel like I have a commitment to the community to read the applications," Alex says. "I still feel like I have a commitment to the board to be providing the city and state agencies with motions too, comprehensive motions. There are residents who really rely on what our role is." However, Alex still demonstrates an understanding of downtown's advanced gentrification that matches that of the residents who protest nightlife. Here she describes young, incoming residents:

> "They don't have that much of an interest in the rest of us."
> "They don't?"
> "I don't think so. I don't think there is any interest in the rest of us. You get this transient population that has no interest in how it affects the actual entrenched population around them."

Residents almost always attend community board meetings as members of groups, some of which are new and some already established.[10] In groups, residents divide responsibilities among their members, such as collecting signatures for petitions against bars, conducting research on the history of a location, writing and sending letters to local politicians and the SLA, making and distributing signs and flyers, and drafting statements to make at meetings. Residents most often attend community board meetings through their own block and tenant associations. These existing groups have added nightlife to their agendas and list of priorities. When they go to meetings, they protest only bars within their own specific area. Downtown Manhattan residents formed these groups in the 1970s and 1980s in response to the damage caused by abandonment, neglect, and destruction in their neighborhoods. Like downtown's many community gardens, they represented grassroots attempts to beautify public spaces and even provide basic amenities and services for streets and buildings, such as planting trees and fixing faulty plumbing. As the area gentrified, streets got cleaned up, and buildings got bought and renovated, block and tenant associations shifted their focus to other issues besides blight and crime. They remain grassroots-level efforts by residents who share similar situations to improve conditions in their immediate area by pooling their limited resources.

As with Alex, the liquor license committee's chair, many residents begin their protests against bars and nightlife through their tenant and block associations. And as with Patti, their acts of nightlife resistance sometimes lead to greater involvement in community activism and depths of understanding of the area's gentrification. Born in Virginia and raised in Tennessee, David moved to the East Village in 1983 after high school, in search of an environment different from the one he grew up in. Its affordability, diversity, and culture drew him to downtown. After a couple of years, he attended college and received his bachelor's degree in history and a master's degree in film studies. Since 1990 he has taught social studies and film at a poor public high school. David lives on East Fifth Street, and his apartment is packed with canisters of old films and decorated with his wife's collages. He had been aware of the nightlife scene's development and affected by the noise outside of his bedroom window, but he only got involved in his block association when he heard about the Cooper Square Hotel, which is located down the street from his building. "I started when this big, giant twenty-three-story, $500-a-night Cooper Square Hotel kind of announced itself onto our block," he says. "We were all completely in shock. Very few people had heard that it was coming. And then suddenly this crane comes there." Using his artistic skills, David began creating posters that graphically represent the scale of nightlife growth. Through his involvement protesting the hotel with the block association, David became educated in the liquor license process and began perceiving the SLA and bar owners the way his neighbors did, namely as threats to his sense of community.

Despite the time commitment ("I realized that this is becoming a part-time job"), he expanded his activism. When he noticed an increase in the number of high-rise and luxury developments on the Bowery, David founded a community group called the Bowery Alliance of Neighbors (BAN), which focuses specifically on historic preservation of the street's physical character. He began understanding the nightlife scene's relationship to advanced gentrification.

> But it's all interlinked, like I was saying. Until we started fighting the bars, I never really even thought about all these things. I didn't know close up how city government worked and so forth. It's really scary when you first start looking. Now I'm, like, coming to terms with it. But it's definitely all interlinked, all of this. The bar issue, as far as I'm concerned, and the whole reason why I felt the need to get involved in this effort to get protective zoning for the Bowery, was the fact that these big towers that everybody in this neighborhood hates, even people that want a lot of development, almost nobody likes these towers that are going up. But the towers are basically three things: they're tower co-ops, they're tower luxury $500-a-night hotels, and they're tower dorms for upper-class kids that go to—I'm stereotyping—that go to NYU. . . . All of that, all of that overdevelopment is feeding into the

number of bars that are going in. Everything is cross-pollinating itself. And it's, of course, it's also affecting the culture in the neighborhood.

While initially David began protesting nightlife because of quality-of-life problems that he feared would be exacerbated by the construction of the large hotel's new nightlife venues, his motives gradually shifted to include such factors as historic and cultural preservation. Through his activism he has constructed an understanding of the community as a place dependent on a built environment of old, low-rise structures and a creative sociocultural world.

Other early gentrifiers have also adopted this preservationist perspective, which they blend with their own nostalgia narrative. But these residents have interests that go beyond their own sociocultural worlds. Virgil, for instance, has constructed a strong nostalgia narrative about his time in the neighborhood. He also interprets downtown Manhattan as New York City's most important historical district in dire need of protection from development. He holds it and its attractions in high esteem:

> If you look at a European city, or if you look at Florence, they have an old sector of the town that's the historical part of town. They would never dream of developing that part of town, building glass, steel structures in the middle of Il Duomo and the Uffizi. It's absurd! You build that stuff *around* the historical part of town, not *in* the historical part of town. *This* is the historical part of town.

Residents like David and Virgil continue to protest bars when liquor license items on their street appear on CB3's agenda, but to them new nightlife has come to resemble the larger threat of advanced gentrification in downtown Manhattan. For them new bars, high-rise developments, and luxury housing do not just threaten their sense of community but also threaten to diminish the area's greater reputation as a historically important place. Their sense of the "public interest" extends beyond their own streets to include the civic good to which downtown contributes.

Along with block and tenant associations, other established groups in downtown Manhattan, such as Good Old Lower East Side (GOLES), a housing and preservation organization that has fought for tenants' rights and affordable housing in the Lower East Side and East Village since 1977, have recognized the relationship between the commercial dimension of gentrification and other issues in these neighborhoods. Jennifer, an organizer with GOLES, explains:

GOLES started at a time when the neighborhood was experiencing a huge amount of disinvestment, and buildings were burning, and landlords were just trying to collect on insurance and collect on their properties. . . . And I think what's been happening here and what's been happening all over the city in the last—depending on how you want to define it—ten, twenty years is that as this neighborhood has become a desirable place, people identify a lot with the culture, the artistic spirit, the history of the neighborhood, and the low rents, the rent-regulated housing units that exist here are all what brought people here. And as the neighborhood, I think a lot of residents feel like as the neighborhood has become a place where more people have wanted to go, the development that has been taken place in the neighborhood has been development that's geared towards meeting the needs of this new incoming population, and it's really not at all focused on or interested in addressing the needs of the existing community and the community that's been here.

As part of GOLES's efforts, Jennifer led a project that worked with local non-nightlife business owners that looked for ways to help them stay in operation. She continues:

As more and more bars and restaurants come into the neighborhood, the neighborhood becomes a lot more of a destination for nightlife. The rents are skyrocketing, and businesses that serve local residents here that are owned by local residents, that hire locally, and that provide a diversity of goods and services at affordable prices are being lost. And so we wanted to step in here where we saw a need and start to find out a little bit more about kind of what businesses are, what their challenges are, what their needs are, what are the issues that are affecting their business, and what we feel would benefit their business in terms of technical assistance or what would help them to remain competitive and profitable amidst those changes in the local economy.

By addressing the issue of nightlife development and linking it with their specific cause, neighborhood nonprofits such as GOLES form alliances with early gentrifiers and their local groups to protest bars.

Finally, residents have also started new groups specifically designed to protest bars and nightlife. Examples include the Save Avenue A Committee, the Lower East Side Alliance (LESA), and the Ludlow Orchard Community Organization (LOCO). Such organized efforts have led to the creation of moratoriums (or resolution areas), the petitioning of local elected officials, and the hosting of a town hall meeting in 2006 that was well attended and covered by the local media. These groups, however, have been ephemeral. They were started with significant enthusiasm by a few active and charismatic residents (such as Patti and Virgil) and even gained a degree of local media coverage, but fizzled out due to infighting between their leaders over the groups' direction, strategies, or priorities.

Despite sharing their frustration with nightlife and their opposition to gentrification, liquor license committee members differ from the residents who attend CB3 meetings in the way they deal with owners and the way they understand the liquor license process. The distinction between committee members and residents stems from the former's role in the process and experience dealing with owners and applicants. Residents usually fight against any liquor license application near their homes. It was their block associations and anti-nightlife groups that developed moratoriums. The liquor license committee members see themselves as mediators between bar owners and residents, and they try, through deliberation, to find common ground between the two sides and to look out for the best interest of the district. Members of CB3 have learned that blanket prohibitions against bars are ineffective. Officials at the SLA ignored CB3's moratoriums because they denied due process to bar owners, who are entitled by law to have their applications read by community boards. The liquor license committee knows that it has to hear what bar owners have to say about their existing or proposed establishments and the members know that they have to provide detailed explanations to the SLA for why they deny licenses.

The liquor license committee also deals with nearly every bar in the district, and its members have a lot of experience with unscrupulous owners and applicants.[11] They therefore view applicants and their applications differently from other residents, who are more likely to disapprove applications out of hand. Michael, for instance, moved to the Lower East Side in 1999, in part because it had hip places to go out to at night. He became more interested in neighborhood issues around when he had children, a few years later, and decided to join the community board in 2005. As a newer resident, Michael does not demonstrate as much nostalgia for his life in the neighborhood as committee members like Alex or as other longtime residents. He had to learn about the issues confronting the neighborhood from complaining residents:

> I've always been sort of an advocate for nightlife, I guess. I mean, I always liked going out, so I never really saw a problem with bars. But I got on the committee and I really started getting sort of the other perspective of what it's like to live next to a bar. Where I live, I don't have any bars next to me,

anywhere close to me, so I really hadn't understood exactly how bad it was. I mean, you'd think I'd be able to see it just by walking around and think, "Oh gee, I wonder what this is like?" But until you're really talking with somebody that's really struggling with it, it doesn't really sink in. So I started to hear some arguments.

The more applications he saw and owners he heard, the more Michael saw patterns that revealed clues about potential problem owners. He explains how he interprets applications:

I also started to see that there's a lot of hyperbole with some people's arguments, and I started to also see how some applicants weren't really, they definitely weren't forthcoming, they were definitely trying to hide stuff. I started to pick up the nuances and—the menu they're proposing is really not a menu for a restaurant, it's really a bar—and looking at the history of the bar. You get a sense of what the potential problem areas are. If somebody comes to you and they have a forty-foot bar in their place, and they have three tables and no kitchen facilities, then you tend to come into it with a bit more skepticism than you would for the four-table little restaurant that serves vegan food with a full menu. So I started to definitely shift away from being as much of an ally, I guess, for nightlife establishments to really being a lot more objective and more critical.

Because of their experience dealing with bar owners and the SLA, the committee members know that having bar owners who are receptive to the needs of their neighbors and are willing to work with them is often the best option they have for achieving their goal of improving the quality of life in the neighborhood. While they understand their role to be in service of the needs of the community and residents, committee members sometimes conflict with resident groups over such licensing decisions.

Many other longtime residents who began their community activism by protesting bars, like David, go on to start or join other groups that deal with different issues of advanced gentrification. Others, like Patti, eventually cease organized resistance altogether. But they still carry a community ideology that nightlife growth and involvement in community board meetings helped trigger. Not all early gentrifiers protest bars through the liquor license process, and more importantly, not all put their community ideology into practice through protest against bars. Bob, the photographer from chapter 3, is an example. Other than when there is an important item on an agenda or a large protest, to which he goes for the photo opportunities, Bob does not get involved in formal community politics. In fact, he is skeptical of the community board because of its limited definition of the community and democracy. "Those folks aren't the community," Bob says in regards to the community board:

> [The street] is where democracy grows from. It's not the Internet, it's not in any other place, it's not in college. It's here, it's people. This is the people's business. They come here and discuss things. They might be wrong, and they argue, and they'll go home and they'll look something up or someone will give them some information, they'll talk about the neighborhood, and they take it seriously. This is theirs, they own it. When you have that sense of neighborhood, they own it, and it matters to 'em.

As we saw, Bob's actions of documenting the neighborhood while rooting himself in a space that features social and physical elements from its past (i.e., public characters, Ray's Candy Store) contributes to his self-understanding as a symbolic owner, which is under threat by the nightlife that surrounds him. Bob practices this ideology nightly through his interactions with the neighborhood's public characters and through his carefully constructed blog posts. The characters themselves, on the other hand, express their community ideology and react to their sociocultural displacement in less subtle ways. They often harass women revelers on the sidewalk with catcalls and call passersby "fucking yuppies."

Bar owners' dealings with the community board presents a different picture from those of residents. Owners do not organize to defend their interests against these groups (or against the police and the local government, for that matter). They go before the community board and confront their neighbors as individuals instead of as a collective. In their arguments, owners do not claim to speak on the neighborhood's behalf, as residents do. Their references to the community in community board meetings revolve around their own personal contribution to the vitality of the neighborhood and its nightlife scene and their self-identity as place entrepreneurs. They have not integrated themselves into existing community organizations, such as the Lower East Side Business Improvement District. Although NYNA is an influential lobbying group, it often represents the interests of large nightclubs, lounges, and restaurants instead of small bars, and it focuses on state government–level concerns rather than local community issues. Few of the bar owners I spoke to were members, and some were critical of NYNA for its inattention to the specific concerns of small bars.

As shown in the previous chapter, downtown bar owners can be critical of their fellow entrepreneurs and sometimes blame them for some of the negative attention that the nightlife scene receives. But in general they act friendly and cordially towards each other at meetings and around their neighborhood. They also sometimes share stories about having difficult neighbors. Still, they do not use their shared experiences in their neighborhood and with residents, or their shared interests as business owners, to organize themselves into a more visible and powerful local force, for a number of reasons. First, they do not always live in their bar's neighborhood, and if they do, they do not always live near each other. Residents derive considerable advantage from their proximity and shared circumstances. The distance makes it difficult for owners to form a formidable local political base. Second, while bar owners appreciate the existence of large nightlife scenes because they attract customers to the area, they still understand their bars to be in competition with each other. They mainly focus on the well-being of their own establishments rather than on issues that concern downtown Manhattan. Finally, as discussed, nightlife regulation of small bars is fairly recent. Bar owners have not historically needed to organize and defend their interests as a group. Furthermore, nightlife scrutiny from local politicians and state authorities ebbs and flows, losing a lot of the momentum from 2006 within three years. Owners also recognize that the police, government, and community board target them as individual "problem owners." For these reasons they appear before CB3 and their neighbors as individuals, with a preexisting animus against them.

IN THE COMMUNITY BOARD MEETING

We can see these ideologies, place identities, and definitions of community in action, the limits of the community board as a form of local participatory democracy, and the ways that conflicts and tensions get reproduced between disparate groups in downtown Manhattan through an analysis of how these actors interact in the liquor license committee meeting. The following sections present episodes that demonstrate how community ideologies and negative perceptions get formed and reinforced through interactions between residents and bar owners during the application process. They specifically focus on how residents use past incidents with bar owners to protest current applicants and reinforce their sense of distrust towards them as well as how both residents and bar owners use their own definitions of community in their arguments against each other.

The Sins of the Past: Reinforcing Distrust

A little past nine o'clock, Alex calls out the next item. The applicants—two young men and a married couple, all in their late thirties—are applying for a sports bar and grill. It is an application to transfer the license of an existing

FIGURE 16   A resident makes her case at a community board meeting. Photograph by the author, 2011.

Spanish restaurant in a northern block on Avenue A that has not had a significant impact on quality of life. The husband, tall and broad-shouldered, is the principal owner and does most of the talking. He and his partners already own a bar in Clinton, a neighborhood on the west side of Manhattan. Like other owners in popular nightlife areas in the city, he wants to capitalize on the buzz surrounding the East Village's well-trafficked scene. The new place will be similar, with ten televisions, an open facade, and a sidewalk café. The owner takes pride in his relationship with the Clinton community and describes how he contributes to it through local charity work (he hosts homeless people at the bar for Thanksgiving). He also claims that his bar deters crime, especially violence, by being an establishment that provides eyes on the street.[12] Following CB3 policy, he has a petition with the signatures of 150 residents in support of his application (he says he stood outside the location for ten hours to collect them).

Alex comments that downtown Manhattan is a different area from Clinton and that violent crime is not an issue here. In fact, she says, the crime that does occur mostly takes place within places like this (i.e., bars that will attract anonymous customers) and that police mostly handle quality-of-life issues.

FIGURE 17 Applicants look on and wait their turn as a resident speaks. Photograph by the author, 2011.

"I understand," he says. "But we're heavily involved in the community at the other bar and we do a good job of managing the sidewalk café."

Reading the application, Nora, another committee member, points out their proposed closing hour of 4 a.m., which differs considerably from the low-key Spanish restaurant. She then rhetorically asks, "Don't you realize people live in this neighborhood?"

Before he can respond, Alex says, "We are overrun with sports bars and most have French doors. I can hear them from blocks away. The main issue on the Lower East Side is noise. You telling me that you will deter crime and that you're involved in the community is like telling me you're a nice guy."

Facing CB3 for the first time, the owner is a bit surprised and speechless. Relying on their history in dealing with owners, the committee members make a mirror out of his application and explanations. They ask questions at the same time as they convey their concerns, particularly the threat of increased noise. They want to hear an honest answer from the applicant on what he intends with his bar. At this point the committee turns to the residents in attendance to protest.

Thirteen residents from the Eleventh Street block association, which represents the block just to the east of the proposed establishment, are at the meeting to oppose the license. Alex calls them out, name by name, from the sign-up list that she has.

"I just wanted to point out," says Janet, the block association's president, to the committee, "that although the front door is on Avenue A, it's still on the corner and people are going to be walking on Eleventh Street. We are a quiet, residential block, and our quality of life has been deteriorating. We already have Landry's [another bar] over there. When we met with him [its owner], he never said he was going to be a sports bar. He said he was going to be a family restaurant."

Janet makes her argument using a mixed strategy commonly used by residents. First, she highlights the direct threat that she feels the bar will have on her block by pointing out the nature of its location. She mentions her area's current condition of a deteriorating quality of life to punctuate this point. Janet then mentions her street's recent history of dealing with another owner, who owns what she feels is an establishment similar to the one the applicant proposes. Most importantly, she states that this owner deceived them before he opened, invoking the board's history of dealing with owners who engage in the "bait and switch" strategy. The owner of Landry's, of course, has no connection with the applicant. But Janet demonstrates how residents make such a link based on their past experience.

Todd, another block association member, furthers Janet's point about the area. "There are already nine bars in the immediate area," he says. "We are saturated ["*Saturated!*" shouts another resident] with nightlife." Todd then mentions some investigative work that he recently did. "I have been to their place in Clinton and people go there for beer, the French doors are open, and the sound bounces off surrounding buildings."

Another of residents' history-based fears is that owners bypass the process, such as by not meeting with them before their meeting. They consider this deceitful and an indication that the owner potentially has something to hide. "He never met with us or reached out to us," says Jason. "We've had a lot of owners open without seeking us out. Just all of a sudden they were [open]! Our quality of life has declined because of this, and I don't see how this place is going to benefit the community."

With this comment Jason brings up community for the first time. Another resident follows up on it and repeats some of the previous statements. "This is going to be insane. We're at a saturation point. This is going to be madness. *The whole area's changed in the last seven years.* Sports bars are not what we should have in this neighborhood. They are places where people go to be loud and get drunk, and then they leave and are drunk outside. What good is that? That's not what this community has ever had."

CB3 learned long ago that the SLA does not consider nostalgia when making licensing decisions. The members therefore never include their narratives of their early days in the neighborhood or their perspective on how downtown Manhattan has changed in their motions to deny or in their deliberations with bar owners. Residents, meanwhile, regularly invoke their nostalgia narrative when protesting a bar, simultaneously asserting their claim as symbolic owners, revealing how their neighborhood has improved from its negative state, and arguing against the changes that nightlife has caused.

A final resident, Patricia, then speaks. She explains that she and her husband have been living in their building just down from the corner of Avenue A for twenty-three years. Patricia talks about her experience with the surrounding nightlife in contrast to her early years in the neighborhood. "We're sleep-deprived, nervous, and feel like we're having a nervous breakdown. We can't afford to move, but we have to coexist. I remember when this was a drug street. I remember when this place used to be a bodega that had gang drug activity. One time, three people were beaten to death there. But we've stuck it out. And at least it was quiet [then]. There's just so much traffic now. We shouldn't have to deal with this."

Visibly frustrated and feeling like a decision has already been made, the owner snaps at the committee, holds up and shakes a copy of his application, and exclaims, "You shouldn't waste people's time by handing these things out if this is how they're going to get treated! I was told I was going to get a fair treatment and that transfers go through."

"Yes, most transfers are approved," says Alex, "but you should not have been told that it was going to be a guarantee."

Michael, the newer committee member without a strong nostalgia narrative, picks up on the sentiment of the block association. He calmly explains their perspective to the applicant and adds his own interpretation of the neighborhood's advanced gentrification. "This community has changed, bars helped change it. But we passed a threshold. These people that requested the resolution [area], they're being priced out now. These people don't recognize who comes here on weekends."

Sam, another committee member, then says to the owner, "You know, after that little outburst, what you said before about working with the community doesn't really seem genuine to me." The committee unanimously votes to deny his application, and he storms out of the room, with his partners following with their heads down behind him.

Being distrustful of bar owners was not new for members of the Eleventh Street block association. They cite times when owners directly deceived them or did not reach out to them, which have led to their wary attitude towards owners and their perception of them as threats to their community. The applicant in this case, who did not know and had no connection to this history, could not offer counterevidence after the committee questioned the relevance of his track record with his other bar in the area and the details of his application. Angered and caught without a defense, the applicant reacted in a highly emotional manner that dismissed any thoughts that residents and the committee may have had of his integrity as a local, community-oriented businessman and reinforced their preexisting perception of distrust towards bar owners. Correspondingly, such interactions contribute to owners' interpretations of residents as irrational actors and inappropriate representatives of the community.

Rebuking Interpretations of Community

At a meeting in October, two men in their early thirties appear before the committee to have a location's existing license to serve beer and wine transferred to them for their new pizzeria. Former owners of a Chelsea nightclub, they want to open on Ludlow Street, one of the densest streets for bars on the Lower East Side. Dressed in designer jeans, half-buttoned shirts, and jackets, they say to the committee that they want to get out of the nightclub business and focus on something more low-key. For the community board, places like pizzerias are ancillary businesses to the nightlife scene. Fast-food establishments succeed because of the large number of revelers who are out until late at night. As with proposed bars, the community board tries to prevent these businesses from having liquor licenses. They feel that not only do these businesses prolong drinking among revelers, they also do not have the means to handle unruly situations, such as by having bouncers.

"We want to cater to the nightlife crowd, but we also want to be a delivery place," explains one of the applicants to the committee. "We want to be for the people who will be staying in the hotels and the new condos that are coming in. They'll benefit from our quality pizza. The other pizzerias around here aren't very good."

"They're not there yet," says Alex.

"They will be, and that's business: looking ahead, not on today."

The committee grumbles at how blunt the applicants are about wanting to cater to newcomers. The applicants acknowledge this by saying that they will also be open during the day to serve people who live in the neighborhood. But the committee sees this as an example of misrepresentation. "Then why didn't you include that in your application?" asks Nora. The committee then starts scrutinizing the application, particularly the petitions, which lack addresses next to the signatures. "You could've gotten these from anyone walking down the street. How can we accept these?" asks Michael.

"I don't understand what you're asking me. I already did what you said," says one of the applicants, referring to the signatures.

"We already have pizza places," says Alex. "This place is not necessary or beneficial to the community."

While laughing and gesturing to the seats behind him, the other applicant asks, incredulously, "Why don't we *ask the community*?" He throws his hands up and meanders around the front of the room, as Michael makes a motion to the deny their application due to the saturation of liquor licenses already on Ludlow Street and misrepresentation on the part of the applicants (i.e., problematic signatures and desired clientele).

While leaving, one of the applicants says to no one in particular, but for all to hear, "This is an advisory board? It's a fucking joke."

It is common at committee meetings for owners to invoke their interpretation of community. Usually they do so in general terms, such as saying they will make a "positive contribution to the community" without specifying whom they mean when they use the term. In this case, however, the applicants directly state which groups in the neighborhood they want to attract: nightlife consumers, visitors, and wealthy incoming residents. They clearly name the sector of the community they seek to serve. Although they say that they also wanted to attract local residents by being open during the day, the fact that they were not forthcoming with this information in their application led the committee to conclude that they were misrepresenting themselves. Recognizing that the community board members are not the people they wish to attract, they rhetorically ask to hear from "the community."

Location and method of operation often signal to the committee members that bar owners have a different definition of community in mind when they apply for a license. One evening, two blond men in their mid-thirties go before the committee for their application for a license to serve beer and wine. They have owned a commercial space on Broome Street for a few years now, which they have mostly been renting to friends as an art space. They were approved for a full liquor license a year ago, but never went through with it after one of their business partners dropped out. The new plan is for an Icelandic-themed restaurant that will be open from 5 p.m. to 4 a.m.

The hours immediately suggest to the committee that they will not cater to a local clientele. Linda, a committee member, begins, "It's unfortunate that you want to open on this block because it already has two restaurants. And since they opened, the noise increase has been incalculable. I could hear it from around the corner on Orchard. And why aren't you going to be open during the day? There are not enough places that accommodate the neighborhood during the day. Night hours are not community hours. They cater to people that are trickling down from wherever." Then, referencing the history of the area, she says, "If you look at pictures of Orchard Street over the past century and a half or however long, it has been a daytime community, not a nighttime community."

The owners exchange glances, unsure of which one of them should speak, or what he should say. One explains that they never considered opening during the day, and adds that they do not want to overload themselves at the beginning by serving breakfast and lunch. Because of the late hours that advertise it as a nightspot, the committee is concerned about the visiting revelers that the place will attract. They are also concerned that since they will be open so late and have a limited menu, they will not really be primarily a restaurant.

But there is an additional issue with the proposed establishment, which is located in a part of the Lower East Side that is near Chinatown and has many immigrant Chinese residents. It is very rare that residents who are not early gentrifiers attend community board meetings to protest bars. But Amy, who is Chinese and the only resident present at tonight's meeting to speak against the application, actively opposes liquor licenses near her home. "This place is on a street of Chinese immigrants that don't speak much English," she explains. "So there is no one to protest, except me." She then speaks at length about her problems with the place opening, which are numerous.

"Broome, Orchard, and Ludlow are small streets that get crowded and noisy easily. There are places like Barrio Chino and Lolita Bar that are already there and noisy. The sanitation trucks come often and wake me up at midnight, 1, 2, and 4 in the morning. Orchard already has many places that have beer and wine licenses. Five or six years ago, there were no bars in this area. It was retail. Then all of a sudden there was this influx. And they came and had places with open doors and windows. And people wait outside and they wait and smoke, and talk, and block the sidewalks, they block the pedestrians. Orchard Street and Broome Street are too small to have all these bars. We have elderly people, infants, children, working people. I think a lot of this is because this is an immigrant neighborhood and people speak Chinese and they don't speak out. And I object."

"Look, my girlfriend is Chinese, so I am sensitive to such things," says one of the applicants.

"This is not going to be a food place, it's going to be a bar place," says Amy, ignoring his attempt at empathy.

"This will be a classy place for the neighborhood, and if the street consists of Chinese immigrants who won't patronize the restaurant anyway, then what daytime community would we be serving?"

"Four a.m. is excessively late. The street is dead by midnight," says Amy, again ignoring him and his point.

"We'll be considerate to our neighbors, and we're helping our building. We really are. And it's better for the neighborhood. Better than it was before."

Amy gives him an incredulous look, and the applicant, with surprise in his voice, says "You don't think so? Isn't it cleaner?"

Amy's argument contains many common elements in residents' arguments, such as quality-of-life complaints, oversaturation claims, misrepresentation and distrust of the owners, and the fact that the proposed establishment is not appropriate for the community. Her definition of the "community," however, differs from that of early gentrifiers. Patti, from this chapter's opening vignette, also refers to the "working people" of the neighborhood in her arguments against advanced gentrification, but she also demonstrates a nostalgia narrative when she discusses the importance of the arts and music scene. Amy refers to the community of Chinese immigrants that populate her section of the Lower East Side. Unlike early gentrifiers, Chinese immigrants lack the social and cultural capital required to navigate the complex worlds of liquor license policies and city politics that facilitate the growth of the nightlife scene. At stake for them is the loss of an environment that is conducive for earning a living as an immigrant, raising a family, and affording a place to live, rather than maintaining a sociocultural world or preserving authenticity and a historical sense of place. The applicants, meanwhile, reflect a common interpretation of community among new nightlife owners, namely a "classy" place that does not cater to the needs of its immediate neighbors.

As the meeting continues, Alex seeks to come to a resolution. The problem is that there is only one person present to protest, the applicants were already approved once before, their application is sound, and the 500-foot rule does not apply. She knows that the SLA will likely approve their application, but she has her natural reservations.

"Well, there have been different views on what the community consists of that have been presented thus far," she says. "I'm torn, because you seem like good people, but you are still new owners who intend to keep long hours and wouldn't be serving the needs of the community by not opening for breakfast or lunch."

To settle the issue, Linda then furthers this last point, which is universal to most downtown Manhattan residents whether they are early gentrifiers or low-income residents. "Look, the issue is the hours. They're geared towards extraterrestrials coming in and not for the community." .

—

Participatory democracy, in which average citizens can meaningfully voice their concerns and formally influence the policies that will impact their everyday lives, serves as a powerful remedy for such processes as those that bring about advanced gentrification. To succeed, participatory democracy must have a structure in place that promotes the principle of deliberation and that grants agency to the local body. The downtown Manhattan's community board structure features flaws, particularly because of its lack of agency. But the focus here has been on how interactions between disparate sets of actors, coupled with ideology, undermine deliberation. In the case of the liquor license committee meeting, true deliberation between residents and bar owners stumbles because of ideological commitments to competing conceptions of community. In many cases the interactions themselves foster these commitments, which lead to further community action and more deeply entrenched ideological concerns. The conflicts and tensions that residents and owners hold towards the other get constructed and reinforced at a forum that exists for resolving them.

UPSCALING NEW YORK

WHAT HAPPENS WHEN AN URBAN NEIGHBORHOOD of disparate groups becomes increasingly upscale? What does it mean for cities when their places that are known for including a broad mix of working-class people, immigrant groups, and creative populations with identities and communities rooted in the actual spaces themselves become home for an exclusive array of phenomena—residents, businesses, cultures, and ideas—that are based on consumption and compete for the same space? In addressing these fundamental questions through the analysis in this book, I aim to raise awareness of the impacts of commercial change on everyday life in today's postindustrial city and to offer insight into what New York City is potentially becoming—a place for upscale living at the center and, at the margins, for lifestyles that range from edgy to impoverished.

In the 1990s and 2000s, many scholars feared that New York City was turning into a corporatized and "Disneyfied" place for amusement, consumption, and tourism. Michael Sorkin famously decried the "end of public space" by claiming that cities were becoming more like theme parks—sanitized, securitized, and homogenized—which threatened their egalitarianism.[1] John Hannigan argued that today's metropolises were becoming more like "fantasy cities" with "urbanoid" entertainment destinations that provide "riskless risk" and safe, branded, and themed amusements for members of the middle class.[2] And in a volume entitled *The Suburbanization of New York: Is the World's Greatest City Becoming Just Another Town?* a group of authors pointed out how the city is losing its unique personality and becoming more like a stereotypical suburb: bland, boring, and soulless.

Global and corporate finance, private security, thematic entertainment, and tourism have surely become more important in postindustrial New York. But as I have shown, these transformations do not explain what has happened in neighborhoods like those in downtown Manhattan. Many areas in the city that are popular to live in and visit hardly resemble a suburb, mall, or theme park. New York does, however, boast several neighborhoods for upscale urban living. But these areas are not like the old elite of Park Avenue, the Upper West Side, or the streets near Central Park. They do not contain haute French cuisine restaurants or classic old hotel bars. And they do not feature opening performances at opera houses or world-class theaters. Rather, the neighborhoods for new upscale living, such as the Lower East Side, East Village, and Bowery, are places that were once marginal to the city's vibrancy but today contain popular nightlife scenes, retail outlets for high-priced and edgy art and fashion, luxury housing, and boutique hotels. Their bars and nightspots, which were once local amusements for marginal groups, are now culturally and economically significant destinations for a range of young revelers that contribute to the city's growth, popularity, and increasing transformation into a place for exclusive urban life.

The downtown neighborhoods of New York City were once living symbols of working-class and immigrant urban life. Today, after a period of gentrification, they are becoming more and more exclusive, and less and less diverse. The reality behind the rejuvenation of these downtown neighborhoods is that people flock to them and use their new spaces to create and reinforce imagined communities based on forms of commercial leisure, taste, and desire at the expense of existing people in actual, place-based communities. These two layers of community—the rootless and the rooted—coexist uneasily in downtown Manhattan today. But the presence of existing residents, their businesses, and their cultures is becoming increasingly unsustainable as life in these neighborhoods advances along with New York City's steady path towards postindustrial dominance.

I have tried in this book to make an argument about how bars and nightlife scenes structure and influence life in downtown neighborhoods that have become, through advanced gentrification, upscale destinations for consumers and residents and prime locations for investment in high-end real estate and business. Commercial establishments like bars—local hangouts with strong tendencies to be neighborhood institutions—are important signs of this process. Bars rest at the intersection between a city's culture and its economy and offer a window for understanding changes in local patterns of socializing, the formation of local identities, and the transformation of neighborhoods. I have therefore used Manhattan's downtown bars merely as a lens for examining the deeper consequences of an upscaling process affecting cities like New York during the postindustrial era.

The proliferation of bars and growth of nightlife scenes alert us to the importance of nostalgia for people in today's postindustrial city of constant, rapid destruction and ever-changing fashions. As I have shown, longtime residents use an exclusive nostalgia-based narrative of a dark period in their neighborhood's past to fuel their continuous protest despite the process's inexorable march towards an upscale status. As a result of threatening conditions—real or perceived—to one's way of life, nostalgia arises amid change. People yearn for a past that they feel has slipped away, or that is in danger of doing so. Many people in downtown Manhattan use their nostalgia as a tool for fighting bars and to preserve what little remains of the neighborhood they knew and wanted. Far from frivolous, nostalgia is a powerful feeling that emerges from within people, unexpectedly and uncontrollably.

In writing this book, I often felt like I was in dialogue with voices and stories from the past. After talking to dozens of longtime and lifelong residents and watching them speak about their neighborhood in public forums, it was clear to me that the past held an almost sacred status for them. Weeping and screaming, they spoke passionately in front of large groups and one-on-one with me about their love for their neighborhood and about what it used to be like to live there. They spoke about its creativity and diversity, its seductive sense of danger, and the feeling the neighborhood gave them that the place was theirs. Their nostalgia was infectious, the stories were filled with urban adventures and colorful characters, and the cultural output from the era—punk rock, graffiti, experimental theater and film, avant-garde art—is indeed inspiring. Their fear is that it is all over, or nearly so, replaced by an uncreative and homogeneous group of consumers. Considering the emotions, it was easy for me to also feel saddened by the end of this period of creativity in downtown Manhattan, even though I did not experience most of it myself, having been a young high school student who occasionally visited the neighborhood in the 1990s.

But nostalgia hides as much about the past as it reveals. The 1970s and 1980s in general are often regarded by the city's cultural critics as especially abundant times in New York City for sub- and alternative cultural production—art, fashion, music, film—much of it emerging from the downtown scene.[3] This scene, along with the gritty images of street crime, litter, and graffiti that characterized New York at the time, came about and were sustained by widespread hardship. Artists, musicians, students, and other young, adventurous urbanites occupied and were inspired by places from the industrial city that were abandoned and neglected, such as downtown working-class neighborhoods like the Lower East Side, East Village, and Bowery. Through their efforts, they inadvertently became early progenitors of an urban transformation that revitalized downtown. The gradual, destructive process of deindustrialization produced far more losers in the city than winners, or to put it another way, the story of downtown's decline is perhaps more about the woes that befell the city's vulnerable populations than about the creativity that arose for a fortunate generation. But this perspective does not generally show up in the tales of nostalgia that many downtown Manhattan and New York City residents tell about the past.

My observations in bars and on the streets and my conversations with young revelers supported many of the attitudes that residents have towards newcomers. Many were visiting the neighborhood to go out, most were not aware of the conflicts and tensions occurring in the neighborhood as they visited bars, and overall the streets were loud at night. However, residents' conception of today's downtown and its newcomers as uncreative is inaccurate. I also observed a considerable amount of behavior besides alcohol consumption in the nightlife scene. For instance, The Dressing Room provides a space for fashion designers to make and sell their items, The Box features well-known burlesque performers, and numerous new bars still double as art galleries and performance venues. Although I have not specifically examined it in this book, downtown Manhattan is also home to numerous restaurants and chefs who are celebrated in the food world and are devoting themselves to making unique cuisines. And as discussed, the nightlife scenes contain numerous establishments that are dedicated to drink cultures—beer, wine, spirits, and cocktails—that strive for quality and precision in the making of their products.

These examples of creativity, of course, are not the "DIY"-style fashions, punk aesthetics, or local cultural products that characterized downtown's previous era. They are not "from the streets," and the people involved with them often do not live in the neighborhoods. They emerged in gentrified, safe, and rejuvenated neighborhoods, not ones that were neglected and abandoned, and they benefit from their reputation as destinations for upscale consumption. Like the nightlife scenes today, downtown's art and music scenes of yesteryear were hardly open to all comers. But the latter's exclusivity was not based on cost, as the cuisines, cocktails, clothing, and other cultural products found in today's downtown in many ways are (tables for burlesque performances at The Box, for instance, start at $1,500). The nightlife scenes appeal to the casual consumer, the connoisseur, and the creative producers of new elite tastes. But their exclusive nature does not set them apart from previous creative scenes in downtown's history. Their upscale nature, in the form of the cultures, tastes, and consumers that compose the scenes, does. And the additional distinction of the economic price tag for today's amusements threatens to remove low-income forms of culture and entertainment from downtown completely.

This contemporary exclusivity in downtown neighborhoods relates directly to growth policies with impacts throughout the city. Downtown's transformation has meant the implementation of an urban growth agenda that produces a commercial scene that appeals to and benefits wealthier newcomers and visitors and prioritizes their desires and needs over those of existing residents. The New York State Liquor Authority has played a direct role in the proliferation of bars and the growth of the neighborhoods' nightlife scene through its interpretation of the law that favors nightlife density. It has done so in spite of active protests from people who live in the neighborhoods and from their community boards. And even as the protests increased in number and became better coordinated while operating within the law, proliferation continued and nightlife scenes grew.

Confronting such a growth agenda has become a reality for people in many neighborhoods around the city and in ways other than the growth of local nightlife scenes. For example, during his twelve-year mayoral administration (2002–2013), Michael Bloomberg rezoned nearly a quarter of New York City, more than the previous six administrations combined (dating back to 1961, the year of the city's last zoning resolution). In many cases, such as derelict industrial areas like the Hudson Yards, West Chelsea, and the Williamsburg-Greenpoint waterfront districts, the goal of the rezoning was to create new market-rate housing in gentrifying neighborhoods by allowing greater residential density. In another example, city officials rezoned a large section of downtown Brooklyn to accommodate a planned mixed-use development of high-rise housing, office spaces, retail stores, and a professional sports and entertainment arena, which opened in fall 2012 as the Barclays Center. In addition, the city used its eminent domain power to seize tenant buildings, private homes, and businesses that were located in the footprint of the proposed development. Given the costs for housing and business in the local real estate markets of these areas, and the luxury style of the new developments and amenities, their rents and costs per square foot are exorbitantly high for most of the existing populations.

In these cases—of helping a nightlife scene to grow, rezoning a neighborhood, and seizing private property and public spaces for a sports arena and new luxury housing—government leaders always stress economic growth from expanding real estate tax revenues and creating employment as justifications. Liquor licensing, rezoning, and eminent domain all are tools that local government officials use to grow and improve their neighborhoods and the city. But they are all highly controversial since they have almost always conflicted with the preferences of existing residents. As with nightlife growth in downtown Manhattan, local groups spent many years protesting these and other rezonings, which promise to radically transform their neighborhoods for decades to come. In each of these and other cases, the local growth agenda resulted in upscale developments: nightlife scenes, luxury housing, high-end retail space, and a corporatized arena. New York City residents who face the effects of a major development in their neighborhoods must increasingly confront a government that bases its decisions to achieve growth in the city on high-end accommodations and amenities that target wealthier outsiders rather than their own needs.

A result has been an escalating amount of civic distrust and animosity towards local government officials and agencies on the part of neighborhood actors. Peter Eisinger points out two potential impacts of entertainment projects that today's city leaders devote more and more resources towards—such as sports stadiums and festive malls and events such as the Olympics—that rarely get acknowledged.[4] First, this allocation of resources skews the civic agenda away from existing municipal services and towards new services for the "visiting class" as well as for wealthier newcomers. Second, in doing so, city officials strain the existing bonds between the leaders and the led. When they target visiting spenders and outside investors, "local elites risk deepening distrust of government, creating deep polarities, and breeding cynicism among residents in the city."[5]

Eisinger refers mainly to large entertainment projects that require considerable political action and intervention on the part of municipal governments, such as decisions over the issuance of bonds or referenda over whether or not public subsidies will be spent on financing the building of stadiums or convention centers. But the case of downtown Manhattan's nightlife scenes presents the impacts that small-scale and uncoordinated economic developments have on local urban populations. Petitioning locally elected officials and government agencies are among the many actions that residents have taken to protest bars. Over time, as they came to realize that their efforts were being unheeded, residents developed strongly negative feelings towards their government representatives and the SLA officials who made liquor license decisions. As a result, some grew disenchanted with their leaders and disengaged from the process.

The politicians who are in a position to pressure such government agencies as the SLA and to create legislation that would protect their districts from such economic developments as nightlife scenes find themselves trapped between two imperatives. Elected officials in the city council and state legislature live among the people they represent. The issues they engage in are often extremely local, such as the condition of a park or a dangerous intersection for pedestrians. In many cases, they were actively involved in community organizing, public institutions, or civic associations in their neighborhoods (including community boards) before they ran for office. Being from and of their neighborhoods, local politicians often enter office with positive expectations and with the trust of people in their local communities. Their primary responsibility is then to serve the needs of their constituents. However, local elected officials are also well aware of the challenges that city leaders face in the postindustrial era. They know they must find ways of increasing revenue, population, and employment in their districts in an urban context in which consumption, knowledge, and specialized services drive growth. As a result, politicians know they must often face a choice between addressing the concerns of their constituents and encouraging the sources of economic growth that the latter opposes. Bars and other nightspots are examples of businesses that cover several bases of local growth: they pay high rents and high taxes (both normal business taxes and taxes on the alcoholic products they sell), they provide employment, they require costly permits and licenses, and they enliven and improve streets and neighborhoods, encouraging consumption and the growth of a commercial scene. Publicly, local elected officials address these twin imperatives by claiming the need to strike a balance between them, or to determine the "right" amount of nightlife in their districts. But their legislative initiatives do nothing to address or prevent the density levels that characterize nightlife scenes and instead target individual "problem owners." Furthermore, these initiatives are reactionary; they have only arisen out of extreme circumstances, namely grisly crimes that received considerable media attention. Downtown residents see these initiatives as halfhearted attempts by their elected leaders to appease their concerns. Instead of using their power to make changes to the way of life of their constituents, they favor a growth imperative that welcomes outsiders and newcomers to come into the neighborhood and consume.

This growth agenda has at the same time weakened the tools that residents have to fight back, namely forms of local democracy at citizens' disposal. I have here tried to expose the liquor license application process and the work of community boards as disempowering and conflict-generating forms of participatory democracy. Community boards were founded to grant citizens a role in the political process once votes had been cast, leaders elected, and commissioners and chairpersons appointed. They represent an opportunity for residents in a neighborhood to voice their concerns and suggestions in an organized fashion, and offer the promise that they can be involved in the decisions that will have an impact on their everyday lives. Who better to know whether an additional liquor license is needed in an area and should be granted for a space that once contained a shoe store than people who live there? Residents get involved in their local community boards—as both board members and attendees at meetings—for these reasons; they want to have a voice and make a difference. Politicians discuss, argue, and debate behind closed doors. But through community boards the people whom they represent have an opportunity to shape the conditions in their neighborhood.

But downtown residents found the promise of empowerment presented by CB3 and the liquor-licensing process to be unfulfilled. Liquor licenses are one of many local issues that community boards in New York City deal with, and that CB3 in particular must devote considerable time to handling. The ABC Law recognizes community boards as the appropriate local bodies for representing the interests of an area's population when it comes to liquor license decisions, just as New York City land use law recognizes them as the appropriate local bodies when it comes to such actions as rezoning. But without formal empowerment, such as in the form of voting or veto power, community boards, as examples of community-based advocacy organizations, lack the ability to truly serve as factors of change in their neighborhoods. They remain beholden to the decisions and agendas of local government officials and agencies. And without such formal empowerment, their deliberations become driven by a mutual distrust with bar owners and result in an abiding animosity between the two groups. An opportunity for local democracy turns into a discordant division.

What would a system of local democracy that did not just allow residents to voice their concerns in an advisory role but granted them the power to actually influence the conditions under which they must live their lives look like? And if people in neighborhoods like the Lower East Side, East Village, and Bowery, where disparate groups of stakeholders vie for and conflict over various resources, were to see such a system implemented, what would be the future direction of the upscaling process that has occurred since their gentrification? The answers to these questions might propose counterweights to the not-inevitable postindustrial growth agenda of commercially based consumption and services that currently play influential roles in the transformation of neighborhoods into upscale destinations through such developments as the proliferation of bars and formation of nightlife scenes.

Related to this skewed civic agenda are the strategies and policies law enforcement officials use to provide the feeling of safety in the postindustrial city. First used to combat disorderly conditions in the New York City subway system in the early 1990s, "broken-windows" policing escalated during Mayor Rudolph Giuliani's administration. Based on the theory of the same name, broken-windows policing attempts to reduce criminal activity by removing symbols of disorder from public spaces, such as graffiti, loitering, and the homeless. The NYPD also implemented the CompStat system during this period to track crime more efficiently. The Bloomberg administration in the 2000s and 2010s continued these policies and expanded them in two key ways. First has been the implementation of the 311 system that links civilian complaints about quality of life and other issues to CompStat, and thereby to local precincts. And second has been the founding of the stop-and-frisk program that give officers the discretion to stop and search a citizen in public based on the former's reasonable suspicion that the latter has committed or may commit a crime. Both broken-windows policing and the stop-and-frisk program have come under scrutiny regarding their effectiveness in reducing crime and their potential to unfairly target people from minority communities by granting the police great discretion to determine which actions qualify as "disorderly" or "reasonably suspicious."[6] But they remain foundational to police work in New York City.

Efficient technology- and statistics-driven policing has come to characterize law enforcement in cities across the United States. Although these policies were never meant for popular nightlife scenes that attract well-to-do revelers, their implementation has meant that the police are held accountable for all sorts of complaints and issues that residents in the city make. In my research I found that the police in downtown Manhattan are forced to deal with the quality-of-life complaints against nightlife, which distracts them from their desire to focus on "real" crimes. Instead of addressing quality-of-life complaints directly, such as by putting more officers in problem areas, local police precincts rely on a variety of private strategies, each of which has become common in a wide range of contexts in postindustrial cities. Namely, the police encourage bar owners to use security cameras, identification scanners, and private security personnel (bouncers) to monitor their patrons and record evidence of any criminal activity. Owners who do not comply with these suggestions risk straining their relationship with the precinct. And those who continue to operate bars that receive regular complaints, which mar a precinct's statistical record, and do not take proper steps to address them, become labeled as problems. Downtown Manhattan's disruptive nightlife scenes represent a nuisance for the police by presenting them with minor issues that take up a disproportionate amount of resources and result in an excessive amount of scrutiny. Police expect owners themselves to find private solutions to remedy the conditions that arise from the growth imperative that constructed the dense nightlife scene.

In 2012, 87 percent of people who were stopped and frisked in New York City were black or Latino, while blacks and Latinos only make up 51.4 percent of the city's population. Under accusations of racial profiling, the NYPD has countered that minority neighborhoods represent the places in the city where the most crime occurs, which it claims explains their targeting of these communities. Rather than carrying lethal or illegal weapons or having an outstanding warrant, the possession of small amounts of drugs is the basis of arrest under the stop-and-frisk program more than any other offense. Despite representing a source of considerable disorderly activity and furtive illegal drug use, revelers in downtown Manhattan are not police targets. Other than two occasions when I witnessed police officers write tickets for misdemeanor criminal behavior for nightlife revelers on the street (one for urinating in public, the other for carrying an open beer bottle), the only times I saw the police take clear action during my fieldwork was when they removed or arrested a homeless person from the street (a regular occurrence), when they monitored and accompanied a planned protest, or when they spoke to bouncers to ask them how the night was going or to question them about a previous incident.[8] The police often obtain information from bars, either through bouncers or from surveillance cameras, about patrons who engage in unlawful behavior (especially drug activity) for their investigations. But they largely allow people to carry on the regular activities of drinking, noise-making, and drug use. The successful downtown nightlife scenes serve as unexpected examples of how contemporary policing policies and programs are implemented unevenly in the contemporary city and in ways that reveal some of today's enduring urban inequalities.

Along with revealing a civic agenda of unequal growth and uneven enforcement, the upscaling of downtown and the rise of exclusive conditions in neighborhoods show the fragility and malleability of former symbols of local stability. Many nightspots that once served as anchors for local socializing for the neighborhoods' diverse populations have either closed or changed, while nightspots with specialized themes that attract more homogeneous populations have replaced them. Earlier, in the chapter that deals mainly with Milano's, Leslie, one of its bartenders, derides young customers who enter the bar with the idea that it will be a dive. Given the media attention that bars like Milano's receive as vestiges of a lost era and survivors of a great transformation, it really is no wonder that newcomers go to the bar with preconceived notions and expectations of what they will find inside. And the experience of their first visit does not disappoint, as they immediately confront dusty shelves, faded black-and-white photographs, yellowed newspaper clippings, and, at certain times, old men. They then peruse the jukebox's appropriate offerings (Willie Nelson, Johnny Cash, the Pogues), learn about the cheap prices and alcohol selections, and stare through dim lighting. Milano's contains enough of the elements that construct the dive bar idea for patrons to recognize and be satisfied with.

The labels that are commonly used to describe local nightspots in nightlife scenes downtown and throughout New York City—dive bar, cocktail bar, lounge, or Irish bar, for example—turn bars in residential neighborhoods into ideas, sometimes before they have an opportunity to become actual places. New bar owners spend considerable time, money, and energy on the design of the actual physical spaces for their bars as well as on the concepts, themes, and special products that will circulate through local media, social media, and social networks. Some promote notions of community while recognizing the impossibility of relying chiefly on local clientele and designing their bars to attract a very specific population. Others purposefully shun local clienteles, preferring upscale crowds. Fundamentally it is a group of people's social attachment to and social construction of a place, rather than a place's ability to evoke a certain set of ideas of place, that make a bar a neighborhood bar. The upscale destination bars in downtown Manhattan resemble the changes that make the neighborhood a place to be for sets of elite consumers. But in doing so they deemphasize the importance of rootedness for places like bars.

Here again rises the issue of nostalgia as a key characteristic of social life in today's postindustrial city. Many people lament that key neighborhood hangouts in downtown Manhattan have vanished and that those that are still around have changed beyond what they remember. These feelings are often intertwined with residents' general feelings of their neighborhood's gentrification. Bars like CBGB and Brownies, which fostered the neighborhood's music scenes, have no place in today's downtown (although the idea of CBGB lives on through merchandise). But this fact does not mean that their replacements lack the ability to integrate strangers or foster a sense of place and community among patrons. Many new bars in the neighborhood have achieved a status as places of great meaning for revelers, who go to them regularly. These places must cope with transience, just as bars from earlier eras had to, although the transience they confront concerns the pressures from shifting tastes rather than those from demographic turnover and gentrification. The point is not that downtown's bars from earlier eras were places of greater creativity and meaning than those today. The point is that the basis for creativity and meaning has become less about a neighborhood's ability to foster local socializing and more about its ability to contain popular and desirable ideas that consumers will continue to want to seek out. In other words, life in the increasingly upscale and exclusive gentrified neighborhood favors the rootless ideas behind today's taste communities rather than the rooted products of their people.

The downtown lifestyle of New York City's recent history will not return to the Lower East Side, East Village, or Bowery in the foreseeable future. An upscale way of life that combines exclusive cultures at escalating prices for distinct groups of urbanites is replacing it. The idea of downtown Manhattan as a place that cultivates creative products from intimate levels of neighborhood-based interactions has disappeared from the cultural maps of New York City, with mere memories filling the void. More importantly, downtown Manhattan's removal from the list of places in New York City for low-income populations to live and survive is intertwined with this reality. What happens when an urban neighborhood of diverse groups becomes increasingly upscale? Neighborhoods open for some but close for others, bars proliferate and thrive but their roots grow weaker, and a place becomes forever transformed. With upscaling comes conflict as well as ephemerality, as anchors of stability lose their strength to ground people amid their turbulent surroundings. The view from the bar, an unserious setting, lets us witness the action, a drink at a time.

METHODOLOGICAL APPENDIX

STUDYING THE SOCIAL ECOSYSTEM OF BARS

AS WITH MUCH QUALITATIVE RESEARCH, the disparities between what I expected to find in downtown Manhattan and what I actually found guided me along many of this book's analytical paths. I began the project because I did not expect to find a bar like Milano's, which maintained a strong connection to the past, in a neighborhood that had transformed as much as downtown had. I was drawn by my inquiry inside the bar to the surrounding area. As I expanded my research and examined other downtown bars and their nightlife scenes, I did not expect to find that residents still protested symbols of gentrification long after the process had made its mark. As I got to know owners and their bars better, and saw how much they focused on being destinations for visitors, I expected neither the former to demonstrate strong pro-community attitudes nor the latter to attract specialized taste communities that stretched beyond their neighborhood's boundaries. And the attitudes of residents and owners towards government officials (the SLA, local politicians, and the police) led me to examine these actors, whom I did not expect to have played such an integral role in the nightlife scene's growth and regulation.

By taking me to the multiple actors who play a role in constructing and regulating downtown Manhattan's nightlife scenes, or whose lives are influenced by it in some way, my research methods eventually led me to the realization that I was examining the social ecosystem surrounding bars. My project was more than just a bar study. Instead, I examined a wide range of groups to understand some of the issues of what I believe is a fundamental upscaling process occurring in today's postindustrial cities. In this appendix, I want to recount the specific work that I did to collect the data upon which this book's analysis is based.

As I have discussed, my fieldwork started in a single bar, Milano's, in February 2004. For more than two years I went to the bar regularly, usually three times a week for at least an hour and a half per visit. There were some weeks when I could not go to the bar at all due to my schedule or because I was out of town. I varied the days of the week and times of day when I went to the bar, to check for variation. The people at the bar conferred "regular of the bar" status upon me, since I had developed relationships with several customers and bartenders.

I also went to the bar at times when I knew people with whom I was friendly would not be there, such as later in the night. I took notes as surreptitiously as possible, in a notebook or on cocktail napkins and coasters, which I sometimes expanded during trips to the bathroom.[1] I then typed them up upon returning home or the next morning. At this phase in my research, which took place when I was a young graduate student, I did not use an audio recorder while in the field. By the end of my fieldwork at Milano's, I had accumulated more than 400 pages of notes; conducted eighteen formal interviews with customers, past and present bartenders, and the two owners (all of which I recorded and transcribed); and documented countless conversations and interactions.

By mid-2006, I was prepared to examine downtown Manhattan's nightlife scenes and began going to other bars and talking to owners, bartenders, and customers. During an interview, an owner who had recently opened his bar casually mentioned the issues he had with his neighbors when he was applying for his liquor license. I inquired further, and after some research learned that the law required bar owners to apply to their local community boards before they applied to the SLA for ultimate liquor license approval. I decided to attend that September's meeting. As I have discussed, most of the important discussions and decisions over liquor licensing occur at the committee meeting, while final decisions are made at the full board. Full board meetings last approximately four or five hours while liquor-licensing committee meetings start at 6:30 p.m. and run well past midnight, sometimes until 2 or 3 a.m. I attended a total of forty-eight of these meetings from September 2006 to December 2008.[2] I also attended seventeen other meetings in downtown Manhattan, such as town halls, public forums, and local community group meetings. I used an audio recorder at some meetings in order to document the dialogue accurately. Otherwise, as in my research in the bars, I relied on written field notes that I typed up at a later time. My research at these meetings resulted in an additional 400 pages of typed notes.

While CB3 meetings are not representative of downtown Manhattan, I argue that they provided me with a necessary setting for fieldwork because of its formal roles as a public forum for residents to express their attitudes towards bars and changes in their neighborhood and as a sanctioned body in the liquor-licensing process. The people whom I did not see at CB3 meetings but whom I regularly saw on the streets, such as Latino residents, led me to seek them out for their perspectives on nightlife, gentrification, and the neighborhood. Since their meetings are open to the public, I did not have trouble gaining access to or embedding myself in the settings of community boards or other community groups. In addition to making observations, I had numerous conversations with residents and bars owners at these meetings. I would usually go up to them casually before meetings started, during lulls, or after their item was finished; introduce myself; and simply talk with them. Since emotions often ran high, I sometimes decided to approach certain bar owners a few days after the meeting, by going to their bars. Board members, who attended every meeting, came to recognize me and would ask me how my project was going. I conducted in-depth formal interviews with several of the residents and owners I met at these meetings as well as with community board members to learn more about their lives and feelings towards nightlife and the neighborhood. From observing the interactions between these groups and from my interviews, I was able to discern the conflicting discourses that they use in their conceptions of their neighborhood. I recognize that focusing on people and activities at community meetings carries limitations to an analysis on neighborhoods. This book surely would be different had I chosen different settings. However, my choices have revealed groups, relationships, and interactions that otherwise would have gone unnoticed.

I targeted a few different actors to learn more about liquor licensing, the growth of the nightlife scene, and the politics of nightlife. I visited the Harlem office of the New York State Liquor Authority to speak to some of its officials about licensing and attend its biweekly full board meetings and hearings where members discuss licensing matters. I attended six of the SLA's full board meetings and two hearings between October 2006 and January 2007. I supplemented this by formally interviewing the chair of the authority and four of its employees at its headquarters in Albany. I also interviewed representatives of local elected officials who either represent downtown Manhattan in the New York City Council and New York State Legislature or represent other areas in the city and have been active participants in the politics of nightlife, whether by serving on task forces, writing letters on behalf of residents, or drafting legislation. These local politicians regularly attend CB3 and other local meetings, where I observed their interactions with residents. These endeavors gave me a broad view of the local government's feelings towards nightlife and the role these actors play in growing and regulating nightlife scenes.

In the two years following my fieldwork at Milano's, I conducted participant observation research at ten other bars in downtown Manhattan to learn more about the people who produce and consume at contemporary nightspots. These establishments included other old neighborhood bars, high-end cocktail bars, craft beer bars, performance venues, and hotel bars. Although I did not spend as much time in them as I did at Milano's, I spoke with and got to know their owners/managers and bartenders well enough for them to share with me their thoughts on downtown Manhattan, their bars, and residents. I also met many revelers from my fieldwork sessions in these bars.

In expanding my fieldwork, I wanted to understand the conditions of downtown's public spaces at night, which is the main source of quality-of-life complaints from residents. I therefore conducted participant observation from April to August 2008 on streets throughout downtown Manhattan, focusing specifically on three areas with dense concentrations of bars: Ludlow Street by Stanton and Rivington Streets; Avenue A and Seventh Street; and St. Mark's Place. In these places I observed a considerable amount of nightlife behavior and spoke with numerous revelers and residents, including Bob and the group he hung out with across the street from Tompkins Square Park. Meeting longtime residents like Bob gave me insight into the attitudes of those people who do not attend community board meetings towards their neighborhood. I also spent a lot of time on the streets observing and speaking with bouncers, particularly at two bars, which showed me how private strategies of nightlife regulation work. Overall, my fieldwork in the nightlife scenes' bars and streets expanded my understanding of who was involved in the cultural production of downtown nightlife and of the sorts of activities that occurred there at night.

My interest in studying bouncers stemmed from what I learned from the police. I attended thirty-eight of the monthly community council meetings of the Seventh and Ninth Precincts of the NYPD in order to understand how contemporary nightlife is enforced.[3] Like the community board, the community council meetings provide the public with a forum for expressing their concerns over neighborhood issues that relate to law enforcement. As I have discussed, bar and nightlife problems constitute a majority of the complaints that both precincts receive. At these meetings police try to mediate between owners and residents, address resident concerns, and discuss some of their nightlife policing strategies. The people at the Seventh Precinct also permitted me to attend the special meeting that it holds periodically for bar owners, as well as a nightlife security class that was held jointly by the NYPD and the New York Nightlife Association, the lobbying group for owners, to educate bouncers in police protocols (I discuss one of these meetings in chapter 5's opening vignette).

I relied on oral histories from interviews with longtime residents as well as archival materials that I requested from the community board to construct a historical narrative on downtown's transformation, the nightlife scenes' growth, and the meanings that people attach to both. I also used the *Cole Directory*, a business and phone listing that has been published annually since 1947, as a resource for tracing the growth of the nightlife scene across time and space and for verifying statements and claims made by participants who relied on their memories.[4] For example, when I asked residents when they recall bars proliferating and becoming a problem in their neighborhood, I compared their recollections with the information I obtained from the *Directory* to test the former's validity. Such directories are excellent tools in qualitative research for "triangulating"—that is, validating by utilizing alternative methods—sources of data and providing an accurate account of an area's transformation, while providing insight into people's perspectives towards this transformation.

In addition to four years of fieldwork and numerous informal conversations with people in these various settings, I also conducted 119 formal interviews for this project. I interviewed: 44 nightlife producers (20 owners, 20 bartenders, 2 real estate agents who work with nightlife establishments, an attorney who specializes in liquor licenses, and a representative from the New York Nightlife Association); 17 revelers of the nightlife scene; 29 residents (early gentrifiers and lifelong residents, some of whom are community leaders members of the community board or other local groups; neighborhood activists; and small business owners); 14 local government officials and representatives; and 15 enforcement actors (3 police officers and 12 people in private security, 2 of whom were former police officers).

I audio-recorded all interviews with participants' permission and transcribed them later for accuracy, except for four that I conducted with people via email (two of which resulted in further face-to-face conversations). They lasted between a half hour and over three hours and were semi-structured and conversational. Participants and I scheduled interviews in advance and at convenient public locations (bars, cafés, restaurants) as well as in private settings such as offices and apartments.[5] Some, such as those with bartenders and bouncers, took place at the field site. For the project in general, in situ conversations with participants were quite common. Very often I would see residents and owners in streets and at meetings, and I would see bartenders, bouncers, and owners in their bars after interviewing them, which gave me the opportunity to talk with them more. These informal follow-ups furthered my understanding of their lives, the neighborhood, and nightlife and allowed me to test the validity of their statements in interviews with their behavior in real settings. I use quotation marks for dialogue throughout the book, regardless of whether or not I audio-recorded a conversation. I only present quotes from people that were not audio-recorded in cases when I was able to write down their words in my notes with considerable accuracy. I respect scholars who choose to indicate in the text when they use transcribed dialogue verses when they rely on re-created conversations.[6] However, given the limitations I placed on my use of such re-creations in this book, my confidence in the accuracy of my note-taking, and the familiarity I established with people's speech patterns in my field settings, I am confident in my decision to use quotation marks consistently.

For this book I changed only some names of people and places (i.e., bars). I honored the requests of participants who did not want their real name to appear in the final version. In cases when I do use a participant's real name, I sometimes contacted them as a courtesy to make sure they agreed to being represented as such. However, I have also included the real names of people at my own discretion, which I have based on such factors as the frequency with which their name is used in the book, their status in the public sphere (i.e., if they are public figures), and my ability to successfully get in touch with them. Occasionally I have altered certain details of people and bars, such as their precise location and some identifying characteristics. Overall, I feel I have provided more than sufficient detail and information for scholars to replicate my study in downtown Manhattan or in other neighborhoods in New York and other postindustrial cities, which is the central purpose of discussing methods in appendices or methodological sections in introductory chapters.

Finally, like other scholars who have conducted research in bars, I regularly consumed alcohol—in small quantities—and used it to start conversations, blend into settings, and further my relationships with customers, bartenders, and owners.[7] In short, consuming alcohol is invaluable to the researcher gathering data in a bar setting.

NOTES

PREFACE

1 See Abu-Lughod (1994), Becker (2009), Cahill (2000; 2007), Martinez (2010), Maffi (1995), Mele (2000), Sites (2003), and Smith (1996) for a sampling of these studies.

2 Grazian 2003.

3 Grazian 2008.

4 Lloyd 2006.

5 See Hadfield (2006; 2009) and Hobbs et al. (2000; 2003) for recent studies on how large contemporary nightlife scenes create criminogenic environments that overburden local law enforcement.

INTRODUCTION: NIGHT AND DAY

1 Sheri Cavan (1966) describes bars as places where people expect unserious behavior to take place. See Johan Huizinga's ([1950] 1971) classic discussion of play as voluntary behavior separate from ordinary life.

2 Most notable of the recent studies on bars are the works of David Grazian (2003; 2008) and Richard Lloyd (2006), discussed in the preface. These works are part of a long tradition in ethnographic research of work on social worlds in bars. Scholars have notably examined social life in African American bars (Anderson 1978; Bell 1983; May 2001), working-class bars (Kornblum 1974; LeMasters, 1975; Lindquist 2002), and dance clubs (Anderson, 2009b; Cressey 1932; Malbon 1999).

3 I derive the concept of the "social ecosystem" in neighborhoods from Sharon Zukin's (2012) use of the term in reference to the role of shopping streets in the construction of an urban cultural ecosystem.

4 See Hannigan's (1998) discussion of the importance of safety in "urban entertainment destinations" in today's "fantasy city." See Sorkin's (1992) volume for its criticisms of how the city has become like a sanitized "amusement park." And see Hadfield (2006; 2009) and Hobbs et al. (2003) for analyses on the criminogenic environments that large nighttime economies create and that local municipalities make efforts to curtail.

5 Several scholars have shown how today's city leaders strive for their cities to have both daytime and nighttime amusements for residents and tourists (Hannigan 1998; Heath 1997; Roberts and Turner 2005). Phil Hadfield (2006) has examined the politics behind the United Kingdom's deregulation of liquor licensing that allows establishments to obtain a license to serve alcohol twenty-four hours a day.

6 See Chatterton and Hollands (2003) for an examination of the use of the nighttime economy as a means of center-city revitalization in the United Kingdom.

7   When they coined this term, Richard Lloyd and Terry Nichols Clark (2001) argued that it represented a more accurate description of the contemporary city's growth agenda than the classic "growth machine" model proposed by Logan and Molotch (1987). In his edited volume, Clark (2004) and other authors expand the concept and support it with considerable quantitative data that show the importance of entertainment spaces and activities in influencing urban growth.

8   For studies that have examined the role of commercial establishments in gentrification processes, see Deener 2007; Levy and Cybriwsky 1980; Lloyd 2006; Patch 2008; Zukin et al. 2009.

9   Sharon Zukin (1983) documents the important role that artists played in revalorizing the manufacturing district of SoHo in the 1960s and 1970s. Writing about the same time period, Richard Kostelanetz (2003) recounts the importance of a new eatery for members of the "artists' colony," while also recalling how the owner of a local working-class Italian bar accepted the creative newcomers.

10 See Richard Lloyd's (2006) discussion of the importance of bars for artists in Wicker Park.

11 Throughout the book I refer to the downtown neighborhoods collectively as an entertainment district in the singular, since the neighborhoods are contiguous and part of the same community district, which I explain later in the Introduction. But I consider each neighborhood to consist of one or multiple nightlife scenes, which have geographic components to their activities. See Silver et al.'s (2010) examination of urban scenes.

12 Grazian 2008; 2009.

13 See note 7 in this chapter for a discussion of Logan and Molotch (1987) and Lloyd and Clark (2001).

14 See Hannigan's (1998) examination of how local governments partner with private actors to create "urban entertainment destinations." Also see Gotham's (2007) analysis of how the French Quarter became a tourist destination in New Orleans.

15 These policies largely stem from Wilson and Kelling's (1982) now classic article on the "broken-windows" theory. For further elaboration on the theory, see Kelling and Coles (1998). For critiques of its application to homeless populations, see Duneier (1999) and Vitale (2008).

16 See Clay (1979) and Lees (2000) for discussions of gentrification's "stages" of development. Hackworth and Smith (2001) refer to three "waves" of gentrification, the third of which is large-scale financial investment in gentrifying neighborhoods. Building from this argument, Lees (2003) refers to "super-gentrification" as the intensified transformation of already gentrified and affluent neighborhoods by a new generation of wealthy gentrifiers (also see Butler and Lees 2006). While they are in an advanced form of gentrification, I do not characterize the downtown Manhattan neighborhoods in my study as undergoing super-gentrification because middle- and lower-income groups continue to live there and wealthier groups are not replacing existing less wealthy groups. As I argue later in the introduction, diversity remains an important characteristic of these neighborhoods.

17 See Deener (2012) and Lloyd (2006) for analyses on how commercial establishments catering to non-locals opened in the gentrified neighborhoods of Venice Beach and Wicker Park, respectively.

18 I explain my exact geographic focus at the end of the introduction.

19 I conducted these counts on foot during the summer of 2007. I walked each street and block and coded every business as either "bars," "restaurants," "fast food," or "other." By "bars" I mean places that primarily served alcohol. They include places for which food sales were ancillary, music venues, and dance clubs. By "restaurants" I mean places that primarily serve food, although most restaurants serve alcohol of some sort in the neighborhood, and some operate more like a bar or club after a certain hour. I included fast-food establishments such as pizzerias in my counts because of the large number of small eateries that have opened alongside nightspots to accommodate the scenes' revelers. I only included places like cafés if their method of operation was as a nightspot in the evenings. These numbers differ from the liquor-licensing statistics that I will discuss later in this book, because an address for establishments like bars, restaurants, or nightclubs may hold multiple licenses if the business has more than one bar (standup or service) on the premises. I recognize a limitation of my counting includes businesses without an apparent storefront, such as places located in basements or on second floors. I also tried to determine if a business that was not open was closed for the day or permanently closed by returning to its block at different times during the day on other days.

20 Grazian 2008; 2009.

21 McSorley's was also immortalized as a classic New York City saloon by writer Joseph Mitchell (1993) in his well-known and highly regarded *New Yorker* essay from 1941.

22 See Ferguson's (1998; 2006) discussion of taste communities in reference to the development of a national French cuisine.

23 This book's geographic focus—neighborhoods within Manhattan Community District 3—consists of thirty census tracts, with only one occupying more than one community district.

24 In his well-known examination of the East Village, Neil Smith (1996) applies his "rent-gap" theory to explain how gentrification in the neighborhood advanced. He argues that gentrification occurs once areas have undergone capital disinvestment followed by reinvestment in real estate. Smith charts this process as it proceeded eastward from western avenues and streets and southward from the East Village area. With some exceptions (such as the Bowery, which gentrified more recently than other areas to its east), the East Village gentrified in this geographic manner. It is not surprising then that the more western areas, which gentrified earlier, contain the wealthier census tracts. Smith also regards Avenue D, the easternmost avenue in the neighborhood, as a natural stopping point for gentrification's advancement, not only because of the East River, but also because of its large row of public housing projects that extend along lower Manhattan's eastern and southeastern shoreline and prevent reinvestment from occurring. In fact, some popular writers have pointed out that once they ran out of affordable places in the east of the neighborhood to move into, young hip urbanites essentially hopped over Avenue D and the housing projects to Williamsburg, located immediately across the river in Brooklyn.

25 Smith 1996.

26 Melbin 1987.

27 See Sharman and Sharman's (2008) research on nighttime workers for whom these meanings are the reverse.

28 Melbin 1987, 15.
29 See Christopher Mele's (2000) discussion of the history of working-class culture in the neighborhood.
30 I discuss my research methods in greater detail in the appendix.
31 "Noho" and "SoHo" refer to "North" and "South of Houston," respectively, "NoLIta" refers to "North of Little Italy," and "TriBeCa" refers to "Triangle Below Canal Street."
32 Mele 2000.
33 Jacobs 1961, 121–29.
34 Small 2009.
35 Becker (1996) makes a similar point in his piece on the epistemology of qualitative research.
36 Small 2009: 17, 21–22; also see Mitchell (1983), as well as Katz's (1997) discussion of "deviant" populations as a warrant for ethnographic research.

CHAPTER 1: THE BOWERY AND ITS BARS

1 Michael T. Kaufman, "Last Call Sounds for Last Gin Mill on the Bowery," *New York Times*, December 25, 1993.
2 Grazian 2003; 2008.
3 Grazian 2008, 13.
4 Grazian 2009, 910 (emphasis in original).
5 Anderson 2009a; 2009b.
6 Oldenburg (1989) refers to such public gathering spaces as "third places," where people can experience forms of Simmel's concept of "pure sociability."
7 See Sanderson 2009.
8 Technically, Bowery ends at Fourth Street, where Cooper Square begins. Originally, Bowery ran to Union Square at Fourteenth Street, and served as the westernmost border for the historical Lower East Side. However, in 1849 wealthy residents of the Union Square area changed the name of their section of Bowery from St. Mark's Place to Fourteenth St. to Fourth Avenue, with Cooper Square (Fourth Street to St. Mark's Place) serving as a buffer zone, in an effort to dissociate it from the lowlier working-class and immigrant reputation of the Bowery (Anbinder 2001). Insofar as this section of the continuous street did not undergo the skid-row transformation as its southern parts did the following century, the name change was successful. Today, Bowery serves as the westernmost border for the Lower East Side and half of the East Village.
9 Whitman 1996, 1210.
10 Whitman 1996, 1241.
11 Caldwell 2005, 112; also see Anbinder 2001; Sante 1991.
12 Maffi 1995.
13 Dowling 2007; Heap 2009; Sante 1991.
14 Chauncey 1994, 33–45.
15 See Anderson (1923). In his account, Anderson, who was once a hobo himself, relied very much on his own experiences. This was the first published book on urban life to come out of the famed "Chicago School" at the University of Chicago.

16 Lutz 2006, 161.

17 Bendiner 1961, 82–83.

18 Estimates vary depending on data sources, such as the number of men officially registered in lodging houses and missions and whether or not locations near but not on the Bowery are counted (Bahr 1973).

19 White 1948, 43–44. Founded in 1736, Bellevue is the oldest public hospital in the United States. It has long been known for treating the poor and uninsured.

20 Bahr 1973.

21 Bendiner 1961, 39.

22 Bahr 1967.

23 Isay and Abramson 2000.

24 Bahr 1967.

25 See Charles Grutzner, "New Name Urged for Third Avenue," *New York Times*, February 7, 1956.

26 The Bowery also features a significant concentration of jewelry stores in its southern section near Canal and Grand Streets. These stores first opened in the early twentieth century and proliferated when Jewish diamond dealers came to New York after fleeing from the Nazis. Today they are located within an expanded Chinatown and run by Chinese merchants. See Jennifer 8. Lee, "No Rings, Brass or Not, for Chinatown Jewelers," *New York Times*, June 29, 2002.

27 Cohen and Sokolovsky 1989.

28 Barbara Basler, "With Skid Row Fading, Change Sweeps the Bowery," *New York Times*, July 29, 1986.

29 Kostelanetz 2003; Zukin 1983.

30 Hager 1986; Taylor 2006.

31 See Deutsch and Ryan (1984) for a discussion of the relationship between art and gentrification during the 1980s on the Lower East Side.

32 Bahr (1973, 141) cites this number, which comes from an unpublished memorandum by George Nash of Columbia University's "Bowery Project" of the 1960s.

33 These are only totals for Bowery the street, not the Bowery area, as George Nash and the Bowery Project's bar totals indicate. Additionally, from searching in the *Cole Directory* I am also unable to determine how many of these bars at the time had patrons who were exclusively Bowery men and were therefore "Bowery bars."
      There were also two documented barber colleges open on the street in 1975. As Bahr (1973) demonstrates, places like barber colleges, as well as thrift shops, pawnshops, and restaurants, are secondary institutions for skid-row inhabitants, providing them with free or cheap services and goods. Both of these colleges were closed by 1985.

34 Michael T. Kaufman, "Last Call Sounds for Last Gin Mill on the Bowery," *New York Times*, December 25, 1993.

35 See Smith (1996) and Sites (2003) for examinations of the city's acquisition of buildings and properties.

36 Kate Millett and her fellow residents fought a battle to remain in the building and even applied to have that region of the Bowery granted historic landmark status. They, along with the tenants of three neighboring buildings, were eventually evicted. See Monte Williams, "Oh, to Be Down and Out Living on the Bowery; Artists' Cheap Lofts, Found Decades Ago, Are Threatened by Development Project," *New York Times*, May 13, 1999.

37 Developer AvalonBay Communities, Inc., has built similar luxury communities across the United States. Avalon Chrystie Place, on Houston and Chrystie Street, is a block from Avalon Bowery Place.

38 Jesse McKinley, "Along the Bowery, Skid Row Is on the Skids," *New York Times*, October 13, 2002.

39 Mission Bar later became a Moroccan fusion restaurant and cocktail lounge called Katra.

40 Excerpted from http://www.danielnyc.com/dbgb.html#dbgb_private, accessed August 7, 2009.

41 The restaurant's name was originally written in the same font used by the legendary rock club. At its first liquor license meeting at Manhattan Community Board 3, a legal representative for the club's owner, Hilly Kristal, declared their intention to sue Mr. Boulud for infringing on trademarks if he did not cease and desist. She added that Mr. Boulud was misusing the meaning behind CBGB and would be profiting off of the East Village image that CBGB helped to create.

42 CBGB's landlord was the Bowery Residents Committee, a social service, housing, and drug treatment agency that has been open since 1971. The Bowery Residents Committee was one of the few new charitable missions to open on the Bowery during this period when its demographics were shifting. See Jon Pareles, "End of a Punk-Rock Institution Whose Attitude Won't Die," *New York Times*, October 16, 2006.

43 Zukin 2010.

44 Carol Vogel, "On the Bowery, a New Home for New Art," *New York Times*, March 28, 2007.

45 Florida 2002; Grazian 2008.

46 Very few Italian residents remain in the area that was once called Little Italy. A number of blocks on Mulberry Street still have Italian restaurants and shops, which cater mainly to visitors and tourists, and several more are scattered on side streets. The northern section of what was once Little Italy is now called "NoLIta," which stands for "North of Little Italy." The section resembles SoHo, immediately to the west, in terms of its upscale clothing boutiques and nightspots and its expensive real estate. The southern sections of what used to be Little Italy are now part of Chinatown.

47 These varying explanations are consistent with those documented by Bahr 1973; Bahr and Caplow 197 4; Bendiner 1961; Bogue 1963; and Cohen and Sokolovsky 1989; as well as many of the personal accounts documented in Isay and Abramson 2000. Incidentally, one of the men depicted in this latter text was a longtime regular at Milano's before his death.

 As with all people in this book, I made efforts to verify the accuracy of certain information by speaking with third parties and researching places, names, events, and incidents. More than most people, perhaps, Bowery men had fuzzy memories and tended to exaggerate, make up, and hide certain facts about their lives. I only include stories from the past about them, the bar, and the neighborhood that I could verify. See Duneier (1999) for his discussion of the ethnographer's responsibility to validate sources.

48   Tommy Milano passed away before I started this project. I was also unable to locate any of his family.

49   Denis is referring to Camp LaGuardia, a shelter for the homeless that the city government (not the church) owned in Orange County, approximately seventy miles north of New York City. In 2006 the Department of Homeless Services closed Camp LaGuardia, which was the city's largest shelter for homeless adults and had been in operation since the Depression in order to free up its funding for new initiatives. The decision also came after many years of local complaints about the residents criminalizing their quiet town. See Chelsea Rudman, "Invisible New Yorkers," *New York Press*, vol. 20, no. 3, January 17–23, 2007; Nina Bernstein, "An Uneasy Coexistence; Tensions between Town and Shelter Flow Both Ways," *New York Times*, May 4, 1999.

50   Phil's comment is not entirely accurate. Bartenders regularly cut off customers who drink too much, and sometimes ask them to leave if they become rude or unruly. They can return if they apologize and behave themselves. There are cases of regulars who no longer go to the bar when a particular bartender is working because she will no longer serve him or her. They simply avoid going to the bar when they know that particular bartender is there.

51   See Hochschild's (1983) influential work on emotional labor.

52   In her classic bar ethnography, Sheri Cavan (1966) uses the term "home territory bar" to describe such settings. Ray Oldenburg's (1989) well-known "third place" thesis also refers to those public gathering places that are regarded by their regulars as like second homes. Also see Katovich and Reese (1987).

53   See Lloyd's (2006) discussion of the importance of nightlife spaces for the formation of the artists' scene in Wicker Park.

54   Katovich and Reese (1987) include "irregular regulars" as one of the identities that customers had constructed at the bar they study, although several of the customers at Milano's also use this term.

55   Chatterton and Hollands 2003, 5.

56   Grazian (2008, 59–62) discusses strategies of staged authenticity, such as not cleaning bathrooms, that some bars engage in to appear grittier than they actually should be.

57   Mitchell 2003, 3.

58   See Grazian 2003; and Joe Bob Briggs, "Last Call," *Time Out New York*, no. 493, March 10–16, 2005.

59   Lofland 1973, 15–16.

60   Tom Waits is a singer-songwriter who regularly sings about drinking and alcohol through a highly distinct raspy, growling voice that has been shaped by whiskey and cigarettes. His lyrics also often create smoky, boozy landscapes for roguish characters that blend well with the image of the dark dive bar.

61   During my research, Milano's only had women bartenders. The only one who did not work at night was Magdalene, who was the only bartender in her forties. The rest were in their twenties or thirties and either worked only at night or split their schedule between the night and the day.

62   Much of what Tugboat told me about himself I had to verify with several people, and some of it I could not verify completely.

CHAPTER 2: GROWING NIGHTLIFE SCENES

1   Councilwoman Mendez's district extends outside of the East Village and covers a wide swath of territory up to Thirty-fifth Street. There were representatives and residents present from that area at the forum, but most were from the East Village.

2   I obtained these numbers from the *Cole Directory*. Published since 1947 by Cole Information Services, the *Cole Directory* is an annual listing of names, phone numbers, and addresses for residents and businesses in major markets across the United States. I searched through the directories from these years and counted the number of listed bars on streets within the study area. I only counted those businesses that were clearly identified as bars. I did not count those I was unsure of, and the directory admits to an 85–90 percent accuracy rate. Therefore, these numbers are conservative estimates intended to be illustrative of the area's transformation.

3   I obtained this number from the State Liquor Authority on April 14, 2008. Most of these establishments have one of two types of liquor licenses—418 are OP, or "full on-premise" licenses, which allow the purchase and consumption of liquor, wine, and beer; and 218 are RW, or "restaurant wine" licenses, which allow the purchase and consumption of only beer and wine. The remaining liquor licenses break down as follows: 27 EB ("eating place beer"), 6 HL ("hotel liquor"), 13 TW ("tavern wine"), 7 RL ("restaurant liquor"), 3 TL ("tavern liquor"). The differences between the types of licenses are based on what type of alcohol they are allowed to serve and what type of business they are.

4   Data from http://www.city-data.com/top2/z52.html, accessed March 9, 2009.

5   Downtown residents regularly cite these statistics in their protests against bars.

6   Smith 1996, 67.

7   As discussed in an earlier footnote, Avenue D is a clear boundary for the nightlife scene because of the large public housing projects between its eastern side and the river.

8   See Brown-Saracino (2009) for an example of a study that counters Smith's interpretation of gentrifiers. And see her edited volume (2010) on debates in gentrification research that provides discussions on different types of gentrifiers.

9   Section 52–61 of the zoning resolution states that R5, R6, and R7 (during the development of the nightlife scene, most of the East Village was R7–2 zoning districts as well as Historic Districts as designated by the Landmarks Preservation Commission are exempt from the two-year non-conforming use discontinuance provision.

10   As Caro (1974) documents, Moses was quite successful in accomplishing a similar project in the Bronx; also see Berman (1982).

11   See Anthony Flint's (2010) work in which he specifically examines this battle between Robert Moses and Jane Jacobs.

12   Harvey 2001, 346.

13   See Zukin's (1995; 2010) work for an examination of BIDs.

14   Greenberg 2008.

15   Harvey 2001, 355.

16   Hannigan 1998, 105; also see Judd and Fainstein 1999.

17 Clark 2004; Lloyd and Clark 2001; also see Judd 2003.

18 See Brown-Saracino (2010) and Lees (2000) for discussions on "supply-side" explanations of gentrification; see Hackworth and Smith (2001) for an analysis of the state's role in gentrification.

19 Zukin et al. 2009, 50–55.

20 The ABC Law breaks down alcoholic beverages in the United States into three categories: beer, wine, and liquor (hard liquor or spirits). Some control states only directly control the sale of liquor, allowing licensed stores to sell wine and beer, and some control the sale of liquor and wine, allowing licensed stores to sell beer. Only one control state (Utah) directly controls the sale of all three.

21 At the start of this project the SLA consisted of three members. However, from late 2007 to mid-2008 the SLA only had two members after one retired. It continued making licensing decisions with two members until mid-2008 when the State Senate approved Governor James Paterson's appointee, Jeanique Greene. As I will discuss in chapter 5, in 2009 Governor Paterson replaced its chair, Daniel Boyle, with Dennis Rosen, in order to expedite the licensing process that had slowed during Boyle's tenure.

22 There are 173 different types of liquor licenses and permits under the ABC Law and many licenses fall under the category "on-premises retail," which means that alcohol can be purchased and consumed on the premises. Most of the on-premises licenses in downtown Manhattan are either OP licenses (On Premises, or full liquor licenses), which permit the sale and consumption of liquor, wine, and beer, or RW licenses (Restaurant Wine), which permit the sale and consumption of only wine and beer. The 500-foot rule affects licenses that fall under Section 64, 64-a, 64-c, and 64-d of the ABC Law, which includes OP licenses (as well as full liquor licenses for hotels, taverns, and cabarets) but not RW licenses.

23 See Silver et al.'s (2010) examination of the concept of scenes and the situated character of urban culture. Also see Straw's (1991; 2004) definitions of cultural scenes.

24 Caves 2000.

25 City leaders often justify investment in entertainment projects to their populations by making such promises of high economic returns. See Eisinger 2000; Hoffman et al. 2003; Judd 2003; Judd and Fainstein 1999.

26 The Department of Transportation is the biggest.

27 These cases occurred in gentrifying Manhattan neighborhoods, some of which are near this book's focus of the Lower East Side, East Village, and Bowery. But their decisions established legal precedents that could be applied to other licensing cases.

28 There are twenty-one total liquor licenses in this section of Ludlow Street—five RW (beer and wine) and sixteen OP (full), which is the type of license that is subject to the 500-foot rule. Two establishments have three licenses each. According to the ABC Law, an establishment needs a license for every counter where alcohol is sold. The two establishments with multiple licenses are larger venues. There are fifteen total liquor licenses on these blocks of Stanton and Rivington Streets—four RW and eleven OP. These numbers are accurate as of April 14, 2008.

29 Half of the fifty community board members are selected from a list of nominees provided by the district's city council member(s).

30 See Sanjek (1998) and Smithsimon (2011) for discussions and examples of a community board's importance in local issues.

31 I obtained data on CB3's structural and voting history from monthly meeting minutes and voting sheets available on its Web site and by requesting photocopies of older versions of such material from the CB3 office, which the district manager graciously provided. I received records from only a few months in 1990, 1991, and 1992, and from every month of every year from 1993 to 2008, with some years missing between one and five months. People in the CB3 office told me that information from these months has been lost.

Due to ongoing nightlife issues, the "SLA Task Force" became the official SLA Committee in July 1998. The two committees—Economic Development and State Liquor Authority—merged into one in 2004. However, liquor-licensing issues dominate the monthly agenda and make meetings last for a very long time. As a result, CB3 is unable to seriously discuss the actions they can take to devise an economic agenda for the neighborhood to counter nightlife. In 2009 they once again split them into two committees: Economic Development and State Liquor Authority and Department of Consumer Affairs Licensing.

32 Abu-Lughod 1994; Patterson 2007.

33 Smith 1996.

34 Because of the sensitivity of these issues, tensions frequently ran high at CB3 meetings during this period. See Andrew Jacobs, "The Wild, Wild Lower East Side: Democracy Is Messy. Does That Mean It Doesn't Work? A Look at Community Board 3," *New York Times*, March 3, 1996; Andrew Jacobs, "Major 'Head-Rearranging' Caps Board 3's Fractious Year," *New York Times*, April 7, 1996.

35 Mele 2000.

36 Both graphs in figures 4 and 5 show the statistics for items that CB3 voted on and the items that were listed on its monthly agendas. I make the distinction because not every item listed on the agenda is an application and receives a vote from CB3. These can include matters like letters of complaint to the SLA, city agencies, and bar owners; budgetary discussions; items that applicants withdraw; and any other issue that CB3 discusses but does not vote on. The top line in each graph, then, reflects the general activity at CB3 and the bottom line reflects the items that CB3 directly voted on that had licensing consequences at the SLA.

We can see how this works in 1997. The bottom line in each graph shows a dip in 1997—in the total and average monthly number of items voted on—while the top line shows an increase. This is because 1997 had a larger number of nonvoting items on its agendas than other years but just as much liquor license and nightlife-related activity.

37 Figure 5 shows the average number of items that CB3 voted on per month, which reflects an upward trend. There is a month missing from the CB3 records of 1993, 1995, and 1999 and three months missing from 1994. To compensate for the missing months in these years, I added the monthly average for the year to the total for each missing month. I then used this number to graph CB3's voting activity.

When necessary, all decimals are rounded off. For 1995, the sum when the average was added to the total from the existing records to make up for the missing month came to 151.8.

38 Again, I adjusted these numbers to account for the missing months in certain years. See note 37.

39 At this time, monthly agendas were not as detailed as they are today. It is possible there were more transfers that were not accurately labeled.

40   As mentioned earlier, transfer applications are not subject to the 500-foot rule. Residents eventually learned this fact, but at the time they did not know about it.

41   CB3 currently has fourteen resolution areas.

42   As I did for figures 2 and 3, I also added the averages for years with missing months for figures 6 and 7.

43   The reason for the sudden dip from 2003 to 2004 and 2004 to 2005 is mostly because of a new CB3 policy in dealing with renewal applications in September 2004. Prior to this date, CB3 required every licensee in the district to appear before it to renew their license. The more bars that opened, the more owners had to renew their licenses and the longer the committee meetings lasted. Because of the excessive length of their agendas and their desire to not make every owner devote their time to sitting in meetings, they changed this policy in September 2004 so that only owners of establishments with complaints were required to appear before the committee, which is still their policy today. This tremendously reduced the number of items on the monthly agenda.

44   I spoke with Tim and some members of his staff about this in formal and informal interviews, but this quote comes from Frizell 2008.

45   In total, Sam was denied three times by CB3—once for the transfer and twice for a renewal—and was approved by the SLA each time before he sold his business in 2008.

46   The SLA divides the state into three zones. Zone 1 consists of New York City's five boroughs as well as Westchester, Nassau, and Suffolk Counties.

CHAPTER 3: WEAVING A NOSTALGIA NARRATIVE

1   Mitchell 1993, 246.

2   In fact, some bar and other business owners have commissioned Power to make a mosaic on their storefronts. Sharon Zukin (2010) understands the contemporary interest in Power and his mosaics as a fascination with local authentic grit that serve as forms of visual consumption.

3   See Weegee's classic collection of photographs, *Naked City* (1945)

4   Here Bob's use of "ghosts" slightly differs, I believe, from Bell's (1997) novel notion of "ghosts of place," in which people feel "*the sense of the presence of those who are not physically there*" (813; emphasis in original). Bob refers to how revelers ignore the neighborhood's public characters, which effectively turns them into ghosts of place.

5   Though Bob began his blog to provide attention towards what he felt was an injustice against Jim Power, he generally documents the neighborhood and does not support causes. However, when Ray encountered rent and legal issues in 2009 and early 2010 and was threatened with eviction, Bob used the blog to help promote fundraising events.

6   The Laundromat was a well-known place to buy drugs in the East Village during the 1980s (see Curtis et al. 2002).

7   Many scholars have looked at a broad array of gentrifiers (e.g., artists, social preservationists, gays and lesbians, whites and blacks, and owners of boutiques and cafés) and focused on their reasons for moving into and opening up businesses in the neighborhood as well as their perspectives towards and relationships with existing residents (Brown-Saracino 2009; Butler 1997; Caulfield 1994; Deener 2007; Lloyd 2006; Patch 2008; Pattillo 2007; Rose 1984; Sibalis 2004). Since gentrification is more a gradual process than a single event, often with identifiable "stages" or "waves" (Clay 1979; Lees 2000; see also Hackworth and Smith, 2000), a neighborhood's conditions at the time of gentrifiers' arrival, as well as their own social position within the neighborhood, help to shape their perspectives towards its gentrification (Brown-Saracino 2010, 170–71). In her discussion of the "marginal gentrifier" concept—an early account of the variety of gentrifier types—Rose (1984) states that scholars must continue to characterize people in gentrifying neighborhoods by their motives and interests (also see Caulfield 1994). Despite the increasing amount of literature on gentrifiers, underexplored is their perspective on the gentrified neighborhood, their attitudes towards its people, their understanding of their own role in its gentrification, and the bases of their local identities, decades after they moved there. Also see Ocejo 2011.

8   Since gentrification occurs gradually and piecemeal, some areas of neighborhoods get gentrified before others. While some areas in the 1980s and 1990s featured renovated housing and new bars, others were still clearly identifiable as working-class "frontiers."

9   Milligan 1998.

10   Schwarz 2010.

11   Maurice Halbwachs (1992) pioneered sociological thought on collective memory in the mid-twentieth century. Also see Anderson's (1991) work on "imagined communities" as well as Hobsbawm and Ranger's (1983) edited volume on invented traditions. These authors discuss socially constructed pasts in societies, but collective memory need not exist on such an abstract or macro level.

12   Milligan 2003; also see Davis 1979; Wilson 2005.

13   Davis 1979; Turner 1987.

14   Kasinitz and Hillyard (1995) examine how a group of old-timers in Red Hook experienced the influx of low-income minority residents as a threat to their community, despite greater macro-structural forces (i.e., deindustrialization) that played a more central role in its demise. Meanwhile, Milligan (2003) shows how a group of college students reacted to the actual destruction and location of their beloved coffee shop.

15   Chernoff 1980; Martin 2007.

16   Deener 2007.

17   Smith 1996.

18   Von Hassell 1999.

19   Martinez 2010; Schmelzkopf 1995; Zukin 2010.

20   Here Doreen refers to the plans that city, business, and real estate leaders had from the 1920s to the 1960s to redevelop the slums of downtown Manhattan into a residential area for the middle class (see Mele 2000; Wasserman 1994).

21   Brown-Saracino (2009) in particular has done much to complicate this image popularized by such scholars as Smith (1996); also see Rose (1984) .

22   Cornwell 2002; 2007.

23   People who are residentially displaced by gentrification are notoriously difficult to locate. Atkinson (2000) describes taking them into account as "measuring the

invisible" (also see Newman and Wyly 2006). Daniel is the only early gentrifier in this book who was residentially displaced, although my participants told me of many examples of neighbors and friends of theirs that were either evicted or forced to leave their apartments due to rising rents. Although he was born in the East Village and did not move there as a young adult, I include Daniel in this analysis because of his orientation towards the neighborhood, and his understanding of the experiences that he had resembles those of the early gentrifiers I spoke with rather than other existing residents.

24 Martinez 2010; Mele 2000; Wasserman 1994.

25 Brown-Saracino 2009.

26 Grazian 2003.

27 Brown-Saracino 2007.

28 Duneier 1999; Jacobs 1961.

29 See Wilson and Kelling's (1982) original formulation of the "broken-windows" concept, and Duneier's (1999) analysis of broken-windows policy and policing.

30 Smith 1996; Vitale 2005.

31 Brown-Saracino (2009) examines the different efforts that social preservationists make to preserve the communities in their neighborhoods they consider "authentic," such as by symbolically linking place identity to old-timers through festivals and theatrical performances, by organizing and protesting, and by shopping at old-timers' establishments.

32 This is not the same Denis who owned the bar.

33 Brown-Saracino 2009.

34 Collective Unconscious is an artist collective that moved to another neighborhood. Condominiums were built on its former site without a commercial storefront.

35 For reflections on downtown Manhattan's cultural scenes made at the time, see Hager (1986) and Musto (1986); for reflections that look back on these scenes, see Maffi (1995), Patterson (2007), and Taylor (2006).

36 Kostelanetz 2003; Lloyd 2006; Zukin 1983.

37 Cornwell 2002; 2007; Kapralov 1974; Patterson 2007.

38 Here she refers to the historical Lower East Side, not just the section that is considered the neighborhood of the Lower East Side today.

39 See Park 1952.

40 Palen and London 1984.

41 Here Beth refers to how SoHo, the neighborhood immediately to the west of the Lower East Side, transformed from an area for small manufacturing into a colony for artists who lived in worked in the abandoned lofts. By the time Beth moved to the Lower East Side, in 1981, SoHo's appeal had spread from artists to the urban middle class, who renovated lofts into a new style of downtown living, which gradually led to the displacement of artists and the neighborhood's arts scene. See Zukin 1983.

42 "Bridge and tunnel" refers to people who take bridges and tunnels (in cars as well as on buses and trains) to get to the island of Manhattan. It is derogatory in the sense that residents view people outside the center—i.e., the outer boroughs, New Jersey, Long Island, or Westchester and Rockland Counties—as culturally inferior because of their suburban status, even though many of these areas are quite urban and many users of the term are in fact originally from similar suburban contexts (Grazian 2008; Hummon 1990).

43 Hannigan 1998.

44 Mele 2000; Musto 1986.

45 See Stack (1973) and Venkatesh (2000) for examples of inner-city populations that rely on each other through informal systems of exchange for survival.

CHAPTER 4: ENTREPRENEURIAL SPIRITS

1 The 500-foot rule does not apply to the type of license for which Sasha is applying. Still, the SLA must take the community's recommendation into account when making licensing decisions.

2 A few months later, Sasha opens the café without a liquor license. More than a year later, he and his business partner apply to CB3 again. They are met with the same resistance from the block association. Eventually, unable to continue to pay the rent by just selling gourmet coffee and baked goods, they close.

3 Sasha later told me that the reason he only allows maximum of five to a group is because with five people you cannot have more than two conversations going at once; more than five and you have three or more. This is one of several strategies Sasha uses to reduce noise and control social interactions in the bar.

4 Oldenburg 1989; also see Lloyd 2006.

5 Grazian 2009.

6 Also see Grazian 2008

7 See Anderson's (2009a) response to Grazian's (2009) finding, in which she discusses different types of communities that exist in contemporary nightlife establishments.

8 Mele 2000.

9 Lloyd 2006.

10 See Clay (1979), Lees (2000), and Hackworth and Smith (2001) for examinations of different "waves," or stages of gentrification.

11 Musto 1986; Taylor 2006.

12 Brown-Saracino 2009.

13 Lloyd 2006; Patch 2008; Zukin et al. 2009.

14 Recall from chapter 1 that when Hilly Kristal originally opened CBGB on the Bowery, his clientele consisted of homeless men. He had to change his method of operation to attract the clientele that he desired, namely creative people in the art and music scene.

15 Jacobs (1961) praises local bars for providing uses and a sense of safety in the neighborhood at night.

16 Building from Jacobs, Patch (2008) refers to new stores opened by women entrepreneurs in a gentrifying neighborhood as providing "faces on the street," or bringing communal and personable spaces to desolate areas.

17 Melbin 1987.

18 I discuss this point in the next chapter.

19 Zukin 2010.

20 Mele 2000, viii.

21   Zukin et al. 2009.

22   Gotham 2007; also see Zukin et al. 2009.

23   Several real estate sources I interviewed and consulted indicate that this is the case. They add that the business that tends to pay the highest storefront rents are banks. As one source explains, in 2007, commercial rents on the Lower East Side for bars and restaurants were $100 per square foot, while for other retail establishments they were $80 per square foot, with these amounts varying depending on the particular street.

24   Currid 2007; Lloyd 2006.

25   I spoke with Continental's owner about this issue on several occasions, but I took this quote from Richard Bienstock, "The Continental Drifts: An East Village Staple Evolves, but Dies a Little in the Process," *Village Voice*, September 5, 2006.

26   Zukin et al. 2009; Zukin 2010.

27   See Ferguson's (1998; 2006) discussions of taste communities in relation to the rise of a national cuisine in France.

28   Hannigan 1998.

29   A muddler is a small wooden stick with a flat bottom that bartenders use to extract juice and oils from fruit and herbs by grinding them at the bottom of the mixing glass. They were obsolete for many years when cocktails were highly simplified. Many bars started using them once the mojito became a popular cocktail.

30   The Southside and Sazerac are both classic cocktails that had long since disappeared from bar menus until they were revived by the cocktail renaissance.

31   Bourdieu 1993.

32   Stuyvesant Town is a large housing development immediately to the northeast of the Lower East Side.

33   Asbury's book originally came out in 1928 and was adapted into a 2002 film.

34   There is a bar not far from Sandee's Whiskey Ward called the Sixth Ward.

CHAPTER 5: REGULATING NIGHTLIFE SCENES

1   Jacobs 1961, 245.

2   The 311 number accesses the city's non-emergency services and information system. I discuss its importance in the nightlife scene later in the chapter.

3   St. Guillen and her friends were initially out at the Pioneer Bar, which was located on Bowery, but on the west side of the street, and therefore in the jurisdiction of Community Board 2, not Community Board 3. They walked a few blocks further west to The Falls, in NoLIta, where she was abducted. Although the incident did not take place there, the Pioneer Bar changed its named to the R Bar shortly afterward due to bad publicity.

4   Moore and her friend were out in Chelsea, a former manufacturing district on Manhattan's west side that has transformed into a popular area for large, exclusive nightclubs.

5   See Greenberg's (2008) examination of how leaders in deindustrializing cities such as New York addressed such crises through branding campaigns.

6   The legality of paid detail has been a contentious issue in New York City. The NYPD have cited sections of the ABC Law that state that police officers are not permitted to be connected with the sale of alcohol. The nightlife industry and local elected officials point out that paid detail units are used at sporting events where alcohol is sold, such as Madison Square Garden and Yankee Stadium. However, the NYPD counter by saying that alcohol sale at these venues is incidental to their primary activities of sports and entertainment.

In two opinions, the SLA has supported both sides of the issue. On the one hand, the SLA maintains that it is illegal for a police officer to have direct or indirect interest in the sale of alcohol. On the other hand, the SLA also acknowledges that paid detail for nightlife establishments and scenes is possible as long as officers, "maintain their complete professional independence." In a 2006 memo, the SLA legal counsel also states that although police officers cannot be hired as a bouncer by a licensee or through a third party, this prohibition "does not apply when the officer is working for, and being compensated by, his/her police department." In other words, the SLA upholds the integrity of the law while recognizing that such a program is possible under certain conditions. Paid detail for nightlife is still in legal limbo.

7   I was not told where they were headed to next when I asked.

8   The aforementioned laws that require places with a cabaret license to have licensed bouncers and security cameras do not apply to bars.

9   Many owners give their phone numbers to their neighbors for this reason. However, many residents complain that the owners are still unresponsive to their concerns and that such a tactic is meant solely as a gesture of appeasement to them and the community board rather than a sincere attempt at a resolution. These sentiments also reinforce residents' view that owners are untrustworthy.

10 A lack of large spaces such as warehouses and different zoning designations explains why downtown Manhattan does not have many large nightclubs. However, a space may obtain a cabaret license in a nonmanufacturing zoning district if the applicant obtains a variance from the city or if the space is grandfathered to have one. There are examples of both in these downtown neighborhoods. See Chevigny (1991) for a discussion of the history of cabaret laws in New York City.

11 Tavern on the Green was an upscale restaurant that was popular for tourists located in Central Park. It closed in 2009 but was open when Mike made this comment. By citing it Mike is implying a double standard in terms of how city agencies enforce their policies against establishments with liquor licenses.

12 The futility of using bouncers, as opposed to uniformed police officers, to prevent noise and sidewalk congestion is a key argument made in support of the paid detail program discussed earlier in the chapter.

13 Lloyd (2006) also discusses the suburban discourse that nightlife scene participants use against outsiders.

14 Vitale 2009.

15 See Noah Marcel Sudarsky, "The Sound and the Fury," *New York Times*, January 21, 2007. In this article, the author uses Heathers to exemplify the quality-of-life complaints against bars that are common in the neighborhood.

16 The Lower East Side Alliance (LESA) was a group of residents during the mid-2000s who fought against bars and other gentrification concerns in the neighborhood.

17   The adults with children carrying banners and signs were holding a protest at this meeting for another item.

CHAPTER 6: THE LIMITS OF LOCAL DEMOCRACY

1   In 2006 Governor George Pataki appointed Noreen Healey, a Brooklyn resident, to be a commissioner of the SLA, which made her the first New York City resident at the agency in recent memory. As Patti implies, residents saw her appointment as an attempt to placate complaining community groups in the city and not as a genuine effort to curb nightlife development. The next two appointees to the SLA, including the chair, were both non–New York City residents. Governor David Paterson appointed both commissioners.

2   Brown-Saracino 2009; Lloyd 2006.

3   CB3 requires all applicants to obtain signatures and addresses on a petition from their immediate neighbors to demonstrate local support for their proposed bars. When neighbors protest, they regularly call into question the names and addresses on the petition, particularly their proximity to the actual bar. They sometimes accuse bar owners of forging these signatures.

4   Several different actors—owners with bars in other parts of the city, liquor license attorneys, representatives from the SLA—expressed this sentiment about CB3's liquor license committee. I also attended the liquor license committee meetings of three other community boards in Manhattan and one in Brooklyn, and while these displayed a high level of organization, were well-attended, and featured a large number of license items, they did not match the CB3 committee's size, engagement, or intensity. I should also note that not every community board has a liquor-licensing committee because nightlife is not a priority in every district. Such districts handle liquor licensing on a case-by-case basis.

5   Fung and Wright 2003; also see Fung 2004.

6   Fung and Wright 2003, 5.

7   Fung and Wright 2003, 17.

8   The number of committee members fluctuated during the course of my research, as did the number of members who attended the monthly meetings. These differences existed because the liquor license committee meetings are by far the longest of any other CB3 committee, members are only volunteers, and the meetings take place on a weeknight. On some nights there were as few as three members present, but on others there were as many as nine.

9   Although the committee handles their applications, the licensing authority for sidewalk cafés is the city's Department of Consumer Affairs (DCA). As with the SLA, CB3 and residents regularly criticize the DCA for granting a large number of sidewalk café licenses despite their protests.

10   See Gregory Smithsimon's (2011, 162–192) work on Battery Park City's community organizing. He documents how new groups formed in the wake of September 11 in the downtown neighborhood while old groups shifted their focus to deal with redevelopment issues at Ground Zero.

11 The only exceptions are those owners who have owned their bars for many decades and have never had any issues and alterations to their bars. In these cases they have never had to apply to or go before the community board.

12 Jacobs 1961.

CONCLUSION: UPSCALING NEW YORK

1 Sorkin 1992.

2 Hannigan 1996.

3 Greenberg 2008; Taylor 2005.

4 Eisinger 2000.

5 Eisinger 2000, 323.

6 See Harcourt (2001) and Karmen (2000) for studies that question broken-windows policing's role in the reduction of crime in New York and other cities in the United States.

7 I obtained the former statistic from the New York Civil Liberties Union's Web site (http://www.nyclu.org/content/stop-and-frisk-data, accessed May 20, 2013). The information is based on police reports. The latter statistic is from the 2010 United States Census.

8 I say "visible" because both precincts use undercover officers in bars to perform investigations and to catch criminal behavior in the act. An example of the latter is the "lucky bag" program, in which an officer leaves a bag containing valuables in a visible place in the bar, then waits with an eye on it to see if anyone takes it.

METHODOLOGICAL APPENDIX:
STUDYING THE SOCIAL ECOSYSTEM OF BARS

1 David Grazian (2003) uses a similar strategy in his fieldwork.

2 Community Board 3 does not meet in August. I did not attend the liquor-licensing committee meetings in July and October 2008 and did not attend either meeting in January 2008.

3 The Fifth Precinct also covers a section of the study area, but it is comparatively small and has fewer nightlife establishments. I chose to focus on the other two.

4 For a discussion of the benefits of business directories for supplementing ethnographic research, see Schlichtman and Patch (2008) and Zukin et al. (2009).

5 I had several phone conversations with participants, but only two were solely phone interviews that did not result in or stem from a face-to-face interview.

6 See Duneier (1999) and Jerolmack (2013) for examples.

7 See Anderson (1978), Kornblum (1974), and LeMasters (1975) for examples.

REFERENCES

Abu-Lughod, Janet (ed.). 1994. *From Urban Village to East Village: The Battle for New York's Lower East Side*. Oxford: Blackwell.

Anbinder, Tyler. 2001. *Five Points: The 19th-Century New York City Neighborhood That Invented Tap Dance, Stole Elections, and Became the World's Most Notorious Slum*. New York: Plume.

Anderson, Benedict. 1991. *Imagined Communities: Reflections on the Origin and Spread of Nationalism*. London: Verso.

Anderson, Elijah. 1978. *A Place on the Corner*. Chicago: University of Chicago Press.

Anderson, Nels. 1923. *The Hobo: The Sociology of the Homeless Man*. Chicago: University of Chicago Press.

Anderson, Tammy L. 2009a. "Better to Complicate, Rather than Homogenize, Urban Nightlife: A Response to Grazian." *Sociological Forum* 24 (4): 918–925.

———. 2009b. *Rave Culture: Alteration and Decline of a Philadelphia Music Scene*. Philadelphia: Temple University Press.

Asbury, Herbert. [1928] 2008. *The Gangs of New York: An Informal History of the Underworld*. New York: Vintage Books.

Atkinson, Rowland. 2000. "Measuring Gentrification and Displacement in Greater London." *Urban Studies* 37 (1): 149–65.

Bahr, Howard M. 1967. "The Gradual Disappearance of Skid Row." *Social Problems* 15 (Summer): 41–45.

———. 1973. *Skid Row: An Introduction to Disaffiliation*. Oxford: Oxford University Press.

Bahr, Howard M., and Theodore Caplow. 1974. *Old Men Drunk and Sober*. New York: New York University Press.

Becker, Kara. 2009. "/r/ and the Construction of a Place Identity on New York City's Lower East Side." *Journal of Sociolinguistics* 13 (5): 634–658.

Bell, Michael J. 1983. *The World from Brown's Lounge: An Ethnography of Black Middle-Class Play*. Chicago: University of Illinois Press.

Bell, Michael Mayerfeld. 1997. "The Ghosts of Place." *Theory and Society* 26 (6): 813–836.

Bendiner, Elmer. 1961. *The Bowery Man*. New York: Thomas Nelson and Sons.

Berman, Marshall. 1982. *All That Is Solid Melts Into Air*. New York: Penguin Books.

Bernstein, Nina. 1999. "An Uneasy Coexistence; Tensions between Town and Shelter Flow Both Ways." *New York Times*, May 4.

Bienstock, Richard. 2006. "The Continental Drifts: An East Village Staple Evolves, but Dies a Little in the Process." *Village Voice*, September 5.

Bogue, Donald. 1963. *Skid Row in American Cities*. Chicago: University of Chicago Press.

Bourdieu, Pierre. 1993. *The Field of Cultural Production*. New York: Columbia University Press.

Brown-Saracino, Japonica. 2007. "Virtuous Marginality: Social Preservationists and the Selection of the Old-timer." *Theory and Society* 36 (5): 437–468.

Brown-Saracino, Japonica. 2009. *A Neighborhood That Never Changes: Gentrification, Social Preservation, and the Search for Authenticity*. Chicago: University of Chicago Press.

———. 2010. *The Gentrification Debates: A Reader*. New York: Routledge.

Butler, Tim. 1997. *Gentrification and the Middle Classes*. London: Ashgate.

Butler, Tim, and Loretta Lees. 2006. "Super-gentrification in Barnsbury, London: Globalisation and Gentrifying Global Elites at the Neighbourhood Level." *Transactions of the Institute of British Geographers* 31: 467–487.

Cahill, Caitlin. 2000. "Street Literacy: Urban Teenagers' Strategies for Negotiating Their Neighborhood." *Journal of Youth Studies* 3 (3): 251–277.

———. 2007. "Doing Research with Young People: Participatory Research and the Rituals of Collective Work." *Children's Geographies* 5 (3): 297–312.

Caldwell, Mark. 2005. *New York Night: The Mystique and Its History*. New York: Scribner.

Caro, Robert. 1974. *The Power Broker: Robert Moses and the Fall of New York*. New York: Knopf.

Caulfield, Jon. 1994. *City Form and Everyday Life: Toronto's Gentrification and Critical Social Practice*. Toronto: University of Toronto Press.

Cavan, Sheri. 1966. *Liquor License: An Ethnography of Bar Behavior*. Chicago: Aldine Publishing.

Caves, Richard. 2000. *Creative Industries: Contracts between Art and Commerce*. Cambridge, MA: Harvard University Press.

Chatteron, Paul, and Robert Hollands. 2003. *Urban Nightscapes: Youth Cultures, Pleasure Spaces, and Corporate Power*. New York: Routledge.

Chauncey, George. 1994. *Gay New York: Gender, Urban Culture, and the Making of the Gay Male World, 1890–1940*. New York: Basic Books.

Chernoff, Michael. 1980. "Social Displacement in a Renovating Neighborhood's Commercial District." In *Back to the City: Issues in Neighborhood Renovation*, edited by S. B. Laska and D. Spain. New York: Pergamon Press.

Chevigny, Paul. 1991. *Gigs: Jazz and the Cabaret Laws in New York City*. New York: Routledge.

Clark, Terry Nichols. 2004. *The City as an Entertainment Machine*. Research in Urban Policy Series, vol. 9, edited by Terry Nichols Clark. New York: JAI Press.

Clay, Phillip L. 1979. *Neighborhood Renewal: Middle-Class Resettlement and Incumbent Upgrading in American Neighborhoods*. Lexington, MA: D. C. Heath.

Cohen, Carl I., and Jay Sokolovsky. 1989. *Old Men of the Bowery: Strategies for Survival among the Homeless*. New York: Guilford Press.

Cornwell, James. 2002. *When Out Was In: The Rise and Fall of the East Village Art Movement*. Winston-Salem, NC: Wake Forest University Press.

———. 2007. "Villains or Victims: Are East Village Artists Willing Agents for Gentrification and the Displacement of the Poor?" In *Resistance: A Radical Social and Political History of the Lower East Side*, edited by Clayton Patterson. New York: Seven Stories Press.

Cressey, Paul G. 1932. *The Taxi-Dance Hall: A Sociological Study in Commercialized Recreation and City Life*. Chicago: University of Chicago Press.

Currid, Elizabeth. 2007. *The Warhol Economy: How Fashion, Art and Music Drive New York City*. Princeton, NJ: Princeton University Press.

Curtis, Richard, Travis Wendel, and Barry Spunt. 2002. "We Deliver: The Gentrification of Drug Markets on Manhattan's Lower East Side." Final report to the National Institute of Justice, grant #1999-IJ-CX-0010.

Davis, Fred. 1979. *Yearning for Yesterday: A Sociology of Nostalgia.* New York: Free Press.

Deener, Andrew. 2007. "Commerce as Structure and Symbol of Neighborhood Life: Reshaping the Meaning of Community in Venice, California." *City and Community* 6 (4): 291–314.

———. 2012. *Venice: A Contested Bohemia in Los Angeles.* Chicago: University of Chicago Press.

Deutsche, Rosalyn, and C. G. Ryan. 1984. "The Fine Art of Gentrification." *October* 31: 91–111.

Dowling, Robert M. 2007. *Slumming in New York: From the Waterfront to Mythic Harlem.* Urbana: University of Illinois Press.

Duneier, Mitchell. 1992. *Slim's Table: Race, Respectability, and Masculinity.* Chicago: University of Chicago Press.

———. 1999. *Sidewalk.* New York: Farrar, Straus and Giroux.

Eisinger, Peter. 2000. "The Politics of Bread and Circuses: Building the City for the Visitor Class." *Urban Affairs Review* 35 (3): 316–333.

Ferguson, Priscilla Parkhurst. 1998. "A Cultural Field in the Making: Gastronomy in 19th-Century France." *American Journal of Sociology* 104 (3): 597–641.

———. 2006. *Accounting for Taste: The Triumph of French Cuisine.* Chicago: University of Chicago Press.

Flint, Anthony. 2010. *Wrestling with Moses: How Jane Jacobs Took On New York's Master Builder and Transformed the American City.* New York: Random House.

Florida, Richard. 2002. *The Rise of the Creative Class, and How It's Transforming Work, Leisure, Community, and Everyday Life.* New York: Basic Books.

Frizell, St. John. 2008. "The Genealogy of Mixology." *Edible Manhattan*, November–December.

Fung, Archon. 2004. *Empowered Participation: Reinventing Urban Democracy.* Princeton, NJ: Princeton University Press.

Fung, Archon, and Erik Olin Wright. 2003. *Deepening Democracy: Institutional Innovations in Empowered Participatory Governance.* The Real Utopias Project, vol. 4. New York: Verso.

Gotham, Kevin Fox. 2007. *Authentic New Orleans: Tourism, Culture, and Race in the Big Easy.* New York: New York University Press.

Grazian, David. 2003. *Blue Chicago: The Search of Authenticity in Urban Blues Clubs.* Chicago: University of Chicago Press.

———. 2008. *On the Make: The Hustle of Urban Nightlife.* Chicago: University of Chicago Press.

———. 2009. "Urban Nightlife, Social Capital, and the Public Life of Cities." *Sociological Forum* 24 (4): 908–917.

Greenberg, Miriam. 2008. *Branding New York: How a City in Crisis Was Sold to the World.* New York: Routledge.

Hackworth, Jason, and Neil Smith. 2001. "The Changing State of Gentrification." *Tijdschrift voor Economische en Sociale Geografie* 92 (4): 464–477.

Hadfield, Phil. 2006. *Bars Wars: Contesting the Night in Contemporary British Cities.* Oxford: Oxford University Press.

Hadfield, Phil. 2009. *Nightlife and Crime: Social Order and Governance in International Perspective.* Oxford: Oxford University Press.

Hager, Steven. 1986. *Art after Midnight: The East Village Scene.* New York: St. Martin's Press.

Halbwachs, Maurice. 1992. *On Collective Memory.* Chicago: University of Chicago Press.

Hannigan, John. 1998. *Fantasy City: Pleasure and Profit in the Postmodern Metropolis.* New York: Routledge.

Harcourt, Bernard. 2001. *Illusion of Order: The False Promise of Broken Windows Policing.* Cambridge, MA: Harvard University Press.

Harvey, David. 2001. *Spaces of Capital: Towards a Critical Geography.* New York: Routledge.

Heap, Chad. 2009. *Slumming: Sexual and Racial Encounters in American Nightlife, 1885–1940.* Chicago: University of Chicago Press.

Heath, Tim. 1997. "The Twenty-four Hour City Concept—A Review of Initiatives in British Cities." *Journal of Urban Design* 2 (2): 193–204.

Hobbs, Dick, Philip Hadfield, Stuart Lister, and Simon Winlow. 2003. *Bouncers: Violence and Governance in the Night-time Economy.* Oxford: Oxford University Press.

Hobbs, Dick, Stuart Lister, Philip Hadfield, Simon Winlow, and Steve Hall. 2000. "Receiving Shadows: Governance and Liminality in the Night-time Economy." *British Journal of Sociology* 51 (4): 701–717.

Hobsbawm, Eric, and Terrence Ranger (eds.). 1983. *The Invention of Tradition.* Cambridge: Cambridge University Press.

Hochschild, Arlie Russell. 1983. *The Managed Heart: Commercialization of Human Feeling.* Berkeley: University of California Press.

Hoffman, Lily M., Susan S. Fainstein, and Dennis R. Judd (eds.). 2003. *Cities and Visitors: Regulating People, Markets, and City Space.* Oxford: Blackwell Publishing.

Huizinga, Johan. [1950] 1971. *Homo Ludens: A Study of the Play Element in Culture.* Boston: Beacon Press.

Hummon, David M. 1990. *Commonplaces: Community Ideology and Identity in American Culture.* Albany: State University of New York Press.

Isay, David, and Stacy Abramson. 2000. *Flophouse: Life on the Bowery.* New York: Random House.

Jacobs, Andrew. 1996a. "Major 'Head-Rearranging' Caps Board 3's Fractious Year." *New York Times*, April 7.

———. 1996b. "The Wild, Wild Lower East Side: Democracy Is Messy. Does That Mean It Doesn't Work? A Look at Community Board 3." *New York Times*, March 3.

Jacobs, Jane. 1961. *The Death and Life of Great American Cities.* New York: Vintage Books.

Jerolmack, Colin. 2013. *The Global Pigeon.* Chicago: University of Chicago Press.

Judd, Dennis R. (ed.). 2003. *The Infrastructure of Play: Building the Tourist City in America.* Armonk: M. E. Sharpe.

Judd, Dennis R., and Susan S. Fainstein (eds.). 1999. *The Tourist City.* New Haven, CT: Yale University Press.

Kapralov, Yuri. 1974. *Once There Was a Village.* New York: St. Martin's Press.

Karmen, Andrew. 2000. *New York Murder Mystery: The True Story Behind the Crime Crash of the 1990s.* New York: New York University Press.

Kasinitz, Philip. 1995. *Metropolis: Center and Symbol of Our Times.* New York: New York University Press.

Kasinitz, Philip, and David Hillyard. 1995. "The Old-Timers' Tale: The Politics of Nostalgia on the Waterfront." *Journal of Contemporary Ethnography* 24 (2): 139–164.

Katovich, Michael A., and William A. Reese II. 1987. "The Regular: Full-Time Identities and Memberships in an Urban Bar." *Journal of Contemporary Ethnography* 16 (3): 308–343.

Katz, Jack. 1997. "On Ethnography's Warrants." *Sociological Methods and Research* 25 (4): 391–423.

Kelling, George L., and Catherine M. Coles. 1998. *Fixing Broken Windows: Restoring Order and Reducing Crime in Our Communities*. New York: Free Press.

Kornblum, William. 1974. *Blue Collar Community*. Chicago: University of Chicago Press.

Kostelanetz, Richard. 2003. *SoHo: The Rise and Fall of an Artists' Colony*. New York: Routledge.

Lees, Loretta. 2000. "A Re-appraisal of Gentrification: Towards a 'Geography of Gentrification.'" *Progress in Human Geography* 24 (3): 389–408.

———. 2003. "Super-gentrification: The Case of Brooklyn Heights, New York City." *Urban Studies* 40 (12): 2487–2509.

LeMasters, E. E. 1975. *Blue-Collar Aristocrats: Life-Styles at a Working-Class Tavern*. Madison: University of Wisconsin Press.

Levy, Paul R., and Roman A. Cybriwsky. 1980. "The Hidden Dimensions of Culture and Class: Philadelphia." In *Back to the City: Issues in Neighborhood Renovation*, edited by S. B. Laska and D. Spain. New York: Pergamon Press.

Lindquist, Julie. 2002. *A Place to Stand: Politics and Persuasion in a Working Class Bar*. Oxford: Oxford University Press.

Lloyd, Richard. 2006. *Neo-Bohemia: Art and Commerce in the Postindustrial City*. New York: Routledge.

Lloyd, Richard, and Terry Nichols Clark. 2001. "The City as an Entertainment Machine." *Critical Perspectives on Urban Redevelopment* 6: 359–380.

Lofland, Lyn H. 1973. *A World of Strangers: Order and Action in Urban Public Space*. Long Grove, IL: Waveland Press.

Logan, John R., and Harvey L. Molotch. 1987. *Urban Fortunes: The Political Economy of Place*. Berkeley: University of California Press.

Lutz, Tom. 2006. *Doing Nothing: A History of Loafers, Loungers, Slackers, and Bums in America*. New York: Farrar, Straus and Giroux.

Maffi, Mario. 1995. *Gateway to the Promised Land: Ethnic Cultures in New York City's Lower East Side*. New York: New York University Press.

Malbon, Ben. 1999. *Clubbing: Dancing, Ecstasy, and Vitality*. London: Routledge.

Martin, Leslie. 2007. "Fighting for Control: Political Displacement in Atlanta's Gentrifying Neighborhoods." *Urban Affairs Review* 42 (5): 603–628.

Martinez, Miranda J. 2010. *Power at the Roots: Gentrification, Community Gardens, and the Puerto Ricans of the Lower East Side*. Lanham, MD: Lexington Books.

May, Ruben A. Buford. 2001. *Talking at Trena's: Everyday Conversations at an African American Tavern*. New York: New York University Press.

McKinney, John C. 1966. *Constructive Topology and Social Theory*. New York: Appleton-Century-Crofts.

Melbin, Murray. 1987. *Night as Frontier: Colonizing the World after Dark*. New York: Free Press.

Mele, Christopher. 2000. *Selling the Lower East Side: Culture, Real Estate, and Resistance in New York City*. Minneapolis: University of Minnesota Press.

Milligan, Melinda J. 1998. "Interactional Past and Potential: The Social Construction of Place Attachment." *Symbolic Interaction* 21 (1): 1–33.

———. 2003. "Displacement and Identity Discontinuity: The Role of Nostalgia in Establishing New Identity Categories." *Symbolic Interaction* 26 (3): 381–403.

Mitchell, J. Clyde. 1983. "Case and Situation Analysis." *Sociological Review* 31(2): 187–211.

Mitchell, Joseph. 1993. *Up in the Old Hotel*. New York: Vintage Books.

Mitchell, Wendy. 2003. *New York City's Best Dive Bars: Drinking and Diving in the Five Boroughs*. New York: Ig Publishing.

Musto, Michael. 1986. *Downtown*. New York: Vintage Books.

Newman, Kathe, and Elvin K. Wyly. 2006. "The Right to Stay Put, Revisited: Gentrification and Resistance to Displacement in New York City." *Urban Studies* 43 (1): 23–57.

Ocejo, Richard E. 2011. "The Early Gentrifier: Weaving a Nostalgia Narrative on the Lower East Side." *City and Community* 10 (3): 285–310.

Oldenburg, Ray. 1989. *The Great Good Place: Cafes, Coffee Shops, Bookstores, Bars, Hair Salons, and Other Hangouts at the Heart of a Community*. New York: Marlowe.

Palen, John J., and Bruce London (eds.). 1984. *Gentrification, Displacement, and Neighborhood Revitalization*. Albany: State University of New York Press.

Park, Robert. 1952. *Human Communities*. Glencoe, IL: Free Press.

Patch, Jason. 2008. "Ladies and Gentrification: New Stores, Residents, and Relationships in Neighborhood Change." *Gender in an Urban World*, Research in Urban Sociology vol. 9, edited by Judith N. DeSena and Ray Hutchinson. Bingley, UK: Emerald Group.

Patterson, Clayton (ed.). 2007. *Resistance: A Radical Social and Political History of the Lower East Side*. New York: Seven Stories Press.

Pattillo, Mary. 2007. *Black on the Block: The Politics of Race and Class in the City*. Chicago: University of Chicago Press.

Roberts, Marion, and Chris Turner. 2005. "Conflicts of Livability in the 24-Hour City: Learning from 48 Hours in the Life of London's Soho." *Journal of Urban Design* 10 (2): 171–193.

Rose, Damaris. 1984. "Rethinking Gentrification: Beyond the Uneven Development of Marxist Urban Theory." *Environment and Planning D: Society and Space* 2 (1): 47–74.

Rudman, Chelsea. 2007. "Invisible New Yorkers." *New York Press*, January 17–23.

Sanderson, Eric. 2009. *Mannahatta: A Natural History of New York City*. New York: Harry N. Abrams.

Sanjek, Roger. 1998. *The Future of Us All: Race and Neighborhood Politics in New York City*. Ithaca, NY: Cornell University Press.

Sante, Luc. 1991. *Low Life: Lures and Snares of Old New York*. New York: Vintage Books.

Schlichtman, John Joe, and Jason Patch. 2008. "Contextualizing Impressions of Neighborhood Change: Linking Business Directories to Ethnography." *City and Community* 7 (3): 273–293.

Schmelzkopf, Karen. 1995. "Urban Community Gardens as a Contested Space." *Geographical Review* 85 (3): 364–381.

Schwarz, Benjamin. 2010. "Gentrification and Its Discontents." *Atlantic,* June (online).

Sharman, Russell Leigh, and Cheryl Harris Sharman. 2008. *Nightshift NYC*. Berkeley: University of California Press.

Sibalis, Michael. 2004. "Urban Space and Homosexuality: The Example of the Marais, Paris' Gay Ghetto." *Urban Studies* 41 (9): 1739–1750.

Silver, Daniel, Terry Nichols Clark, and Clemente Jesus Navarro Yanez. 2010. "Scenes: Social Context in an Age of Contingency." *Social Forces* 88 (5): 2293–2324.

Sites, William. 2003. *Remaking New York: Primitive Globalization and the Politics of Urban Community*. Minneapolis: University of Minnesota Press.

Small, Mario Luis. 2009. "'How Many Cases Do I Need?' On Science and the Logic of Case Selection." *Ethnography* 10 (1): 5–38.

Smith, Neil. 1996. *The New Urban Frontier: Gentrification and the Revanchist City*. New York: Routledge.

Smithsimon, Gregory. 2011. *September 12: Community and Neighborhood Recovery at Ground Zero*. New York: New York University Press.

Sorkin, Michael (ed.). 1992. *Variations on a Theme Park: The New American City and the End of Public Space*. New York: Hill and Wang.

Stack, Carol B. 1973. *All Our Kin: Strategies for Survival in a Black Community*. New York: Basic Books.

Straw, Will. 1991. "Systems of Articulation, Logics of Change: Scenes and Communities in Popular Music." *Cultural Studies* 5 (3): 361–375.

———. 2004. "Cultural Scenes." *Society and Leisure* 27 (2): 411–422.

Sudarsky, Noah Marcel. 2007. "The Sound and the Fury." *New York Times,* January 21.

Taylor, Marvin J. (ed.). 2006. *The Downtown Book: The New York Art Scene, 1974–1984*. Princeton, NJ: Princeton University Press.

Turner, Bryan. 1987. "A Note on Nostalgia." *Theory, Culture, and Society* 4 (1): 147–156.

Venkatesh, Sudhir Alladi. 2000. *American Project: The Rise and Fall of a Modern Ghetto*. Cambridge, MA: Harvard University Press.

Vitale, Alex S. 2005. "Innovation and Institutionalization: Factors in the Development of 'Quality of Life' Policing in New York City." *Policing and Society* 15 (2): 99–124.

———. 2009. *City of Disorder: How the Quality of Life Campaign Transformed New York Politics*. New York: New York University Press.

Von Hassell, Malve. 1999. *Homesteading in New York City, 1978–1993: The Divided Heart of Loisaida*. Westport, CT: Greenwood.

Wasserman, Suzanne. 1994. "Déjà Vu: Replanning the Lower East Side in the 1930s." In *From Urban Village to East Village: The Battle for New York's Lower East Side*, edited by Janet Abu-Lughod. Oxford: Blackwell.

Weegee. 1945. *Naked City*. New York: Da Capo Press.

White, E. B. 1948. *Here Is New York*. New York: Little Bookroom.

Whitman, Walt. 1996. *Walt Whitman: Poetry and Prose*. New York: Literary Classics of the United States.

Williams, Monte. 1999. "Oh, to Be Down and Out Living on the Bowery; Artists' Cheap Lofts, Found Decades Ago, Are Threatened by Development Project," *New York Times,* May 13.

Wilson, James Q., and George L. Kelling. 1982. "The Police and Neighborhood Safety." *Atlantic,* March, 29–38.

Wilson, Janelle L. 2005. *Nostalgia: Sanctuary of Meaning*. Lewisburg, PA: Bucknell University Press.

Zukin, Sharon. 1983. *Loft Living: Culture and Capital in Urban Change*. New Brunswick, NJ: Rutgers University Press.

———. 1991. *Landscapes of Power: From Detroit to Disney World*. Berkeley: University of California Press.

Zukin, Sharon. 1995. *The Cultures of Cities*. Oxford: Blackwell.

———. 2010. *Naked City: The Death and Life of Authentic Urban Places*. New York: Oxford University Press.

———. 2012. "The Social Production of Urban Cultural Heritage: Identity and Ecosystem on an Amsterdam Shopping Street." *City, Culture, and Society* 3 (4): 281–291.

Zukin, Sharon, and Ervin Kosta. 2004. "Bourdieu Off-Broadway: Managing Distinction on a Shopping Block in the East Village." *City and Community* 3 (2): 101–114.

Zukin, Sharon, Valerie Trujillo, Peter Frase, Danielle Jackson, Tim Recuber, and Abraham Walker. 2009. "New Retail Capital and Neighborhood Change: Boutiques and Gentrification in New York City." *City and Community* 8 (1): 47–64.

INDEX